Robert S. Mulliken

Life of a Scientist

An Autobiographical Account of the
Development of Molecular Orbital Theory
with an Introductory Memoir by
Friedrich Hund

Edited by
Bernard J. Ransil

With 33 Illustrations

Springer-Verlag
Berlin Heidelberg New York
London Paris Tokyo

ROBERT S. MULLIKEN

Editor

BERNARD J. RANSIL, M.D.
Department of Medicine, Beth Israel Hospital,
and Harvard Medical School,
Boston, MA 02215/USA

Cover photograph by B.J. Ransil, 1968.

ISBN 3-540-50375-7 Springer-Verlag Berlin Heidelberg New York
ISBN 0-387-50375-7 Springer-Verlag New York Berlin Heidelberg

Library of Congress Cataloging-in-Publication Data
Mulliken, Robert Sanderson.
  Life of a scientist.
  1. Mulliken, Robert Sanderson. 2. Chemists—
United States—Biography. 3. Molecular orbitals.
I. Ransil, Bernard J. (Bernard Jerome), 1929–
II. Title.
QD22.M75A3   1989   540'.92'4 [B]   88-34897

Typesetting: TCSystems, Inc., Shippensburg, Pennsylvania.
Printing and Binding: Edwards Brothers, Inc., Ann Arbor, Michigan.
2151/NY30-543210—Printed on acid-free paper.

Editor's Preface

It was Prof. Mulliken's intention for many years to write a book about molecular orbital theory. That this intention motivated him, in part at least, to undertake the writing of his scientific autobiography, I have little doubt. But at the same time he very much wanted to write an accurate history of how the molecular orbital theory originated and evolved, as he remembered it.

In the origin of the molecular orbital theory, Friedrich Hund played an essential and pivotal role, as the reader of this book will learn from one person in a position to know. Originally referred to as the Hund-Mulliken theory, the MO theory slowly became identified with Mulliken over his 50 years of almost continuous development of it, interrupted only by World War II. Despite their close association during the early years, Hund and Mulliken never wrote a joint paper. Rather, they interacted and stimulated one another by visits and lively discussions, by corresponding and reading each other's papers.

As I listened to Hund's account of those early years via a video-tape cassette specially prepared for the First Annual Mulliken Memorial Lecture at the University of Chicago on May 9, 1988 by the Institut für den Wissenschaftlichen Film (Göttingen), I was struck by how closely the two men's histories corroborated one another; and at once decided to request Prof. Hund's permission to include his memoir as an introduction to that of his old colleague and friend. In a subsequent exchange of letters, Prof. Hund graciously agreed. The result is hopefully a volume that will be welcome and useful alike to the student, the scientist, and the historian of science.

The text has been printed in two type sizes to distinguish the non-scientific history from the scientific, thereby enabling the reader to follow one or both lines of narrative. If the scientist-reader disagrees at times with allocation of the material, I beg his indulgence: the dilemma, at times, was not unlike that confronting the surgeon who would separate a pair of Siamese twins.

I think it safe to say that those who knew Prof. Mulliken will recognize him in these pages. It is an accurate account, as far as it goes, of the man, his life and times as he perceived them, and his work. It is not a complete account by any means, because he believed there were limits to what a man ought to divulge about his private life and beyond these he would not go. His voluminous archives at the University of Chicago's Regenstein Library are a treasure trove awaiting the historian of science interested in the origin and evolution of molecular orbital theory, and the men who contributed to its development.

Boston, MA
December, 1988

BERNARD J. RANSIL

Recollections of Robert S. Mulliken

FRIEDRICH HUND

This brief reminiscence of Robert Mulliken was presented by Prof. Hund via videotape cassette at a dinner following the first annual Mulliken Memorial Lecture at the University of Chicago on May 9, 1988. We wish to thank both Prof. Hund and the Institut für den Wissenschaftlichen Film, Göttingen, for permission to include it in this volume.

Ladies and gentlemen:

You have invited me to be present at the inauguration of the Robert Mulliken Memorial Lectures and to contribute some reminiscences from the early days of molecular spectroscopy and from my association with Mulliken. I appreciate the honour you have accorded to me with your invitation, and I would like to express my deep gratitude to you; but I am too old to attend in person. Therefore, allow me at least in this way to pass on some recollections of my colleague and friend Robert S. Mulliken.

Mulliken and I were born in the same year, 1896. During the First World War we both had to do some scientific work connected with it; so we had fortunately no occasion to shoot at one another. Mulliken got his PhD in 1921, I my Dr. degree in 1922. Both theses had nothing to do with molecular spectra. I began to lecture in 1925, he became assistant professor in 1926. I cannot remember Mulliken's short visit to Göttingen in 1925, but we certainly noticed one another in the following year. I had had some success in understanding the complex atomic spectra with the moment of momenta vector model of Russell and Saunders; I was proud of it, and I hoped then to understand the electronic terms of molecular spectra in a similar manner. In a paper I discussed the coupling of rotation with electron motion in diatomic molecules using, as examples, the rich empirical results Mulliken had obtained. I especially noticed his comparing the spectra of isoelectric molecules. After my paper, Mulliken understood his results better and published new analyses.

The Schrödinger equation appeared in 1926, and now it was rather trivial to interpolate the electronic quantum states of a diatomic molecule between the limiting case of two separated atoms and the other limiting case, where the positive electric charges of the two nuclei were united to one. I wrote a paper on it, and in the summer term of 1927, I gave a course of lectures on molecular structure at Göttingen. Mulliken, then for some months at Göttingen, heard at least a part of it. We had lively discussions, we became good friends, and Mulliken joined me on a hiking trip in the Black Forest. I fear he had to put up with some unusual ways of cooking meals and several uncomfortable nights' lodging.

With our respective approaches to molecules (Mulliken's wide experimental skill and overview and my perhaps somewhat clearer understanding of the theory), each of us was a good complement to the other. From then on our paths ran parallel. Mulliken was quick to comprehend the possibilities that quantum mechanics opened up—the meaning of orbits and quantum numbers. He systematized and explored molecular spectra by assigning quantum numbers to the individual electrons. I independently did the same, and in summer 1928, I had just handed a paper to the editor when I received a copy or a proof sheet of Mulliken's paper. I immediately saw that in some examples, Mulliken's interpretation was more convincing. So I requested back my manuscript and wrote a new one, which combined Mulliken's and my reflections.

Of course, Mulliken has the priority of systematizing the simple molecular spectra by assigning quantum numbers to the individual electrons. Mulliken's concept of the "promoted electron" and my schedule for correlating the electron states with the two limiting cases were the germ of what was later called the correlation diagram.

The following year (1929) I gave lectures at Harvard on molecu-

lar structure (John Slater, among the audience, gave valuable comments.) Mulliken and I then met in Chicago. A picture (above) shows us in front of the Ryerson Physical Laboratory: In the first row you see Heisenberg, Dirac, Gale and Hund; in the second A.H. Compton, Monk, Eckart, Mulliken, and Hoyt.

At this time it became urgent to establish a unitary nomenclature for molecules, the symbols σ, π, δ for orbitals, capital $\Sigma^{\pm}$, Π, Δ for terms, g,u for symmetry, etc.. Mulliken and I discussed the possibilities in the long train trip between Chicago and New York; then other colleagues agreed. A picture (below) I took during a meeting of the American Physical Society in Washington shows Morse, Crawford, Mulliken, and Dennison, and has the note "Einigung

IX

über die Bezeichnung der Molekülzustände" (agreement on the nomenclature for molecular states).

We had not invented Quantum Chemistry. Heitler and London began this discipline in 1927. Both Mulliken and I had some difficulty in understanding them within the framework of molecular orbitals. It was Gerhard Herzberg who explained chemical binding in a simple and convincing manner with bonding and antibonding electrons, where an antibonding electron could counterbalance a bonding electron. Of course, Mulliken's early concept of promoted electrons came near to the idea.

Chemists got interested in the physicists' explanation of chemical binding and so Mulliken and I were invited to the meeting of the Bunsen-Gesellschaft (German Association for Physical Chemistry) at Heidelberg in 1930 and we had to give lectures. Mulliken perhaps was much more impressed by the evening festivity in the Heidelberger Schloss close to the famous Heidelberger Fass (a tremendous cask for wine), where Walter Weizel contributed to the amusement. Mrs. Mulliken designated it later on in the evening as the wildest party of her life.

But back to molecules. For Mulliken all this was only the beginning of a lifelong research in molecular structure. You know the rest. The thick volume of selected papers edited by Ramsay and Hinze bears witness to it.

Now at the end of my speech I hope the memorial lectures will contribute to keep alive Mulliken's merit. To Gerhard Herzberg (who probably is present) my special regards and compliments may be given.

Author's Foreword

When I approached the age of 82, I fell to wondering, what shall I do with the rest of my life? Until this time I had continued with co-workers to carry on research on molecular structure and spectra, but finally, I had fallen behind in acquaintance with some of the newer developments and did not want to turn back, as I could have, to still worthwhile earlier activities such as the analysis of molecular spectra which had now become pretty routine. I thought possibly I might take up watercolor painting, but thought I should do so only after some fairly intensive training, even though one summer many years ago I had done some good watercolors of nature with no training whatsoever. However, I never seriously pursued this idea.

I thought I might do something to help nonscientists understand science and scientists better. One day, when he was visiting, I told Prof. Thomas Kuhn of my dilemma. His immediate response was to the effect that there is a very great lack of autobiographies by scientists. I took this as a recommendation for me to write an autobiography. By "a great lack", I assumed that he meant for people concerned, like him, with the history of science. I had always thought that some people should work in this field, but I wanted, myself, to do something new, to be a pioneer in research, but now this course no longer seemed feasible for me.

As for writing an autobiography, I thought, what have I done that anyone would want to read about? However, after some contemplation, I decided to try it. I started writing and soon produced over

200 typed pages. Some of this I thought was good and would interest nonscientists as well as scientists. After some additions and changes suggested by wise editors, the present version is now ready and is presented in the following pages.

Arlington, VA   ROBERT S. MULLIKEN
January, 1986

Contents

Contents

Contents

Robert S. Mulliken
Life of a Scientist

I

Early Life in Newburyport

On one of my shelves I have copies of three different American editions of *Conversations on Chemistry*, by Mrs. Jane Marcet (1). These had belonged to family members and a cousin in the early 1800's. I had found them in the old family house in Newburyport, Massachusetts. One, published in Hartford, Connecticut, in 1930, is "the twelfth American Edition, from the last London edition . . . ." The book consists of a series of animated and very instructive dialogues between "Mrs. B" and two young ladies, Emily and Caroline. At first Emily and Caroline were very skeptical about chemistry, but soon Mrs. B had their interest as they pursued the subject together. Mrs. B (Mrs. Marcet) explains in the preface that she attended a number of the famous popular lectures and demonstrations by Sir Humphrey Davy at the Royal Institution in London, but did not properly understand them until she had discussed them with a friend. She then decided to write a book to explain chemistry to other women.

On the title page of the Hartford edition of *Conversations* is the signature of my paternal grandfather, Moses Jonathan Mulliken who was born in 1816. I surmise it was about 1832 when he inscribed his name. Also, dated 1879, is that of my father, Samuel Parsons Mulliken, born in December, 1864. I added my signature in 1980. On the fly-leaf is drawn in, by hand, an anchor. I presume this was done by Moses.

My grandfather's father, Samuel, was born in 1769. He was married to Phoebe Parsons in 1798 (she was born in 1776) and had a comfortable new two-story house built in 1810 with plenty of light, and a fireplace in every room. The cost was $2,750.

This house at 46 High Street still stands. I was born there, as were Moses and his two brothers and six sisters, and his son and two daughters. Recently it became mine and I gave it with some repairs but no remodeling to my older daughter Lucia. The name Lucia has been transmitted from aunt to niece for several generations.

My great-grandfather hoped that his son Moses would go to college, but instead at the age of sixteen Moses joined the crew of a new clipper ship just built in a nearby shipyard. I assume that the anchor in my grandfather's copy of *Conversations on Chemistry* symbolizes his feelings at the time. Life on a ship at sea would be vastly more exciting than talk about chemistry by girls.

Newburyport, at the mouth of the Merrimac River, was then a rival of Boston as a center of international trade by sailing ships, many of which were built there. In fact, only Boston, New York, and Philadelphia surpassed Newburyport in population between the Revolutionary War and the War of 1812.

The country around Newburyport is hilly and scenic. Extending south for eight miles from the Merrimac river mouth is Plum Island, with sand dunes and the ocean on one side and salt marshes and Plum Island river on the other. The novels of a native author J.P. Marquand give many glimpses of how life was in Newburyport.

My grandfather Moses was the successful captain of many ships in trading expeditions all over the world. At the time of the gold rush in California about 1849, he more than once made the difficult and dangerous trip there around Cape Horn. Later came voyages to India. In Calcutta, about 1858 a Cape Cod captain named Sears showed Moses a letter from his niece Sarah Delia Gibbs. Although over 40 at the time, Moses had never married. But now he was fascinated by the letter from Sarah Gibbs. Soon they entered into correspondence and in 1860 he made her his bride after returning with gifts from a voyage to France and St. Petersburg (2). My daughter Lucia has the samovar which he brought Sarah Gibbs. She was from Sandwich on Cape Cod, a region where cranberry bogs flourish. Several of her ancestors had come to Plymouth on the Mayflower.

When my father was a young man, times had changed; the lure of great sailing ships was past. Thus it happened that at the age of perhaps fourteen or fifteen his interest in chemistry was aroused when he came upon his father's copy of *Conversations on Chemistry*. In high school, he and his friend Arthur A. Noyes did chemistry experiments alternately in the "woodhouse chamber" (3) of the Mulliken house and in the Noyes family house. Still later, each of them attended MIT (the Massachusetts Institute of Technology) and then went to Leipzig for a Ph.D. in chemistry, and afterwards both became professors at MIT. Noyes later went to Pasadena and was instrumental in developing the California Institute of Technology there.

Although many facts about chemistry were well described in Mrs. B's book, there was then really no satisfactory theory to help in understanding many of these facts. By the time my father and his friend Arthur Noyes were studying chemistry at M.I.T., however, the major elements of an understanding in terms of atoms and molecules had been worked out. It was now agreed that matter, whether solid, liquid or gas, is basically composed of extraordinarily small atoms in utterly vast number. In gases, small or moderate-sized groups of atoms are combined to form molecules.

Chemistry was now actively developing in many countries, especially in Europe, notably in Germany. Many Americans, among others my father and Arthur Noyes, went there for advanced study and research. My father's Ph.D. thesis in Leipzig in 1887 was on the making and the properties of an "organic" molecule called chlorcinnamic acid. The name indicates that it has some relation to cinnamon; many organic molecules can be obtained from natural products.

My father's sister Sarah was the family genealogist, and traced most of my father's ancestors back at least to the time they came to this country. Very nearly all came from England to Massachusetts, beginning in 1620. The one who arrived last was Robert Mulliken (he spelled it Mullicken). He is supposed to have sailed from Glasgow in 1680. He was in Boston as early as 1686 according to the Brattle Street Church record. From the spelling of his name it is probable, according to my aunt, that he came from the very northern part of Scotland, or that his family did. However, I think it more likely that he was Scotch-Irish, that is, one of those people who, although originally of Scotch ancestry had settled in the north of Ireland. Some of the later Mullikens were noted for making excellent grandfather clocks.

An early ancestor was John Gyles whose parents and their children once lived in Pemaquid, Maine. In 1680, the family house and other property were burned, and his father killed, by the Indians who cooperated with the French in a war against English settlers. John Gyles became a slave of the Indians. He lived with them between the ages of 8 and 16. His master was relatively kind and finally sold him to a French settler. Later John Gyles was released and went to Boston. A charming novel about his life with the Indians was published in 1966. It greatly embellishes a brief account which Gyles had reluctantly been persuaded to write (4) many years after his return from captivity. In reading this, I felt that I knew my ancestor almost as a friend.

My mother, a distant relative of my father, was also a Mulliken descended from the original Robert. Her father Elijah Sanderson Mulliken was from a family who had lived in Lexington since before the American Revolution. Before she married she had studied art at the Pratt Institute in Brooklyn, New York, had had a studio and done many oil paintings, and had taught piano and singing. She tried to each me to play the piano, but although I very much appreciated listening to good piano music, I rebelled at the tedious exercise and never learned to play myself.

My aunt Sarah was a great storyteller and often the children of neighbors visited her to be entertained by her stories, some of which were also published in book form (5). They were largely about the doings of people back in the colonial days before the American Revolution. Interwoven were tales about family members. As a child and even afterward I called Aunt Sarah "Narnie."

One of the ancestors in whom my aunt was especially interested was the Rev. Jonathan Parsons, pastor of the Old South Church on Federal Street, a Presbyterian church which is still there. His sermons were bound in six volumes which I now have. I confess that I have never read them. Jonathan Parsons was the grandfather of Phoebe Parsons, for whom, when he married her, my great-grandfather, Samuel Mulliken, built a house about which I have already written. In a sermon in 1775 Jonathan Parsons called on the men of his parish to take part in the American Revolution against the British. Jonathan Parsons was a friend of the English evangelist George Whitefield, who sometimes preached at the Old South Church. My aunt told me that the bones of both Jonathan Parsons and his friend Whitefield were placed in a crypt in the church pulpit and could be seen there. I myself, perhaps feeling this rather too gruesome, never went to look at them. Some years later they were removed to a more conventional resting place.

4

Prominent in maritime affairs in Newburyport was Captain Jonathan Parsons, son of Reverend Jonathan. I have a silver snuffbox that was his. It is gaily and beautifully fashioned, which suggests something of his life.

About my early years, before high school, I seem to remember rather little. I vaguely recall my early awakening, at perhaps three or four years, to the immense delight of being alive in this extraordinary and wonderful world, as it then seemed to me. At that time I joyfully assumed that the world was made for humans, to make them happy. Later I learned that Nature is not quite so generous as I had then believed.

Another thing I remember is that one night my father awakened me to tell me that the world was just starting on a new century. On another occasion that seemed momentous, he told me that Queen Victoria had died. A few years later I saw my first automobile.

Still another thing I remember from my earliest years was that my parents insisted that if I wanted something I should always say "Please", and, if my wish were granted, I should always say "Thank You." Having learned these things, I went one step further and, when I wanted something seriously, I said "Please-Thank You-MUST!!" I don't remember how effective this early verbal effort was, but perhaps it helped.

My father with his wife and children lived at first in a rented house on Bromfield Street only a block from the old family house on High Street, which I visited often. Primary school was a few doors away up Bromfield Street. One summer I skipped a grade by learning the multiplication table. During school years I read some children's books, but don't remember when. These certainly included *The Five Little Peppers, The Wizard of Oz,* and *Alice in Wonderland.* I did not read the Bible, or Shakespeare or grown-up books in general. I played with a few children, including my sister Katherine, who was two years younger than I; and later there was also my brother Gyles, who was seven years younger than I. Also we often saw the Berry family, who lived next door.

In summer, among other things, I turned the crank to make ice cream in the freezer. My father cultivated a vegetable garden. Occasionally, the family took the trolley car which ran alongside the Merrimac River to Plum Island. Here we settled down for lunch on the sand where we could watch the ocean waves roll in, meantime doing justice to a supply of freshly boiled lobsters which we had brought along. In winter, I often roamed the countryside

5

on snow shoes. At home, once, I built a snow house and froze my ears.

The country about Newburyport was fascinating in many ways, and I explored it thoroughly. The trolley car to Plum Island passed by large areas of salt marsh—and clouds of mosquitoes if you went into the marshes, and horseshoe crabs. But first we passed a region by the river on the east end of Newburyport which was called Joppa. Here with some fascination I sometimes saw men skinning eels they had caught. There were also clams in the mud-flats, and sometimes I went out there to dig some. One could find them because of columns of water which they spouted. Another trolley car led to Parker River, where the first settlers of Newbury had arrived. Close by was Oldtown Hill, 200 feet high.

Another trolley car led inland through delightful country to Byfield, where there was a boy's school (and still is), past Jack Frost's ice-house (Jack Frost was his real name), where ice cut in the winter from a near-by pond was stored and delivered to customers in Newburyport; this was before the days of refrigerators made by General Electric. Another trolley car went to West Newbury where there were covered bridges across the Merrimac River. Another trolley from Newburyport went north across the river to Ring's Island, Salisbury, and Salisbury Beach, with more vistas of salt marshes along the way.

For hiking in the country, one could go to Devil's Den with its interesting serpentine, asbestos, and other minerals. Nearby was the old swimming hole in Little River, with depth that varied as the tide came up from Parker River. Nearby was Devil's Pulpit, and half a mile away was Devil's Basin, where we went in early spring to find the first flowers, the hepaticas. There were also many surrounding small towns to visit, each with a town common and old churches. Some of these were across the Merrimac River in New Hampshire, beyond Salisbury.

Among friends whom we often visited were the Littles of Little's Lane. A mile or so down High Street from our old family house, they had a magnificent house dating back to the 1600's. Nearby, they carried on farming on broad acres bordering the Plum Island marshes.

When I was probably about eight, I played sometimes with a girl of whom I thought highly. But sometimes in a discussion, she put me down, perhaps because of her superior wisdom or sophistication. Anyway, my male ego was sometimes deeply wounded. On one such occasion, I thought I would like to kill her and bury her in the sand. But then I reasoned that if I did that, the government would kill me, and I didn't want that. After further thought, I concluded that this policy of the government was wise, for it would never do to allow people to go around killing other people. It was probably these reflections which led me to a belief in capital punishment for premeditated murder, which I still maintain.

After several years the family moved to a three-story house near the center of town, at 6 Harris Street. Half a block away at the corner of State Street stood the historic Wolfe Tavern.

With the Harris Street house came fruit trees, a barn, and a steep slope which permitted sliding down hill on a sled in winter. The house belonged to Cousin Margaret Stone, a first cousin of my father, who grew up there and later kept a school there. Her mother was great-aunt Sarah, who had married Captain Gyles P. Stone.

In the house, my mother worked very hard with cooking and keeping us fit for school; she now had very little time to keep up her art. She made delicious bread, popovers on Sundays, and baked beans on Saturday night. On alternate years the crabapple tree bore abundant fruit, and then she made excellent crabapple jelly. This was stored in glass jars in a room in the cellar.

My mother belonged to the Women's Club and the Choral Union, which once a year sang the Messiah. She was a member of the Unitarian Church, which has a beautiful building with a tall spire on Pleasant Street. Many times she got me to go there with her on Sunday. I absorbed the Judeo-Christian ethos and ever since have thought it good, but I finally got tired of going to church and listening to sermons. My father did not go with us—his family church had been Congregationalist. That church and the ancestral burying ground were located a moderate distance down High Street in the town of Newbury. I assume he went to that church as a boy.

While I was growing up, my father was writing his lengthy well-known treatise on *A Method for the Identification of Pure Organic Compounds,* in four volumes. This was the standard work in the field for many years. The first volume contains a set of two standard color charts which were prepared through home labor by myself and my sister. We had small gummed squares of all the various colors; one of each color had to be stuck in its proper place in the chart. We were paid for each completed chart. Another activity which I carried on was proof-reading of my father's books. I

7

remember doing a great amount of this, which accustomed me to the complicated chemical names of the compounds described, but I think did not excite me to any special interest in chemistry. The publisher of the books, William O. Wiley, was a friend of my father who referred to him as WOW.

Financially, we were not well off. My father's salary, plus some consulting, did not bring in much income; but I think he was also helping out his mother and sister in keeping up the old house. (My grandfather had died in 1903). Perhaps for this reason, social life with the more influential members of the community was largely lacking. This may account for a deep-seated inferiority complex which I have had, especially toward people in authority, but *not* toward scientists. Tennis was an unheard of luxury then, but later I enjoyed it. I never played or had any interest in baseball. I dabbled a little in football. Nowadays, I find following the stock market a very good indoor sport.

When Arthur Noyes left MIT for the California Institute of Technology at Pasadena, he tried to pursuade my father to join him there. But my father refused, I suppose because of loyalty to his mother and sister and the old house. My own life would have been different if we had moved.

I never had really intimate talks with my father. However, while I was growing up, we made expeditions together in a row boat on the Merrimac and the Plum Island Rivers. Exhibiting a sense of humor, he named the row boat Eile mit Weile (Make haste slowly). Once or twice after going through the Plum Island River we went up the Parker River to the spot where the first settlers in Newbury had landed. Later with a motor boat I accompanied my father in excursions off the coast of Maine, sometimes navigating in deep fog and once, some miles in the ocean to Monhegan Island.

My father was very interested in Pemaquid, Maine, where our ancestor John Gyles had been captured by the Indians and lived with them from ages eight to sixteen. I made many hiking trips with my father on the Presidential Range in the White Mountains of New Hampshire. I also spent a little time helping him at MIT with some laboratory experiments in which he was trying to make a paste that would be very, very sticky. In view of my father's career as a chemist, it is natural that I became interested in science although I was strongly tempted to move in other directions, such as philosophy or other humanistic fields. I don't recall that my father tried to persuade me to become a chemist, but I am sure he was happy later when I became successful in scientific research.

I was much more empathetic toward my mother, who inculcated in me a sense of beauty and of justice. This includes beauty in nature and art and in character, but I have little of the feeling of beauty in the scientific laws of nature which other scientists often express. I have sometimes experienced very strong feelings of intimacy with nature, as I will explain later, but not of beauty in its laws. My mother had a strong influence on me. One day I repeated to her one of those four-letter words which are not in the dictionary that I had learned from a schoolmate. My mother came down on me with such terrific force that ever since my language has remained free—perhaps too free—of at least the most offensive of these words.

In my grammar school years, I was an avid stamp collector. American stamps I obtained largely from old letters which had accumulated in the old family house in Newburyport. There were stamps of various denominations from successive issues, fascinating in their changing variety. Particular treasures were stamps commemorating the World's Fair—the Columbian Exposition—in 1893 in Chicago. Of interest also were special delivery stamps. Most abundant of course were two-cent stamps which for some years were all that were needed for ordinary first class letters. The design of these changed as time went on. But even at any one time, careful scrutiny shows a small fraction of the two-cent stamps to differ in certain details. In particular, some of them showed a small cap over the number two. As it happened, someone who had lived at 6 Harris Street before we had, had left a whole dresser drawer filled with hundreds or thousands of two-cent stamps which he (or she) must have soaked off from letters. I searched through these assiduously and plucked out a small number which displayed the cap over the two.

In addition to the domestic stamps, I had many foreign stamps, which I think I got mainly by sending to stamp companies which sold packets of stamps. Also I got some by exchanging with other boys who collected stamps.

After building up a substantial collection, I finally after some time wondered whether it would not be more sensible to sell them instead of keeping them. Soon I found someone to buy them. I seem to remember that he was a distant relative who had no scruples in offering me a very modest sum for my collection. Although I felt that I was probably being very foolish, I naively and fatalistically accepted this offer without discussion. My stamps were now gone, but at any rate, I had had some fun.

While we were living on Harris Street, often in the afternoon after school I would walk up Park Street (a short, sloping street which began opposite our house) to High Street. Then I would go down the length of High Street to the old family house at Number 46 to have a visit with my grandmother. We would play Parchesi, and I would also visit the cookie jar. On the wall there was a fine oil painting done in Antwerp, of one of my grandfather's ships, the Anna Schmidt. When it became mine, I gave it to the Newburyport Marine Society for their museum.

On the walk up High Street, I greatly enjoyed looking at the many distinguished and beautiful old houses. These are largely three-story brick buildings built in the early 1800's for the merchant traders in the shipping business who flourished then. Although our family house, staunchly constructed of wood, is very attractive, commodious, and sunny, it is not so noble as some of the architectural masterpieces which I admired. The beauty of the old houses owes much to the fact that they were built by the same master craftsmen who designed the great ships that sailed from Newburyport. High Street to me was a parade of beautiful houses, interspersed, to be sure, by some that were more prosaic. The houses were shaded by many magnificent elms most of which are now gone, victims of Dutch elm disease. Other streets of course held architectural treasures, but High Street was, and is, rather special.

Before going on, let me mention an unusual young man with red hair named Gillis who for a time was a classmate at the Jackman Grammar school in one of the years before I entered high school. He did not like having to go to school and spent little time there. As a result, he dropped several times from one grade to a lower one, until before long he was in the same grade as my brother who was seven years younger than I. In a book about him, he is quoted as saying that "my worst trouble is that I got my lessons done too quick." It would seem that he was capable of good school work because later he successfully completed high school in three and a half years. He soon became popular and well-known for his unconventional exploits. Generally known as Bossy Gillis, he was before long elected mayor of Newburyport.

I. Early Life in Newburyport

In 1909, at age thirteen, I graduated from the eighth grade of the Jackman grammar school on Prospect Street and in the fall began four years at the Newburyport High School. I remember rather little about the years before high school, but recently in looking over the mostly very boring "themes" I did in the English course as a freshman at MIT, I found in one of them a relevant comment. This says that when I entered the High School, it "seemed a place of great interest, pleasure and privilege, and from it I had more enjoyment than in all the previous schools."

II

Newburyport High School

Newburyport High School was an excellent school on High Street not far from our house on Harris Street. The curriculum included a classical and a scientific course. The scientific course perhaps owed its existence to the fact that there was a "Wheelwright Fund" which enabled qualified young men of Newburyport to study science or engineering in Boston or Cambridge, usually at MIT. The resulting economic stimulus reinforced the scientific side of my interests, and I took the scientific course in preparation for going to MIT. My father and his friend Arthur Noyes had been the first to go to MIT on a Wheelwright Scholarship.

The scientific course in high school included biology, physics, French, German, and of course English. I think most students took the classical course. I do not recall that anyone thought it strange that I took the scientific course. My feeling probably was that everyone chose what he (perhaps influenced by his parents) liked or thought he could do. Or perhaps he let someone choose it for him.

I had good teachers, women in biology and English, a man, Dana Wells, in physics. I do not remember who taught French and German. However, a little later when I went to MIT, I found that my knowledge of German was so good that I did not need the MIT course. As an extra in high school I took one year of Latin which I subsequently found to be very valuable in the understanding of modern European languages and their origins. Another minor activity in high school was predicting the weather. Each morning I read the official forecast in the Boston Herald, looked at the barometer and at the sky, and on the basis of this information prepared a forecast which was published in the local afternoon paper, the *Newburyport Daily News*. Official forecasters might have disapproved of this, but I enjoyed it, and perhaps it was useful as education.

As a high school student, I was briefly interested in philosophy, but soon concluded that since no two philosophers agreed, all are probably wrong. Hence I returned to science, where the test for correctness for both experimental work and explanatory theory is agreement between different workers. Later it seemed to me that the scientific study by Nature by experiment, and by theory deduced from experiment, forms the truest basis for philosophy.

I also became interested in the forms of the words used in language. I once went through a French dictionary and culled out a list of irregular verbs, those which have abnormal, often archaic, forms for their different tenses. I also enjoyed some poetry.

In my studies, I was greatly influenced by the theory of evolution, the evidence for which was so convincing that for me evolution long since became a fact, not a theory, and has remained so, in spite of controversies over details. I don't recall how I first encountered it; probably in the biology course, followed by avid reading and thought.

I was especially fascinated by accounts of recent developments in science. I recall books by Robert Kennedy-Duncan as especially stimulating. Some of them dealt with life and its origin as well as with physics and chemistry. I was privileged, as having the second best record in the class, to present an essay at the graduation ceremony in 1913. I talked about "Electrons: What They Are and What They Do." Much of my later research has been concerned with aspects of that same subject.

Another subject on which I wrote a theme for my English class was "A Trip To The Moon." This was rather up to date in that the initial impulse for the trip was supplied by a powerful explosion.

In my high school days, when spring came, I got out my bicycle and took long rides. At that time automobiles were still scarce, so bicycle riding was a pleasure. Starting at 4 A.M., before sunrise, I could easily make twenty miles before breakfast and school. Often I heard the birds wake up and express their joy at the return of the sun. Also, taking up a hobby of Aunt Sarah's, I became an amateur taxonomist, getting acquainted with the local wild flora. I was especially fond of the pitcher plants, the sundew, and other bog plants.

Later in the season I was much interested in the goldenrods, genus Solidago, and other members of the family Compositae, especially the fascinating and varied species of sunflowers and asters. I found the study of weeds and water plants rather fascinating too. Based on the occurrence of intermediate forms, I concluded that one ubiquitous species of goldenrod, S. rugosa, forms hybrids with several others, including the very different salt-marsh goldenrod S. sempervirens. These observations and conclusions were perhaps an early example of my development of a scientific viewpoint.

All this was entirely independent of high school work. In high school there were no expeditions outside the school. In vacant lots extending a few blocks from the river bank, the hemp plant Cannabis sativa used to be abundant. The seeds must have come from ships which had visited the East Indies. In recent years, when it was learned that these harmless looking weeds were marijuana, they must have been ruthlessly exterminated. For, in visits to Newburyport since then, I have found no trace of them.

Across the river from Newburyport was an idyllic spot which I called Paradise. For my freshman English class at MIT, I once wrote an essay about this place. In returning the essay the professor had written on it, "A mystic philosopher sans confidence."

This essay shows how much at the time I felt in touch with nature, and I now quote a few paragraphs from it:

"Across the river in Salisbury is a tract of wooded land which to me seemed the most delightful place near Newburyport. To reach it we leave the road and go through a few trees and across some land where rocks and boulders everywhere jut from the barren soil, but with a grove of tall yellow pines on one side. To the left is a little pond overhung with tangled greenbriar and stiff alders, and with a few pines growing up from mossy rocks on another shore. The pool is confined by a grass-covered ridge of rock, which barely rises above the level of the water that runs out, when it wishes, through a little crevice in the rock."

"Leaving the pond, we approach our goal over some marsh land which was once salt marsh but now is cut off from the tides by a dike. Through the marsh are scattered several rocky islets from whose red cedars and junipers come the varied and cheerful notes of the song-sparrow, like a wild canary, while from the distance the meadow larks answer one another with sweet, plaintive song."

14

II. Newburyport High School

"When we have passed the islands and jumped over a stone wall, a gentle slope rises before us, covered with interlacing yellow pines. Underneath, the blocks and ridges of rock are strewn with pine needles and overgrown in the corners and damp spots with velvety green moss. After a few steps into this, there is nothing to indicate the nearness of civilization."

"Going on, we may sit down under a mossy boulder, by whose side the greenbriar, growing up from the border of an oozy place, climbs up into the branches of a red cedar tree and forms a natural drapery of green. . . ."

Some of my Nature expeditions I made in the company of two family friends, Amelia and Margaret Little or of a young man, Charles Stockman, of about my age, who was interested in animals and was preparing to become a zoologist. Although he was in the following year's high school class (1914), I found him especially congenial. He was wiser than I about what to expect from life, but later became more disillusioned than I. He taught me enough about animals in the wild so that later, on one solitary bicycle ride, I put a non-dangerous milksnake into my pocket to take home. But when I got home, only the body of a mouse was there.

I was reasonably friendly with my high school classmates, but not close to them; I think there was only one, Tom Knowland, whom I visited at his home. A few girls I found decidedly attractive but I never took any of them to a movie or on a date. I do not recall any serious discussion with a classmate about the purpose of human life or what to do about it. Once my mother enrolled me in a dancing class, but at that time I was so frightened at getting close to a girl that I refused to take part in the class. Eventually I got over this phobia.

In the summer of 1914, some family members and I visited the picturesque house of a cousin in North Conway, New Hampshire. I was then eighteen. We climbed some mountains during the visit. I was much upset by the beginning of World War I, because people would be killed and, less distressing but still important, houses and other buildings which had been constructed with much human care and labor would be destroyed. But I never became a pacifist. Sometimes war has become necessary to defend ourselves or our friends.

During two or three years up to 1914 I knew as a school friend a German boy about my age named Kurt Schambach. He and my sister Katherine seemed fond of each other. His father was a business man temporarily in Newburyport, but when the war broke out they returned to Germany and never came back. Afterward I was afraid Kurt was lost in the war. His father said this about me: "Er hat's faustdick hinter den Ohren." This German phrase evidently represented a complimentary appraisal of my potentialities. (6)

In high school, under the influence of meditations on science, particularly on evolution, I developed in my private thoughts a highly deterministic point of view. In this I dehumanized myself and felt similarly about the surrounding human and animal world, looking on people and animals as basically animated machines, with every action determined by the joint effects of heredity and environment. Sometimes I thought of people as *things,* coldly, cruelly, as the military have to do toward a war-time enemy. Some years later when Bertrand Russell was visiting Chicago, I mentioned to him this aspect of my views on life at age sixteen. He said *he* had felt that way at age eight.

Although this private dehumanization did not prevent me most of the time from having normal human feelings toward other people, I think it acted as a damper on those feelings. I think that in the later years of my life I have been in the process of rehumanizing myself, in other words, learning to empathize and sympathize.

Although my dehumanization was activated largely by thoughts on biological processes of evolution, I felt that biological phenomena, including mankind, were merely secondary results of some admittedly amazing but obscure operations of chemistry and physics. This influenced my choice to go into physical science which, as compared to biological science, seemed more primary or fundamental. Here one's aim is to find out whatever he can about the basic principles of the universe.

From the point of view of the Universe, I thought perhaps life is just a minor aberration. Or, contrariwise, perhaps via mankind, it gives the Universe a means for understanding and becoming conscious of itself.

As I prepared to enter college, there was still a question as to whether I should specialize in physics or in chemistry, or possibly something different. However, without much hesitation I settled for chemistry, perhaps because I was more familiar with it, since my father was a chemist. There was in my mind little question of what college to attend, since I thought that my financial support, coming from the Wheelwright Fund, pointed to MIT. Actually, I might have preferred to go to Harvard with the hope of gaining broader viewpoints and possibly even going into something different than science. However, I did not have the temerity to raise the question of whether the Wheelwright Fund would support me for study at Harvard (7). Further, I was in no way prepared to try to get a job to help pay for my education. As a boy, I had never earned money on an outside job. Once I did accept a job at a pottery but ran away from it before I had done anything. In short, I had been in the regrettable habit of expecting to be supported.

Before entering upon a description of my life at MIT, I will review my general ideas about science, which were probably pretty well formed in high school. First of all, I was enthusiastic about the progress science was making in our understanding of the world in which we live. Of course most of what I learned was from books and teachers but a little was from my own direct experience. I generally trusted the correctness, within reasonable limits, of what the teachers and books taught me. Along with this learning I did my own thinking. What I read about the factual evidence for the theory of evolution convinced me absolutely and totally that this evolution is a *fact* of nature. This fact, combined with extensive thinking and possibly some reading, led me unhappily to the dehumanization I have described above.

In all this, I placed my faith in a scientific attitude wherein supreme value is attached to objective truth. Here I am speaking of scientific truth about Nature, including human nature, the world, the universe. There are of course very many other kinds of truth which are important for human beings, but I don't want to elaborate on these humanistic truths here. In the pursuit of scientific truth however, honesty, a humanistic virtue, is indispensable and becomes almost automatic to the practicing scientist. In those rare cases where a scientist has cheated about his results, he has soon been discovered, condemned, and ostracized by other scientists. This is especially true in the more exact sciences. I should add that of course in his day-to-day activities, the scientist is less constrained to be honest, but I think (and I hope) is often impelled by his scientific habits of honesty.

From the vantage point of hindsight, I learned enough about science in high school, mostly from books, that it became almost a religion for me. I was enthusiastic about its progress and it was thus only natural that later on I undertook to take part as a research scientist in that progress.

But before that, I needed to learn very much more about the

existing body of knowledge, including that on human affairs, and also on the practical techniques of my chosen field of science. Among other things, I learned how to make two kinds of chemical analysis, qualitative and quantitative. In quantitative analysis, the exact amounts of the components of a mixed sample are determined. Quoting from a talk I once gave, "In quantitative analysis, which by the way I hated, I learned discipline. I was brought face to face with the unpitying relentlessness of Nature in the form of some brute facts of chemical technique." Endless patience was required to save and weigh every little crumb of material derived from the sample in a series of manipulations and operations. Discipline is thus essential in learning to be a scientist, although of course the need for it is not at all unique to scientists. Real success in any field, be it politics, ballet, music, painting, or business, requires discipline." (8)

III

MIT: Chemistry and Chemical Engineering

In high school I was perhaps the best in the class. But at MIT I learned that there are many other bright people. Also there was one subject—I think it was descriptive geometry—which I couldn't cope with, and I think it was charity that I received a passing grade. Perhaps this ties in with the fact that as a boy I was never interested in machines, or in dismantling and reassembling a mechanical object, such as a watch or a car. In this respect I was an exception to most successful physicists and chemists.

In chemistry I did well. I think I can say that I loved molecules in general, and some molecules in particular. In physics we had a textbook, Duff's *Physics,* which as I remember it, I found almost impossible to understand. When I began to read a page, I would very soon come to a sentence which, as it seemed to me, could have either of two different meanings. The same trouble occurred with the next sentence, and the next. So I was soon hopelessly lost amid a plethora of alternative possible meanings. Other students didn't seem to have this difficulty; somehow they knew which was the correct meaning. I have often wondered how to explain this phenomenon. It seems that I have a compulsion to look at all possibilities, both probable and improbable. While this habit has hindered me in learning, especially in physics, perhaps it has helped me find original ideas in the course of my research.

The undergraduate chemistry program at MIT included carrying out one or two pieces of research. My first experience in this activity was an assignment by Professor Arthur Noyes to do some

19

work with complex ions. I do not now remember just what I should have done, but what I think I did was just to prepare a very long list of molecules or ions, an activity which had no research value and which greatly disappointed Professor Noyes. It also made my father very unhappy. He apparently had had high hopes that I might turn out to be a good research chemist.

Later, in my senior year, however, I did carry out a satisfactory small piece of research in organic chemistry with Professor J.F. Norris. The results were published in 1920 in *Journal of the American Chemical Society*. Although the work (combining alcohols with halogen acids to form chlorides or bromides) was pretty simple, it was fun. I also found it interesting to smell the various compounds and to look for resemblances or differences in the odors of similar or related compounds. I have always been fond of colors and odors and, for the latter, I feel I am somewhat of a dog.

For a while I wondered whether I should stick to chemistry, or perhaps go into chemical engineering. As a result, I took two courses in the latter subject area, and rather enjoyed them. This experience certainly broadened my views, even though eventually I settled on pure science.

In those days, the only way to get to MIT from my home in Newburyport was by public transportation. First I commuted to Boston on the Boston and Maine Railroad. There were through trains to Boston from Portsmouth, New Hampshire and points further north in Maine and New Hampshire. The line to Boston ran through Salem and Lynn and other Massachusetts cities nearer to Boston than Newburyport. One day, returning home, the train went through the middle of a conflagration which destroyed much of the city of Salem, while leaving the tracks sufficiently clear so that the train could get through. Somedays I went to Boston on the "western division," a slower alternative to the main line. This went through especially attractive scenery and several interesting small towns.

After arriving at the North Station in Boston, I took the subway to reach my classes. These were in Boston for the first two years, then in Cambridge after MIT had moved there across the Charles River. The subways were relatively new and had a fresh smell which I enjoyed. My father likewise commuted to MIT during the many years when he was a professor there.

During perhaps my last summer at MIT, I had a delightful experience in the Chemical Engineering Practice School. This consisted in spending a week at each of several industrial sites where chemical operations were carried on. At a chemical factory near Boston, sulfuric and hydrochloric acids were being made. In those days, atmospheres were not regulated as now, and on entering the sulfuric acid department, the air was suffocatingly loaded with sulfur dioxide, perhaps a hundred times what the law now allows in our cities. In the hydrochloric acid department, the air was so loaded with acid that it actually tasted sweet. Another visit was to a coke-oven site. Here coal was roasted to make into coke plus a variety of organic chemicals which were driven out by the heat. In Maine we visited a sulfite pulp mill where logs were ground up and the resulting soup spread out to make paper. Again in Maine, we visited a plant where chlorine and caustic soda (sodium hydroxide) were made from salt. Caustic soda solutions can chew up wool, and one amusing sight on the side of a big pool of caustic soda solution was a pair of flannel trousers with the legs half gone where the caustic had eaten them. All these industrial establishments had their characteristic odors which I greatly enjoyed, and there were many fascinating details of construction and operation. This valuable experience broadened my outlook on business and industry. However, I decided to go on for a Ph.D. in basic research.

While I was at MIT, I wondered at times, as no doubt everyone does, what life is all about. I discussed this one day with a sympathetic professor, a very fine person, W.K. Lewis, one of whose classes I attended in chemical engineering. In class a favorite comment of his was "hell's bells." Apparently this seemed to him a suitable characterization of some of the suprising things that nature exhibits in some engineering processes. I was disappointed in my discussion with him about life. He suggested that I adopt a pragmatic attitude. I think I concluded that I had been too idealistic and decided to make the best of things in my still largely dehumanized condition.

IV

World War I

At the time I graduated from MIT in 1917, this country had entered World War I. I then accepted a wartime job at American University in Washington, D.C. which at that time seemed appropriate for a chemist. The work was with poison gases, probably to try to improve the chemical steps in their manufacture. J.B. Conant, later well known as a chemist and administrator, was in charge. If I remember correctly he was then in uniform as a lieutenant in the Chemical Warfare Service (CWS). I think I had some good ideas about the chemical preparation of mustard gas, but was too timid to talk to him about them.

The laboratory consisted of one not very large room. It contained samples of a variety of poison gases, including sneeze and tear gases, chlorine, hydrocyanic acid, and mustard gas. Most of these are not really gases, but liquids or solids which became gaseous on heating. Hydrocyanic acid is a volatile liquid. A supply of it was kept in a large open bowl. One day I took in a deep breath of the vapor above the bowl, but then breathed it out quickly. No harm resulted, but undoubtedly my action was indiscreet.

I was a civilian in this laboratory for some months, but was finally put into the CWS. This meant that I got an ill-fitting uniform and had to go out and drill every day. My father was a major in the CWS dealing with the handling of classified reports. He was stationed at some other location, so that I rarely, if ever, saw him.

Meantime a few things had happened. I lived in a boarding house with some of my fellow-scientists. Somewhere I met a very lovely girl whom I hoped to see more of. All I remember now is one happy canoe trip on the Potomac River. Fate cut off further meetings. It took the form of an accident, one day, when I was working with mustard gas. My technique was inexcusably faulty; I was not a good experimenter and did not properly exercise the discipline that I thought I had learned in quantitative analysis. As a result, I spent six months in the hospital recovering from a very severe burn, which required a skin graft.

That summer at the hospital it was very hot, going up to 106°F one day. This was before the time of air conditioning. I had as an amiable roommate a policeman whose foot had been badly mangled in a traffic accident. Every now and then his doctor, a police doctor, came in to see him. Some other doctors came in occasionally, and it was clear that they disapproved of the management of my roommate's case by his doctor. These other doctors very evidently thought that an amputation should have been performed before the gangrene went further. But apparently the police doctor was not convinced. Finally he let things go until my roommate died. I surmised that it was medical ethics (Alt.: medical courtesy. Ed.) which prevented the other doctors from doing anything about the situation.

After I got out of the hospital, I was assigned to a different laboratory where we studied the size of suspended particles as related to the intensity of a Tyndall beam. Several of us published a paper on the results. Among other carriers of suspended particles, we used cigarette smoke.

When Armistice Day arrived, we and our allies celebrated it with an avid and immense relief of a quality and intensity which one cannot now conceive. We felt most deeply that we could resume normal life again.

However, soon the very severe 1918 influenza epidemic appeared and I was again in the hospital for some time. After that, I was discharged from the CWS as a private first class. Why "first class" I did not know. Formally at least, I was now a veteran of World War I. Now I was ready for a job.

V

A Job with the New Jersey Zinc Company

Soon I was working as a chemist for the New Jersey Zinc Company in Palmerton, Pennsylvania. This was in "Pennsylvania Dutch" country. A young woman and I had the job of doing chemical analysis. I hoped my work was satisfactory but I longed to do something more like research. The laboratory director was very kind when I told him about this and soon I was doing experiments mixing carbon black or zinc oxide into rubber, and testing the results. I don't remember the details but I rather enjoyed the work.

I lived in a boarding house which perhaps belonged to the company. While there I learned to play poker and bought a share in a used car. I had a roommate who was generally reasonable but finally persuaded me to lend him $50 which he never returned. Occasionally there were dances attended by company managers and employees and wives or girl friends, and I took part in some of these. On the whole, my life was enjoyable.

In my private thoughts from time to time I went on from my high school dehumanized point of view. I decided that life rationally considered seems pointless and futile, but still it is interesting in a variety of ways, including the study of science. So why not carry on, following a path of scientific hedonism? Besides, I did not have the courage for the more rational procedure of suicide—I have never understood why suicide by a healthy person is classified as cowardly. Some brilliant young men *have* had the courage. And also, I thought, just possibly the other people who think that human life accomplishes something worthwhile may be wiser than I. Incidentally, I feel rather certain that if I had been born in an age of faith, I would have become an eloquent preacher like my ancestor Rev. Jonathan Parsons. (9).

VI

The University of Chicago

Meantime, having tentatively settled my views on human life, I made arrangements to go to the University of Chicago to obtain a Ph.D. In high school I had discussed electrons in my graduation essay, but it now seemed to me that the subject that most deserved attention was that of atomic nuclei. Rutherford in England had recently shown that an atom contains at its center a small heavy nucleus around which electrons must move, and Bohr had presented some very important ideas as to how the electrons in an atom may move in orbits like planets around the sun. Atomic nuclei should have been a subject of interest to physicists, but in this country the only person I knew of who had shown interest in atomic nuclei was a physical chemist, William D. Harkins, at the University of Chicago. I don't know why American physicists were not yet interested in atomic nuclei. For one, I think physicists at that time in general, and as students at MIT, had somewhat old-fashioned training.

Somehow I had learned that Chicago was one of the best places for graduate work. I must then have sent them information and an application for admission to the graduate school. I don't remember having written to Harkins. But with help from favorable recommendations I got a fellowship to help support me at the University of Chicago. I arrived in Chicago in the fall of 1919. The New Jersey Zinc people expressed disappointment at my leaving them.

Central to chemistry is the periodic table of the chemical elements. Bohr, using his ideas about electrons in orbits in atoms, had

26

recently given a brilliant general explanation of the periodic system which I had read with great interest. Appproximately 90 chemical elements were then known. Every atom has of course a definite weight, but some of them had been shown, especially in the work of the mass spectroscopist F.W. Aston, to consist of two or more isotopes. (Isotopes are atoms with the same number of protons but different numbers of neutrons, thereby differing in atomic weight. Ed.) For example, chlorine has two isotopes of atomic weights 35 and 37 on a scale in which the weight of the lightest known atom, the hydrogen atom, is approximately 1.

Professor Harkins had studied the weights of the known atoms and also their abundances on earth and in the sun and had been reaching interesting conclusions on how the heavier atoms might be built in part out of lighter particles, such as hydrogen nuclei or other particles of mass 1. Later the neutron, of mass 1 but with no charge, was discovered as just such a building block in going from one isotope to another. In my reading of Harkins' papers, it seemed to me that he almost (but not quite) saw the neutron as such a building block.

Harkins was interested in the possibility of partially "separating" (really of unmixing) the isotopes of an element like chlorine (Cl) which is a mixture of isotopes (10). I have been told that his interest may have been aroused by a suggestion from the well-known physical chemist Washburn. When I arrived in Chicago, a student was already working with Harkins on the separation of the chlorine isotopes by letting chlorine diffuse through a porous tube. Or rather, he mostly used hydrogen chloride (HCl), which served the purpose better because it contains just one chlorine atom. Although chemically they are practically identical, the HCl molecules containing the light chlorine isotope move faster than those with the heavier isotope and should get through a suitable diffusion membrane, that is, a thin porous wall or sheet, in relatively greater number. This is shown by well-established and thoroughly understood theory. Thus the collection of molecules that got through should be enriched in the lighter isotope, and those that remained behind should be enriched in the heavier isotope. By repeating the process many times the enrichments can be steadily increased. By such a process uranium can now be enriched to increase the amount of the lighter isotope U^{235} which is active in nuclear fission.

When I arrived at Chicago, I told Professor Harkins that I would like to work with him, but did not explain why. As a result, he set

27

me to work on a project concerned with surface tension. Besides his work on atomic nuclei, he was very interested and a leader in this quite different field. Apparently I was too timid to object and tell him I wanted to work with something more related to nuclei. So at first I worked on surface tension.

While this was not uninteresting, I finally told Harkins what I really wanted to do and he then proposed that I try to check and perhaps improve on some recent work of Brönsted and von Hevesy in Denmark. They had obtained a partial unmixing of the isotopes of the well-known element mercury, a liquid metal which can be evaporated by moderate heating. Mercury has several isotopes ranging from 197 to 204 in atomic weight. The accepted atomic weight of ordinary mercury is 200.61, which is an average of the atomic weights of the several isotopes, each weighted by its abundance.

I proceeded with enthusiasm to undertake this project and also to study and further work out the theories for several methods of isotope separation. Here, as already mentioned, a better word than separation would be enrichment. In any process of partial separation, what is really done is to separate the original material into two samples, in one of which the lighter isotopes are enriched and in the other, the heavier isotopes. While working on these theories I was also, with important advice from Professor Harkins, designing equipment to do isotope-enrichment experiments on some very carefully purified mercury. I designed, but following normal procedure, the Chemistry Department's glassblower with his special experience and skills, actually made the apparatus. It was of pyrex glass and was relatively simple. The apparatus most used is shown in Fig. 1. Liquid mercury was placed in the basin B of a hollow vessel. All possible air was pumped out at A, through which also the mercury could be put in. F indicates a large glass cylinder filled with ice surrounding C. The mercury at B was then heated by a flame which caused it to evaporate and rise to be condensed on the roof C. The slope of C was made sufficient so that the condensed mercury did not fall back into B but ran into a circular trough indicated by D. The trough had an exit attached to a receiver E. The fraction of the original mercury collected in E (the "condensate") had been enriched in the lighter isotopes while that which remained in B (the "residue") had been enriched in the heavier isotopes. The theory back of this non-equilibrium evaporation is that, in the absence of any air or any accumulation of mercury vapor, the atoms evaporating from B go directly to C and are

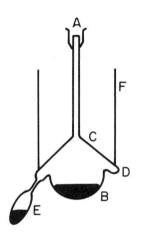

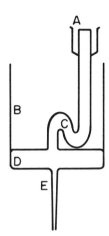

Fig. 1. Cross section of evaporator for the separation of isotopes.

Fig. 2. Cross section of efficient evaporator for the separation of isotopes.

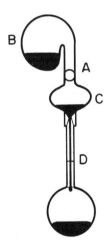

Fig. 3. Pycnometer.

condensed there, under which circumstances the lighter isotopes move faster than the heavier ones so that more of them get to C. Fig. 2 shows a more efficient apparatus which, however, proved to be too expensive to use very much because it required something colder than ice water for condensing the evaporated mercury.

The problem of comparing the atomic weights of the condensate and residue atoms was solved, as proposed by Professor Harkins,

29

by using a pycnometer (Fig. 3). This was so constructed that a definite known volume of mercury could be placed in the pycnometer bulb and then weighed. Samples of equal volume from (A) the original material, (B) the condensate, and (C) the residue could easily be weighed to high accuracy, and showed differences as expected: increased weight in the residue and decreased weight in the condensate. The ratios of these weights to that of the original material are rather obviously proportional to the atomic weights of the three samples and therefore show the extents of enrichment of the heavy and light, residue and condensate, samples. In a typical run, the atomic weight of the light fraction was decreased 29 p.p.m. (parts per million or 29 millionths) at the beginning of the run, while if half the sample was evaporated (a "cut" of 2), the atomic weight was decreased about 20 p.p.m. for the light and increased about 20 p.p.m. for the heavy fraction. The pycnometer measurements were accurate to about 1 p.p.m. By subjecting the material from a single separation operation to further similar operations, larger increases and decreases were obtained. By making four successive cuts of approximately 2, on both light and heavy fractions, a decrease of 64 p.p.m. or 0.013 units of atomic weight, was obtained in the lightest fraction, and a corresponding increase of 69 p.p.m. or 0.014 units on the extreme heavy fraction.

This work resulted in a long article, "a paper," which was sent to the *Journal of The American Chemical Society* about September 1, 1921, and soon published there (pages 37 to 65) in the January 1922 issue. As is customary with scientific papers, the Journal first sent it to a reviewer for possible criticism and an appraisal as to whether it was worth publishing. Evidently in this case the reviewer must have approved it very quickly. In sending the manuscript to the Journal, the authors were listed as Robert S. Mulliken and William D. Harkins with my name first indicating that I had done most of the work. Of course it was right that Harkins' name was there too, since he had made the original suggestion of doing the experiment on mercury, and later contributed important advice or suggestions.

The second half of the paper described the experimental work and results, while the first half dealt with the "theory of resolution of isotopic mixtures by diffusion and similar processes." It contained some useful new equations and definitions applicable to isotopic mixtures in general. The theory for mixed isotopes diffusing through a suitable membrane is practically identical with that for non-equilibrium evaporation. I also discussed other methods requiring different theories.

The article just described was accepted by the Chemistry Department in 1921 as fulfilling their Ph.D. requirements for a piece of good original research. However, I had also to pass an examination on my knowledge of chemistry, especially physical chemistry, since my research was in that part of chemistry. Nowadays there are both written and oral examinations before a student is granted a Ph.D. What I remember is only an oral examination. On this I thought the examining professors were disappointed, especially in my understanding of thermodynamics. However, they recommended me for a Ph.D. "cum laude." When I started work for the degree, I had said I would like to get through quickly, and that was accomplished. However, as I realized afterward, it might have been better if I had stayed longer to build a better understanding of physical chemistry.

Before I had finished the Ph.D. research, I began to think what I should do next. At that time the National Research Council was awarding a few postdoctoral fellowships to promising candidates to do independent research. Each candidate made a proposal describing a plan of research and telling where he would like to go to do it. I was enthusiastic about extending my Ph.D. work to get bigger isotope separations with mercury using more elaborate equipment and methods. I proposed to stay at Chicago to do this. The Council awarded the fellowship, with an adequate stipend and so I went ahead. From this experience I learned that working as an independent postdoctoral fellow, not supervised by a professor or anyone else, is one of the best routes toward becoming a successful research scientist recognized all over the world. I will postpone telling what I did until I have told something more about my life in Chicago in 1919–1923.

After first arriving in Chicago, I became a member of the Gamma Alpha graduate scientific fraternity, and lived and had meals in the Gamma Alpha house. Other members were working in various branches of science. The arrangement was a happy one. After lunch I usually played bridge, which I found an interesting game, although I finally gave it up as too time consuming. I continued to live there as a postdoctoral fellow. Nowadays (1981) Gamma Alpha still goes on, but admits women graduate students as well as men. While I was a student, hold-up men tried to rob me. The first time, they (two men) got $2. The second time when I had $15, I walked past the would-be robber, who seemed slow-witted; also there were people only half a block away.

As a student I was greatly interested not only in separating

31

isotopes, but also in the ideas of the great chemist G.N. Lewis, then a professor at the University of California at Berkeley. I went to the chemistry library where I read Lewis' papers on the shapes of atoms and how they form molecules by sharing or transferring electrons. I also read related papers by Langmuir. Some people spoke of the Lewis–Langmuir theory, but really, I concluded, it was mostly Lewis' although Langmuir was rather assertive. Although I was now interested with Harkins in nuclei, I was also still very interested in electrons as I had been in high school. Now, with G.N. Lewis as a guide, I could learn more about what electrons were doing in molecules, a subject which later led me to work which won a Nobel prize.

I attended a regular series of lectures on organic chemistry by Professor Julius Stieglitz but felt I had already learned at MIT most of what he had to say.

I needed very much to learn more mathematics but most unfortunately never did. To be sure, I did attend one course given by Professor A. C. Lunn but which unfortunately consisted only of a rather useless series of commentaries. Harkins told me that Lunn had sent in a paper to the *Physical Review* which contained the essence of the new quantum mechanics, but that it was turned down. He also told me that Lunn never tried to get it published elsewhere which I thought very regrettable.

At that time Professor H. I. Schlesinger was doing interesting work on the then little-known boron hydride, B_2H_6; this was then a puzzling molecule as to its structure but also was difficult to work with experimentally. I also particularly enjoyed a very informative course, or series of seminars, by Professor Schlesinger on a great variety of oxides of nitrogen which at the time greatly stimulated my interest in strange molecules.

As a student, among other things I took two physics courses with Robert A. Millikan, a Nobel prize winner. He introduced me to the old quantum theory, which seemed to me an awful mess, but Millikan was full of enthusiasm. Actually, the old quantum theory was an awkward but valuable transition stage toward the revolutionary new theory called quantum mechanics. This first appeared in 1925–26, and is now accepted as correct by all scientists because its explanations and predictions have fitted the results of innumerable experiments.

Being interested in isotopes, I went over to the Physics Department one day, where Professor A.J. Dempster had a mass spectrograph with which individual isotopes of various elements could be identified, as J.J. Thompson and F.W. Aston had done in England. But as already mentioned, this could be done only with a few atoms at a time, and so could not be used for separating isotopes on a large scale. I believe it was Dempster who first discovered the uranium isotopes U^{235} and U^{238}, of which it turned out later that U^{235}, present in small proportions, was the isotope needed for nuclear fission. When Dempster found that I was working with Harkins, he refused to show me his apparatus. He apparently thought I was a spy for Harkins, who sometimes undertook research on things that were usually done by physicists.

Harkins was a very good scientist, who I believe was not appreciated as much as he deserved (11). The reason was, I think, that he too often got into disputes with other scientists working in the same field, in particular, in surface tension and related matters, and claimed that they had not given him proper credit for his work. I think that his concerns were exaggerated and created unnecessary antagonism. Sometimes he was accused of plagiarism. I believe that this was incorrect, but Harkins was often very quick to adopt methods used by others. This could perhaps be called very eager imitation or quick pursuit of new methods, but not plagiarism. Soon after Lawrence invented the cyclotron, Harkins built one, the first in Chicago.

Most research scientists when writing articles to report their work are careful to mention others who have already done similar or related work. Science grows largely by a scientist building on the previous work of other scientists, making improvement, additions, or innovations, often small, but sometimes large. Quite naturally scientists like to have their contributions appreciated and acknowledged. Sometimes this is not done and there are arguments or disputes. Regarding Harkins, one man who did express appreciation of his ideas on the constitution of nuclei was the famous Sir Ernest Rutherford in England, the leader in experiments which greatly advanced our understanding of atoms and their nuclei. Near the end of his life, when I was again in Chicago, I often had lunch with Harkins. One day he spoke of my success in research as greater than his own. I am not sure he was right, but in any event I felt that one should not judge him by his earlier complaints that he had not been given proper credit for some of the things that he did. He was a very good scientist, and I am sure I learned much from him.

As a National Research Council (NRC) postdoctoral fellow at Chicago, I set out eagerly to get much increased separation (or enrichments) of the mercury isotopes, and had considerable success. The paper I then wrote was called "Application of Systematic Fractionation in a High-Speed Evaporation-Diffusion Apparatus." For this work, I devised a new type of apparatus, which combined irreversible evaporation with diffusion. I had six like units to increase the rate of progress. In each unit, I heated and evaporated the mercury in the same way as in Fig. 1, except that instead of condensing it on a cold roof I let it go on up into a water-cooled cylindrical glass tube, inside of the middle section of which was a tube made from a thin sheet of filter paper, a type of porous paper used by chemists. Through this, part of the mercury vapor could diffuse and, after being condensed on the surrounding water-cooled glass tube, could run down and be collected below. The lighter atoms diffused more rapidly than the heavier ones through the paper membrane and the resulting diffusate was collected in a trough below, much as in the earlier experiments illustrated in Fig. 1. The theory for diffusion is practically the same as that for irreversible evaporation. The remaining undiffused vapor went on up, was cooled and condensed on the water-cooled glass top part of the tube, above the paper membrane, and fell back into the basin from which it had been evaporated. After a time the operation of the unit was interrupted. The diffusate and residue were then emptied and put into bottles, and later introduced into appropriate units of the apparatus for further treatment. The final result was a collection of increasingly heavier and lighter fractions. Each of the units combined two isotope separation effects—a not very efficient separation in the evaporation step followed by a more efficient separation in the diffusion step. The combined operation gave a higher over-all efficiency than either step alone.

The whole thing I called an "isotope factory" and I was very proud of my progress in collecting more and more samples of heavier and lighter mercury. I felt at this time that I had at last become a respectable experimental scientist. Also I thought that perhaps in building a set of six units with systematic procedures for using them in cooperation, I was benefitting from my two courses in chemical engineering at MIT.

During the year of my postdoctoral fellowship, I also wrote several papers besides the one on the isotope factory. They were all soon published. I was much interested in considering various isotope separation methods which might be useful. One paper was on "The Separation of Isotopes by Thermal and Pressure Diffusion," in which I discussed thermal diffusion but concluded it was not very promising. Instead, I advocated the use of a centrifuge. The heavier isotopes could concentrate on the periphery of a rotating centrifuge and the lighter ones in the middle. I tried the method in a simple experiment which was unsuccessful because of vibration. But subsequently centrifuge methods were used successfully to separate the isotope U^{235}.

I also wrote on "The Separation of Isotopes by Distillation and Analogous Processes." I was surprised to find that when mercury is distilled without special precautions and even in the presence of air, there is an easily measured enrichment of the lighter isotopes in the distillate and of the heavier ones in the residue. The effect was greatest if the mercury surface in the distillation flask was dirty—the dirt apparently acted like a diffusion membrane. The flask used was a glass vessel with a spout which was water cooled to condense the vapor as it came out.

Being very enthusiastic about getting big separations from my isotope factory, I asked the National Research Council if they would renew my fellowship for another year. They replied that I had been separating isotopes at Chicago long enough and indicated that they might renew my fellowship if I would do something different and in another place. Anxious to continue independent research of some kind, I proposed to go to Cambridge, England, to work in Lord Rutherford's laboratory; I suggested work on β-ray spectra. The fellowship board wrote back that I didn't know enough about the experimental work needed, or about physics, for this, but indicated that I should suggest something else.

A friend, Norman Hilberry, who was studying physics, helped me with some suggestions which led me to look for isotope effects in the spectra of molecules.

A spectrum is a record made by a spectrograph, an instrument of which there are many varieties. This instrument sends light of different wave lengths or frequencies into different locations on a suitable recording instrument which in most of the work I shall describe was a photograph. The light may be visible light of any color or invisible light of either longer (infrared or microwave) or shorter (ultraviolet or x-ray) wave length. But most of what follows concerns visible or ultraviolet light.

The photographic spectrum of a diatomic molecule usually contains a series of lines in groups called bands. Some bands do not consist of sharp lines but are continuous. Each line is really an image of a short narrow slit through which the light has entered the spectrograph. The instrument sends images for different frequencies of light to different locations on the photographic plate, where the various images appear as lines. The positions of these spectrum lines are then carefully measured and compared with some standard lines which are included in the spectrum. One also makes a note of how strong each line is.

Then using the quantum theory, the energy equivalent of each line is interpreted as that for a jump between two of the usually very numerous energy levels of an atom or molecule. Each spectrum line is a result of the atom or molecule jumping from a higher to a lower energy level, or vice versa. Spectra in which the jump is down to a lower level are called emission spectra (black lines); those when it is up are called absorption spectra (white lines on a dark background). The former are obtained by observing light which comes from a hot or electrically excited source. The latter are obtained by seeing what wave lengths are removed from a beam of light on passing through the substance being studied. When the spectrum is suitably analyzed, energy values are obtained for some of the energy states of the molecule.

In the case of diatomic molecules (molecules made up of 2 atoms, such as N_2 and O_2) their quantized states have in general a three-fold character: (1) besides the lowest (ground) state, there are electronic levels in which one or more electrons are excited from their condition in the ground state of the molecule; (2) for each electronic level, there are many states of vibration of the molecule, each indexed by a vibrational quantum number which can vary in steps of 1; (3) for any electronic and vibrational level, there is a rotational quantum number which measures the extent of rotation of the molecule. Then in many cases there are other finer details.

When electrons are excited, the resulting spectra, called electronic spectra, are usually in the visible or ultraviolet region. It is possible, however, to have a spectrum in which only vibrations and/or rotations are excited. Spectra which involve only such excitation are exemplified by vibration—rotation bands in the infrared region. Polyatomic molecules have much more complicated spectra, some of which I studied after I had become well acquainted with those of diatomic molecules.

Isotope effects had already been found in 1920 by F.W. Loomis in this country and A. Kratzer in Germany in the infrared absorption spectrum of HCl (hydrogen chloride). The HCl spectrum showed two distinct sets of spectrum lines for the two isotopes HCl^{35} and HCl^{37}, where Cl^{35} and Cl^{37} are the isotopes of chlorine with respective atomic weights 35 and 37. Just such an isotope effect was predicted by the old quantum theory.

It now occurred to me that isotope effects might be found also in some diatomic *electronic* spectra. After looking at published papers on molecules whose atoms were known to have isotopes, I found one by Wilfred Jevons, an English physicist, on a visible spectrum of boron nitride. Now boron was known to have two isotopes, B^{10} and B^{11}, with relative abundance 1:5. There were strong bands which Jevons had identified, and weaker ones which he had not classified. I concluded that the stronger bands belong to $B^{11}N$ and found that the weaker bands then fitted very well into corresponding sets for $B^{10}N$. The isotope effect is a manifestation mainly of the fact that the vibrational levels of the two isotopes must differ since they depend on the vibration frequencies. These should differ considerably for $B^{10}N$ and $B^{11}N$ because, although their electronic constitutions and the forces between B and N should be practically identical, the different masses of the two boron isotopes would necessarily result in different frequencies of vibration.

VII

NRC Postdoctoral Fellowship at Harvard, 1923–1925

I therefore proposed to the National Research Council that I should go to the Jefferson Physical Laboratory at Harvard to investigate isotope effects in boron–nitride bands and other band spectra, as diatomic molecular spectra were then called. This time they agreed. I chose Harvard because the the well-known spectroscopist Professor F.A. Saunders was there and the Physics Department had good spectrographs including one with a 21-foot grating; also because Professor E.C. Kemble, an expert on quantum theory and interested in my project, was there. In fact, Professor Kemble with co-authors R.T. Birge of the University of California at Berkeley, F.W. Loomis of New York University, W.A. Colby of the University of Michigan, and Leigh Page of Yale were preparing a report for the National Research Council on the status of work on diatomic molecular spectra. Various authors (especially Deslandres and Fortrat in France, and Hulthén in Sweden and Birge in America) had already made important experimental and interpretive contributions to the subject, but it was still in a disorganized, early stage of development, including features not understood by the old quantum theory. Although on arrival at Harvard in 1923 I knew practically nothing about spectroscopy, Professor Saunders showed me what to do, and I was soon at work making, measuring, and interpreting diatomic spectra. I was lucky that the subject was just ripe for such work and for the development of new understanding, which I soon undertook.

I was also lucky in knowing how Dr. Jevons got his BN spectrum. Namely, he produced it by letting a little BCl_3 (boron chloride) into a stream of "active nitrogen." This is produced from ordinary nitrogen gas, which can be easily obtained in a tank under high pressure, after it has flowed through a tube in which it has been subjected to a suitable electrical discharge. The gas is then led into another tube, the afterglow tube, where it glows with a bright yellow color. Active nitrogen is now explained by the fact that the electrical discharge breaks up many of the diatomic molecules (N_2) into nitrogen (N) atoms. These atoms gradually recombine to N_2, giving out the yellow glow, which is part of the usual N_2 spectrum. After the discharges many atoms remain for some seconds or even longer to give the afterglow. Then if another substance is introduced these atoms attack it to make new molecules. These are in excited states and give out bright spectra.

Figure 4 shows the arrangement of the apparatus. The nitrogen is let into the long pyrex glass tube at the right, going in through the lower of the two stopcocks. The lower side of the long tube (the "discharge tube") has two bulbous attachments into each of which is sealed a piece of tungsten wire. The two wires are connected to a source of electricity which sends a current from one to the other through the nigrogen gas which is flowing rapidly to the left through the discharge tube. It then passes through the light trap T and into the afterglow tube at left. The light trap removes some unwanted light of the normal N_2 spectrum produced in the discharge tube.

At the near end of the afterglow tube the window Q is sealed with hard wax. Beyond this is attached a bulb B containing the substance

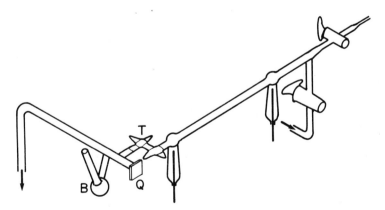

Fig. 4. Arrangement of discharge and afterglow tube for exciting spectra by means of active nitrogen.

which is to be introduced into the active nitrogen in the afterglow tube. As I was very lucky to learn, many different spectra can be obtained by introducing various substances. This was not my discovery; I learned it by reading (as Jevons did) about Lord Rayleigh's earlier experiments. I used it to obtain a number of interesting spectra, some showing isotope effects.

Depending on whether the substance to be introduced into the active nitrogen is a solid or a liquid, bulb B is heated or cooled to control the rate at which the substance enters the afterglow tube. Near the point where it enters there is a bright glow like a flame. A spectrograph is lined up so that this glow enters it through the window Q and its spectrum is photographed. This spectrum also contains some N_2 and NO bands from the afterglow spectrum but these are relatively weak and can be allowed for and so usually cause no trouble. In the work with BN, liquid BCl_3 was placed in bulb B and cooled so that it evaporated slowly. In another investigation which I did, solid CuI (copper iodide) was placed in B and heated very strongly. In this case the spectrum produced was that of CuI including several sets of bands of the two isotopes $Cu^{63}I$ and $Cu^{65}I$ together with many spectrum lines of the copper (Cu) atoms. Since the wavelengths of these atom lines are well known, they were used as standards in making the measurements on the CuI bands.

One of the first things I did at Harvard was to make new photographs of Jevons' BN bands, and to measure and analyze them. My measurements generally agreed well with his, but I found many additional bands, especially of the lighter isotope. I devised formulas which reproduce the frequencies of the bands of each isotope in terms of vibrational quantum numbers. Each individual band is characterized by two vibrational quantum numbers, one (n') for the upper and one (n'') for the lower electronic state. Each band can then be labelled by n', n''. Of special interest is the "origin" or (0,0) band. This is often called the "null line." This band, involving no vibration, might have been expected to have practically the same frequency for the isotopes $B^{10}N$ and $B^{11}N$. However, that was not quite true here. I found, instead, that if we assume that the smallest vibrational quantum numbers are not 0 but $\frac{1}{2}$, the difference in frequency between the origin bands of the two isotopes, now called $(\frac{1}{2}, \frac{1}{2})$, was explained. With this change, and a like addition of $\frac{1}{2}$ for all the vibrations, all the $B^{10}N$ bands fitted fairly well into a formula differing from that for the $B^{11}N$ bands just as predicted by the quantum theory. The coefficients in this formula involve the frequencies of the vibrations, which differ for the two isotopes in a way that can be calculated from the atomic weights of the atoms present (10 and 11 for the boron isotopes, and 14 for nitrogen).

However, I found that there was a very much better fit for the isotope effect if I assumed that the molecule concerned was BO and not BN. For the oxygen atom the atomic weight 16 was used. The change to BO was a surprise but it could be explained by the presence of a little oxygen as an impurity in the active nitrogen. Also if the nitrogen was made unusually pure, the BO bands got much weaker. The results showed that boron atoms even in the presence of many N atoms have a great preference for O atoms and seek them out.

So I had discovered two things: (1) the supposedly BN bands are really BO bands, (2) vibrational energy, at least in BO, comes in half quanta and is never less than one $\frac{1}{2}$ quantum. As people often did at that time when they obtained interesting new results, I sent a letter about them to the editor of the English magazine *Nature*. This was published in 1924. Before long (1925–56) the successful new quantum theory called quantum mechanics had shown that the half quanta and the so-called zero-point energy (i.e., a minimum of $\frac{1}{2}$ quantum) are to be expected for all molecules.

From the preceding discussion of the BO spectrum, I intentionally omitted, for the sake of simplicity, one important fact. Namely, the spectrum contains two types of bands which differ in several ways. The totality of bands of each type is said to form a *band system*. The two BO systems are called α and β systems. As was recalled earlier, every molecule has a ground or normal electronic state, and a number of excited electronic states, each electronic state having an assembly of vibrational and rotational energy levels. The bands in a particular band system differ with respect to their upper and lower vibrational quantum numbers n' and n'' but all belong to the same electronic jump or transition. The α and β bands of BO have different upper electronic states but both have the ground electronic state as lower levels.

Each β band has a single head, but each α band has four heads, in two rather close pairs. A comparison with the spectra of atoms is instructive. For example, the Na (sodium) atom spectrum has a pair of yellow lines which correspond to transitions from two related upper states called $^2P_{1/2}$ and $^2P_{3/2}$ (together, ^2P, to be read as "doublet P") to the ground state called ^2S (doublet S). The explanation of the four heads of the bands of BO is two-fold: (1) The upper electronic state of the molecule is a doublet state later called a $^2\Pi$ state, somewhat similar to the ^2P state of the Na atom; (2) for each of the two components of the $^2\Pi$ state, namely $^2\Pi_{1/2}$ and $^2\Pi_{3/2}$ there are two heads which can be explained as belonging to two "branches," an R and a Q branch.

A "branch" is a series of band lines all alike with respect to the *jump* which the *rotational* quantum number makes. The rotational number jump is 1 for an R branch, 0 for a Q branch. The rotational quantum numbers for each vibrational state have whole or half number values, starting from a small number near the null line and increasing by 1 from each line to the next. Whole or half integral values occur depending on whether the number of atoms in the molecules is even or odd. At first the lines in a branch get stronger, up to a maximum as we move away from the null line; and then get weaker until they fade away. Besides the R branch there is also a P branch with jump -1. In our bands the P branch does not form a head, but is made up of the band lines on the side of the null line away from the head that is seen. In a typical band, the lines get closer and closer together in either the P or the R branch until a head is reached, after which the lines start coming back toward and perhaps beyond the null line. In some bands the P branch forms a head, in others the R branch. The theory shows that the spacings of the band lines depend on whether the molecule has a larger or smaller distance, R_e, between its two nuclei in the upper or in the lower electronic state. By measurement of the positions of the band lines, it is possible to deduce the R_e of the molecule in both of these states. The band systems of all diatomic molecules contain P and R branches, but only some of them contain a Q branch or branches. The β bands of BO, and the SiN bands, have only P and R branches.

Besides the BO bands, Jevons had studied a set of SiN (silicon nitride bands. I made a new photograph of these bands, and found that they were best obtained with very pure nitrogen, so they could safely be attributed to SiN. According to Aston, silicon's main isotope is Si^{28} but there are also small amounts of Si^{29} and Si^{30} (this was doubtful). On my photographs, I found both $Si^{29}N$ and $Si^{30}N$ with the former slightly stronger. They can be seen on favorably located bands. In others, they are covered up by the much stronger Si^{28} bands.

In Fig. 5, vibrational quantum numbers $n'n''$ are given for each band. As is typical for diatomic spectra, each band usually starts with a "head" consisting really of several sharp lines which are so close together that the photograph can not show them separately. Then there is a gap, followed by a large number of band lines which in some cases can be seen distinctly, in other cases are largely run together because of crowding in the photograph. Figure 5 shows a number of examples of these effects. The gap is a region where really only one lines is missing (the "null line") but the neighboring lines on both sides are so weak that they do not register in this photograph. In several of the bands in Fig. 5 (most clearly in the 4,5 and 5,6 bands) two weak $Si^{29}N$ and $Si^{30}N$ heads are seen to the left of the main $Si^{28}N$ head. Their positions agree with those calculated from the theory of the vibrational isotope effect.

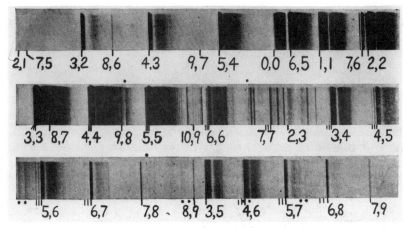

PLATE 1. The entire band spectrum of SiN from λ3986 (top) to λ4800 (bottom).

Fig. 5. SiN spectrum. (Reproduced from Physical Review 26, 319–38 [1925].)

At this point I should mention that the diatomic spectra which have been recorded and analyzed have always been of molecules in the state of gas or vapor, so that each molecule is unaffected by its neighbors, or nearly so. The molecules involved fall into two classes: (1) those that are chemically stable and exist as gases, for example N_2 (nitrogen), CO (carbon monoxide), NO (nitric oxide) and HCl (hydrogen chloride); (2) those often called "radicals" which are only fragments of chemically stable molecules but can be obtained from the latter by the action of thermal excitation, electric discharge or other disrupting mechanism, e.g., active nitrogen. These can exist in excited states long enough to give out spectra, but are very soon removed as a result of chemical action. BO is a radical, so is CN, whose spectrum is easily obtained in active nitrogen or in some electrical discharges. Among other radical spectra are those of positive ions, that is, molecules or radicals which have been deprived of an electron and so have a positive charge. A familiar radical ion is that of CO^+ which gives rise to some well-known band spectra. One group of CO^+ bands is that of the "comet-tail" bands, so-called because they have been seen by astronomers in the spectra of the tails of comets. They are also known in spectroscopic laboratories on earth.

My NRC Fellowship at Harvard was renewed for a second year (1924–25). After that I stayed for one more year with the support of a fund obtained by Dr. Kemble. Holding an NRC Fellowship for three years as I did was unusual. Ordinarily one or two years is considered enough, after which it is time to get a position somewhere.

During part of 1924–26, two other NRC Fellows, F.A. Jenkins (later a professor at the University of California at Berkeley) and H.A. Barton (later Chairman of the American Institute of Physics for some time) came to work with me on band spectra. "Pan" Jenkins, like me, had obtained his Ph.D. with Harkins, but a little later. He had great natural talent as an experimentalist and showed his artistry also in writing.

We worked together on the "red" and "violet" bands of the CN radical, analogous to the α and β bands of BO. We obtained the red bands by introducing CCl_4 (carbon tetrachloride) into active nitrogen, and the violet bands by introducing C_2H_2 (acetylene). The results were published in the *Physical Review*, partly in 1927; later on the violet "tail" bands (Jenkins) and the red bands in 1931–32 (Jenkins, Roots, and Mulliken).

We and Harry Barton obtained the β (visible) and γ (ultraviolet) band systems of NO (nitric oxide) by letting a little air into active nitrogen. The oxygen (O_2) in the air supplies the oxygen content in NO. The β bands are of the type $^2\Pi \to {}^2\Pi$, that is, both the upper and lower electronic states, though different, are of the same type $^2\Pi$. Like the $^2\Pi$ states of BO and CN, each $^2\Pi$ state comprises two subsets, $^2\Pi_{1/2}$ and $^2\Pi_{3/2}$ differing somewhat in energy. The lower of the $^2\Pi$ states is the normal state of the NO molecule. In the spectrum, only $^2\Pi_{1/2}$ to $^2\Pi_{1/2}$ and $^2\Pi_{3/2}$ to $^2\Pi_{3/2}$ transitions occur, each with a P and an R branch, and also a very weak Q branch. The Π bands are of the type $^2\Sigma \to {}^2\Pi$, ending on the same normal-state $^2\Pi_{1/2}$ and $^2\Pi_{3/2}$ states as the β bands.

The molecule NO, which also is found in the exhaust from automobiles, is unusual in being stable even though it has an odd number of electrons. Most other so-called "odd molecules" (e.g., BO, CN, SiN) are chemically unstable radicals. One characteristic of these is that they are all magnetic. Another familiar magnetic molecule is oxygen, O_2. Although not unstable under ordinary circumstances, it becomes chemically active and produces fire when the temperature is high enough, as everyone knows.

During 1926, F.H. Crawford and I photographed a well-known spectrum of the CO molecule (the "Ångstrom bands") under the influence of a magnet. Changes in any spectrum caused by a magnetic field are called the Zeeman effect, after a well-known Dutch physicist. This causes spectrum lines to be slightly split up or shifted, and gives new information about the molecule. Professor Kemble was especially interested in what happened, and discussed the theoretical explanation in a paper which we published jointly with him.

Louis Turner of Princeton and I collaborated on some aspects of the atomic spectra of iodine and mercury. One day we excited the mercury spectrum by introducing mercury vapor into active nitrogen; it had interesting and rather special characteristics, including a cut-off of the spectrum lines above certain energies. But the next morning when we came back we found to our astonishment that the tube we had been using for the experiments just wasn't there anymore. Our conclusion was that mercury nitride must be explosive.

By 1925 or 1926 I had become rather well known as a leader in the understanding of band spectra. I had become a member of the American Chemical Society in 1918, and of the American Physical Society a little later, and gave talks on my work at some of their meetings.

A procedure which I, like other scientists, often followed before sending in a paper for publication was to give a brief presentation at a society meeting, first sending in an abstract which was published with the notice of the meeting. In 1924–26, however, I sent several brief papers to *Nature* and to the *Proceedings of The National Academy of Sciences.* From 1925 on I sent off abstracts of many of my papers on diatomic spectra and structure which were to be presented at Physical Society meetings.

I especially enjoyed going to the spring meeting of the Physical Society which for a good many years was held in rooms at the Bureau of Standards at its former location on Connecticut Avenue in Washington, D.C. I went there to give a paper and to listen to other people's papers, but also to lie on the grass and talk with fellow scientists and sometimes to go inside to talk with scientists at the Bureau. Of special interest to me was the atomic spectroscopy laboratory presided over by William F. Meggers. Here with the collaboration of Charlotte Sitterly, the important tables of atomic energy levels obtained from atomic spectra were prepared for publication. Others whom I visited at the Bureau were Paul Foote and F.L. Mohler who had written a fascinating book called *The Origin of Spectra,* discussing the current state of knowledge of quantum phenomena and their explanation. I also visited the excellent infrared laboratory of Earle Plyler and other laboratories dealing with atomic and molecular phenomena. In 1966, the Bureau moved to a more spacious location in Gaithersburg, Maryland.

Places near Washington at which I visited spectroscopic laboratories included the University of Maryland at College Park, Maryland and the Naval Research Laboratory. Also not far away in Baltimore was Johns Hopkins University.

I was also invited to give two lectures at the University of Toronto, and perhaps other places. One time (perhaps at New York University) I gave a colorful exhibition of active nitrogen, leading it in tubes around the room glowing yellow, but at several points introducing substances into it to give a variety of bright colors.

At one rather prominent eastern university, the head of the Physics Department told me that in general, according to his impressions, only one research project out of a very large number turned out to be successful. I was astonished because in my experiences the success rate seemed to me usually very high, although often with unexpected changes of outcome.

In contrast to my otherwise very modest behavior, I gradually became scientfically aggressive. That is to say, I had no hesitation in promoting scientific ideas which I had, or presenting analyses of band spectra, even when they disagreed with what other well-known spectroscopists had published. Also, I had no hesitation in getting in touch with the most famous spectroscopists and other scientists.

Although I spent much of my time measuring or analyzing band spectra which we at Harvard had photographed, I did much reading to learn what people at other places had done. I had learned enough French and German in high school so that I could readily understand scientific articles in those languages. I looked for, and often found, improvements on previous analyses or interpretations. Through this reading and study, I developed a broad general familiarity with, and understanding of, band spectra as interpreted by the old quantum theory.

Very helpful was a chapter on band spectra in the book *Atombau and Spektrallinien (Atomic Structure and Spectral Lines)* by Professor Arnold Sommerfeld of Munich, Germany. This chapter also helped point the way for me toward an exploration of the relations between molecular and atomic electronic states. Two examples which Sommerfeld cited as showing resemblances of molecular to atomic spectra were certain series of bands in the spectra of the H_2 (hydrogen) and He_2 (helium) molecules.

Much of my attention in 1924–26 was devoted not only to analyzing but also to classifying the bands of various molecules with respect to what types of branches were present in the bands. The process of classification was in terms of answers to the following: (1) were Q branches present as well as P and R branches; (2) was each branch composed of a single set of sharp lines, or was each line a narrow double (or sometimes triple); (3) what pattern or formula did successive lines in a branch follow with respect to intensity as well as frequency; (4) after the null-line which, as already discussed, is a vacant position in a band branch, there are one or two other missing lines; if so, the theory shows that their number and positions give some reliable information as to the kinds of electronic states involved in the band system; (5) does the band system show multiplet structure as in the α bands of BO? Besides the characteristics described above, band branches often have various other special features which give information about the molecular states involved. One such feature is the occurrence of irregularities ("perturbations") in the spacings of the band lines.

Some of the papers I published on these matters in the *Physical Review* in 1926–27 were entitled "Electronic States and Band-spectrum Structure in Diatomic Molecules" with various subtitles referring to CuH, CH, and CO, and other band types, and to intensity relations. Other papers were on the ZnH, CdH, and HgH (zinc, cadmium, and mercury hydride) bands and on the He_2 bands.

Also in 1926 I published a paper in the *Proceedings of the National Academy of Sciences* giving a classification and partial diagnosis of the He_2 bands, based on information which had been published by W.E. Curtis. In interpreting the bands, I assumed that in each band every other line is missing as was first suggested by Dr. Rudolf Mecke, then at Bonn, Germany, later at Freiburg-im-Breisgau. Without making this, at first sight strange, assumption, one would have had to believe some unreasonable things, including incredibly small distances R_e between the atoms in the He_2 molecules. The absence of every other rotational line was a little later explained by quantum mechanics as being a characteristic of molecules composed of two like atoms whose nuclei have zero angular momentum.

Other molecules composed of two like atoms, notably N_2, as shown by Birge, show a similar but less extreme effect, namely an alternation of strength from one line to the next (stronger, weaker, stronger, . . .) in each branch of each band. The extreme case of alternate missing lines occurs only for nuclei with zero angular momentum, as in He_2. In general, the ratio of strengths of alternate lines, as was shown later, can be used to determine the nuclear angular momentum. This quantity differs for isotopic atoms. A molecule composed of two isotopic atoms, e.g., ^{14}N and ^{15}N, shows no alternating intensities.

My efforts toward a better understanding and classification of the structures of bands led naturally to attempts also to understand molecular electronic states as more or less like those of atoms. At first it looked as if the lower energy levels of CN, SiN, CO^+, BO, and others are analogous to those of the sodium atom, and I wrote a paper entitled "On a Class of One Valence Electron Emitters of Band Spectra," published in the *Physical Review*, in November 1925. The sodium atom has one outer valence electron, in addition to electrons in inner shells, and I argued that the molecules mentioned are similar to it. Likewise I pointed out that molecules like CO and N_2 have two valence electrons like the atom Mg (magnesium), and that NO has three like the atom Al (aluminum). Mecke in Bonn, Birge in California, and Sponer in Germany advocated somewhat similar ideas. Incidentally, Birge went so far as to postulate that the electronic states of diatomic molecules could be characterized by symbols ^2S, ^2P, ^3S, ^1S ^1D, etc., the same as those of atoms, and with similar meaning. Although it was not really justifiable, I temporarily adopted this type of symbol for molecular electronic states. Attention to the above-mentioned analysis, developed while using the old quantum theory, soon began to be replaced by a new and really valid understanding of molecules, obtained at first largely by Friedrich Hund, using the new quantum mechanics. By 1928 attention turned to the "aufbau" or "building-up principle" for the allocation of electrons in the structures of diatomic molecules.

Here I should say something about less scientific aspects of my life at Harvard. During my first year there (1923–24) I had two other research scientists as roommates, one a geophysicist, Louis Schlichter, the other Samuel K. Allison, who had obtained his Ph.D. with Harkins shortly after I did and now held a NRC Fellowship to work on X-rays in research related to that of Professor William Duane. Although roommates, we were working in entirely unrelated research fields and were not much together except at mealtimes and bedtimes.

For the next two years (1924–26) John C. Slater and I occupied neighboring rooms at an interesting place near Harvard Square. Our rooms were adjacent to a rail yard where electric cars came in, and their trolleys as they made contact often gave out a bright green light whose spectrum was that of the copper atom. Slater in 1924 had just returned from Europe after spending a year there, mostly at the Theoretical Physics Institute of the great Niels Bohr in Copenhagen. He had obtained his Harvard Ph.D. the year before. We had many scientific discussions and later we both went on to establish well-known laboratories devoted to molecular or atomic problems. In 1925–26, Dr. Harold C. Urey and I had at first planned to room together but our rooming plan fell through at the last moment because he was offered and accepted a position at Johns Hopkins University. Dr. Urey soon became well known for the discovery of deuterium, the heavy isotope of hydrogen for which he received a Nobel prize, and later for studies including the production by electrical discharges of various molecules which might plausibly be responsible for the origin of life on earth.

Other scientists at Harvard in 1923 included John H. Van Vleck, an expert on magnetic phenomena, at that time a recent Harvard Physics Ph.D., and later the recipient of a Nobel prize. My friend Slater in the opinion of many should also have been awarded a Nobel prize, but died in 1976, I believe just too soon. Another physicist who received his undergraduate Harvard degree while we were there was J.R. Oppenheimer.

VIII

England and Europe, 1925

I often corresponded with Professor R.T. Birge in Berkeley on problems and ideas about band spectra. He had been the foremost American worker in this field. In the course of my work, as I have already mentioned, I reported in letters to the magazine *Nature* on my results and conclusions on the BO bands. After I had written that the bands are due to BO, not to BN as Wilfred Jevons at King's College, London had originally supposed, Jevons sent a letter to *Nature* saying that of course the bands are BN not BO. I wrote Birge that I must send another letter to *Nature* emphasizing the reasons why the bands are BO not BN. Birge wrote back "Why don't you write a letter to Jevons instead of to *Nature?*"

Meantime I had been saving for a trip to Europe in the summer of 1925. So I wrote Jevons suggesting I come to see him and talk things over. Before long, after an exciting but tiring steamboat trip over the ocean, I was in London talking with him. Somehow I had also arranged for visits to nearly everybody in Europe who had been doing worthwhile research on band spectra, as well as to other scientists who had been leaders in work on atomic spectra and quantum theory. They were all very kind in welcoming me.

In London, at King's College of the University of London, I met R.C. Johnson, known for his work on certain CO^+ bands, and W.E. Curtis, an authority on the He_2 bands. Johnson later went to the University of Melbourne, Australia and Curtis to the University of Durham at Newcastle-on-Tyne where I visited him later, in 1927. As I was reminded recently on finding an old letter to Curtis in my files, he and I and my old high school friend Charles Stockman hiked together in 1925 through some charming villages along the coast of Cornwall.

Jevons arranged for me to meet Lord Rayleigh, the man who had done much of the early work on active nitrogen. I met him and his young son at breakfast at Rayleigh's house in Russell Square. When I visited Jevons he explained that his proposed letter to *Nature* advocating BN was not really his own idea, but that the department head put him up to it; so we got this matter straightened out. Jevons introduced me to various other spectroscopists in England. I called on A. Fowler, Professor of Astrophysics at Imperial College; he and H. Paschen in Berlin were the leading atomic spectroscopists on that side of the Atlantic. At Oxford, I looked up the distinguished spectroscopist Professor T.R. Merton, who besides being a spectroscopist was a country gentleman. At Cambridge, besides meeting other scientists at various Colleges, I had a pleasant visit with F.W. Aston, with whom I discussed our common interest in isotopes. He also gave me a demonstration along one wall of his college of the techniques of rock-climbing, on a ledge only one foot above the ground.

In France I looked up Dr. F. Baldet at the astronomical observatory of Meudon, near Paris and discussed with him the comet-tail bands of CO^+ on which he had done so much work; there were also the Baldet–Johnson bands which both he and R.C. Johnson had studied. In Paris I became acquainted also with other spectroscopists and their wives: often husband and wife worked together, which besides contributing to science helped them make a living.

My visit in Germany was particularly comprehensive with respect to the number of spectroscopists and other atomic and molecular people whom I met. In Bonn I met Professor H. Kaiser, the author of a well-known many-volume *Handbuch der Spektroskopie (Handbook of Spectroscopy)*. Also at the Physics Institute at Bonn, I met Mecke, whom I have already mentioned, and had some good discussions with him. Finally, there was Professor H. Konen, author of the book *Das Leuchten der Gase und Dämpfe (Lumination of Gases and Vapours)*, which, when I was learning spectroscopy at Harvard, I had found to be an exciting source of most interesting information. Professor Konen invited me to dinner at his house. During dinner a Moroccan soldier walked through the dining room. Professor Konen apologized for this, saying that it was not a matter of his choice, but that a French officer and his orderly had been billeted in his house. This was while the Rhineland was still under French occupation after World War I. From Bonn I went to Munster where I looked up Professor A. Kratzer who in 1920 at the same time as F.W. Loomis, first found the isotope effect in the infrared HCl spectrum. He had also published several other papers on molecular spectra and had cooperated in Sommerfeld's chapter on band spectra.

In Göttingen Professor James Franck was extremely hospitable. I had first learned of the important work of Franck and his friend Herz reading *The Origin of Spectra,* a book written by Foote and Mohler, both of whom at that time were at the Bureau of Standards in Washington, D.C. This book, delightfully written and illustrated, was a splendid source from which at that time to learn of the current state of knowledge on quantum phenomena and their explanation. Professor Franck, as always, was most kind in welcoming me on this visit to Göttingen and introducing me to other members of the brilliant constellation at that university. Associated with Franck's institute were Otto Oldenberg, Hertha Sponer, the Sunshine of the Institute, always cheerful and energetic and filled with ideas, Heinrich Kuhn (subsequently Professor of Spectroscopy at Oxford), and other spectroscopists.

In Max Born's Institute of Theoretical Physics, I was especially interested in talking with Friedrich Hund, who was then Born's assistant. I talked with him extensively about what I had learned about molecular spectra. Hund in 1926–27, while on an International Educational Fellowship in Copenhagen at Bohr's Institute used the then new theory of quantum mechanics to put this and related information into up-to-date forms based on quantum mechanics. In a 1927 paper he described his now well-known cases a, b, c, and d for diatomic rotational energy levels and thereby brought clarity to the problems of band spectrum structure with which I had been struggling using the old quantum theory. He also in this and two further papers brought forward a quantum-mechanical model for molecular electronic states, and what later were called molecular orbitals. This incorporated the ideas that Mecke, Birge, Sponer, and I had put forward in 1925 on the electronic levels of BO, CN, etc.; no doubt I had talked with Mecke about these in 1925. Hund's papers used a united-atom approach, by which is meant thinking in terms of the atoms that one could imagine obtaining by somehow pushing together the two nuclei of the molecule to form a single nucleus.

In Berlin I visited the famous atomic spectroscopist Paschen at the Technische Hochschule. I remember entering the building through some tall, massive doors, and have a recollection of high-ceilinged laboratory rooms where Professor Paschen very kindly showed me around and told me about what he was doing. At the University of Berlin I visited Professor Peter Pringsheim, who was doing some very interesting things with the iodine molecule spectrum, to which in later years I gave much attention. I also met there Dr. Boris Rosen; he was working in association with Professor Pringsheim. I knew him later at Liège, Belgium, where he worked actively and wrote a book on molecular spectra.

In Copenhagen, I found that Professor Bohr was not at his Institute but was at his seaside home in the country. However, he invited me to come up to see him there. Bohr came to the railroad station on his bicycle to meet me. We walked back from there to his house, where I met his five stalwart sons and his charming and remarkable wife, known for her hospitality and sympathy to the many scientists who have been at Bohr's Institute. I asked Bohr's opinion about certain highly excited states of molecules called Rydberg states. (I had been looking into the Rydberg states of the helium molecule and comparing them with those of the helium atom, following up earlier work of Curtis and Fowler.)

From Copenhagen I crossed on the ferry to Lund in Sweden to meet Erik Hulthén, who was then professor at the university there. We talked about band spectra, and he also showed me the ancient cathedral with its massive columns, and especially impressed me with a visit to a cafe where we had all kinds of wonderful drinks (notably Schnapps), and he had the orchestra play the "Star Spangled Banner." I inquired about T. Heurlinger, whose university dissertation in 1919 showed great promise for an understanding of molecular spectra, but learned that he had unfortunately become insane. I was extremely sorry to learn this, but thought I could understand why it could happen, because even before the new flow of insight offered by quantum mechanics, there was already such an overwhelming vista of exciting possibilities of new research and understanding using the old quantum theory.

In my contacts with European scientists in 1925, I always found it easy and natural to establish friendly relations on the basis of our common interest in a better understanding of molecular spectra, especially those they or perhaps we had been working with. In short, this common interest made us comrades, regardless of country, or language or social background. I found it very interesting in this way to meet people of quite varying backgrounds from lords to very ordinary people, and belonging to one country or another. Mostly we talked English; in England of course, but elsewhere too because they could talk English better than I could their language. However, in Germany I was to some extent able to talk in German. In fact, one night I dreamed a little in German. Naturally, besides science, I asked questions about life and opinions in the various countries, and thereby broadened my understanding.

The glorious summer of 1925 ended with a mountain excursion in the Dolomites conducted by Hermann Mark, who has long since been a well-known professor at Brooklyn Polytechnic Institute. His wife Mimi went along, but found it very tiring. Sam Allison, an old friend of Mark's, also went on this excursion, after arranging for my participation.

IX

Assistant Professor of Physics, New York University at Washington Square, 1926–1927

In the fall of 1926, I became Assistant Professor of Physics at the Washington Square branch of New York University (NYU) as a result of a suggestion by Norman Hilberry. I was glad to get started on a normal university career with teaching and research opportunities, and with students. I was not worried about the future. I knew it was good for me to be teaching some courses, thereby learning some things I needed to about physics. Hilberry and I roomed together in the nearby Hotel Earle. The hotel and the university are on the edge of Greenwich Village in Manhattan. This proved interesting. At the time, the 18th amendment to our Constitution made the consumption of alcoholic beverages illegal. However, enforcement was inadequate until finally the amendment was voted out.

At the same time Barton, Jenkins, and I finished up papers on the work we had done at Harvard on the NO bands. I was also writing more theoretical papers on interesting relations among observed spectra.

At NYU I gave some physics courses and had three graduate students doing experimental research on diatomic spectra. We had a good grating spectrograph in the basement. However, everyone working there had to bend over because the head room was only four feet. Of these students, Walter F.C. Ferguson received a Ph.D. in 1929 for work on the SnCl (tin chloride) bands, carrying further some research done by Jevons; and Roger S. Estey received a Ph.D. in 1930 for work on some of the CO (carbon monoxide) bands. A third student, Harold T. Byck, worked on some intriguing CN bands, but got a Ph.D. only later at Johns Hopkins University. However, he came to me still later at Chicago to do research as a National Research Fellow (1930–31).

While I was at NYU, F.W. Loomis was the head of the Physics Department at both branches of NYU, one farther north at "The Heights" as well as that at Washington Square. He and other scientists made an expedition occasionally to an establishment at fashionable Tuxedo Park, N.Y., belonging to Alfred L. Loomis who, besides being a banker in New York, was much interested in physics and biology. He later made important contributions to science, especially in radar as World War II developed. I must have visited his laboratories more than once, but remember just a few small things about a visit or visits there. Running around freely were some green monkeys which the Rockefeller Institute had given to Loomis because they were no longer useful there, having had all the diseases the Institute was studying. I never knew what Loomis might be learning from them. However, I noted that at one time when Professor Duane from Harvard was going through a doorway, one of the monkeys reached down from above and playfully tweaked his nose. At the end of the day we went into the living quarters where Mrs. Loomis presided over a more excellent and elegant dinner than I was accustomed to.

Among others present was the well-known spectroscopist R.W. Wood from Johns Hopkins University. He was a friend of Loomis, and made use of a good spectrograph which he had set up in Loomis' laboratories. Wood was noted for some things besides spectroscopy. One of these is his little book *How to Tell the Birds from the Flowers*. Not all the entries are recognizable as birds or flowers; for example, one of them is how to tell the gnu from the newt. Then there is the story about how after dust had gathered in his spectrograph, he sent the cat through to clean it out. Another story tells how he astonished some idlers at a curb-side in Balti-more after a rain. As he came by, he popped a small piece of metallic sodium into his mouth, but spat it out very quickly into a puddle, resulting in a flash of fire. The bystanders were astonished, impressed, and mystified.

R.W. Wood had very cultured and beautiful daughters. I probably met some of them at the Loomis laboratory. In New York, I once invited one of them to go to the theater with me. The lovely Miss Wood was beautifully dressed for a pleasant occasion, but I was too inexperienced to do all the right things for a happy evening. For example, we walked on wet pavements instead of taking a taxi. But perhaps it was all right. I had never had an adequate social education.

In 1925 and 1926 there were developments of enormous importance in the understanding of matter and the particles of which it is composed. These for the first time made the spectra, structure, and behavior of atoms and of crystals clearly understood, and laid the ground work for a similar understanding of molecules and their formation from atoms.

Until about 1925, much was known experimentally about the nature of atomic spectra, but much was still obscure, including what were called inner and outer quantum numbers. Although the revolutionary new quantum mechanics soon gave a basic explanation of the principal phenomena, two essential rules had to have been discovered and fitted into our knowledge of atomic spectra and structure: (1) the fact that every electron always has an intrinsic spin angular momentum of $h/2\pi$; 2) the Pauli principle, which declares that no two electrons can have all their quantum numbers the same, including those for electron spin. In any pair of electrons, the two electrons must differ at least in having their spins pointed in opposite directions. These two rules helped very much in the understanding of atomic spectra. A book by Hund published in 1927 was very helpful in presenting and explaining the two rules and in using them to explain the periodic system of the elements. Naturally I was much interested since the same two rules must also apply to the electronic states of molecules.

Meantime the new quantum mechanics was rapidly being developed. This at first took more than one form. One of these was the wave mechanics of Erwin Schrödinger in Zürich, building further on ideas of Louis de Broglié in Paris for which de Broglié had received a Nobel prize in Physics in 1929. Wave mechanics obtained wave functions for atoms or molecules; also for the individual electrons in these. The latter I later called orbitals. The Pauli principle now applied to electrons in orbitals. A second form was the matrix mechanics of Werner Heisenberg in Göttingen, owing much also to Max Born. Then there was the formulation of P.A.M. Dirac in Cambridge, England.

All these emphasized various aspects of quantum mechanics. All the men just mentioned were awarded Nobel prizes in physics after some delay: for 1932, Heisenberg; for 1933, Schrödinger and Dirac jointly. The delay resulted I think from the fact that at first the Nobel prize was given for the discovery of things such as new particles but not for a new theory. The new quantum mechanics was of such absolutely fundamental importance that the policy of the prize committee was changed to include the recognition of major advances in theory. In 1954, Born, the importance of whose contribution to the development of quantum mechanics was not adequately recognized earlier, shared the prize with W. Bothe. Niels Bohr of Copenhagen, who had received a Nobel prize in physics in 1922 for his notable pre-quantum-mechanics work on the structure of atoms, and several others, also made important contributions to the understanding of the new theory. A major characteristic of quantum mechanics, and the related uncertainty principle, is that small things like atoms and electrons use a different language than we humans. In other words, they behave in ways that seem impossible or contradictory according to our human experience with larger objects.

X

Europe Again, 1927

My next visit to Europe was in the summer of 1927. I had no special program in mind, but planned to talk with spectroscopists and theorists about the problems of molecular structure and spectra, especially with Hund, and perhaps to do some writing. Probably I ought to have devoted more attention to an intensive study of quantum mechanics, but I was satisfied with a general knowledge of its methods and principles sufficient to help me understand particular molecules or types of molecules and their properties; especially their spectra. In short, I was more interested in getting better acquainted with molecules than with abstract theory about them. Also I wanted to get better acquainted with old and new scientific friends and acquaintances.

In those days we necessarily went by ship to Europe. Two days or so after our ship left, we heard that Lindberg had started across the ocean in his plane. We could visualize him coming nearer and nearer, passing overhead and going ahead of us. He arrived in France two days before we did. The celebrations of this first crossing of the Atlantic by plane were still going on in Paris when I arrived there on the way to Göttingen to spend the summer. Hund was now there and we had many conversations about molecules and their spectra.

While in Göttingen that summer, I lived at the house of Frau Goeppert, widow of a well-known pediatrician. She had a daughter, Maria, who was then a student at the University. One day Maria asked me if I would like to go with her to a social event at the University. Churlishly perhaps, I declined the invitation.

59

In June 1930, another American scientist, Joseph Mayer, who had stayed at the Goeppert pension, married Maria and took her to America. They later worked together and published important scientific papers and books. For some years they were colleagues of mine at the University of Chicago. But before that I had kept up friendly relations with them and had sometimes visited them.

Maria was a brilliant scientist in physics and chemistry. For her work in explaining the internal structure of nuclei she and J.Y. Jensen of Heidelberg were jointly awarded a Nobel prize in physics in 1963. Regrettably she died in 1972. I sometimes wondered how we would have done if I had married her. Her knowledge of mathematics and quantum mechanics was far better than mine, and together we might have done well. Scientists often marry other scientists, and this can make for efficiency in their work. In Paris in 1925 I met some husbands and wives who were both scientists and worked together; they told me that this was also an important help in meeting the cost of living. But in those days, most scientists were men whose wives took care of the household and family. My own feeling was that to marry a non-scientist was better for a scientific man than to marry a scientist because it would help to give him broader perspectives and interests.

While in Göttingen in 1927, I had a bicycle and took numerous rides into the neighboring country. At the end of the summer Hund invited me to go with him and some friends on a memorable hiking trip in the Schwarzwald (the Black Forest).

After that I visited Zürich, where I went to call on Erwin Schrödinger. He told me that two men were working at his Institute who had some results which he thought would interest me; he then introduced me to W. Heitler and F. London, whose important paper on the chemical bond in the hydrogen molecule (H_2) was published not long after. This paper was the first of many using the "valence bond method." This method explained the structure of molecules in terms of atoms linked together by quantum-mechanical "exchange" forces. Chemists had long talked about valence bonds between atoms in molecules, but could not explain the forces involved. The paper of Heitler and London on H_2 for the first time seemed to provide a basic understanding, which could be extended to other molecules. Linus Pauling at the California Institute of Technology in Pasadena soon used the valence bond method in his book, *The Nature of the Chemical Bond*. This book discussed the structures of molecules in general, and also of many individual molecules. As a master salesman and showman, Linus persuaded chemists all over the world to think of typical molecular structures in terms of the valence bond method. For polar molecules, however, he had to add a percentage of ion-pair structures. One may recall that an ion is an atom with one electron added (anion) or one subtracted (cation); an ion-pair is composed of an anion and a cation clinging together. Linus received a Nobel prize in Chemistry in 1954 for this work. He also in 1962 received a Nobel peace prize. It should be recognized also that his work on the determination of the structure of crystals was outstanding.

Being human, I was not especially enthusiastic about the Heitler–London or valence-bond method since Hund and I had a rival and perhaps broader method for dealing with the structure of molecules, by putting each electron into what later (1932) I called a molecular orbital (MO). Similarly in atoms, each electron is assigned to an atomic orbital (AO). In quantum mechanics, orbits are not possible, but the word orbital was intended to mean "something like an orbit" or, something which, according to quantum mechanics, an electron occupies instead of an orbit. One important advantage of our MO method was that for polar molecules we could describe the polarity in the forms of the MOs, instead of having to add an extra ion-pair expression as in the valence-bond method.

Actually, an orbital is simply a mathematical function which satisfies Schrödinger's quantum-mechanical wave equation. The word orbital is really just an abbreviation for "one electron orbital wave function." There are many different orbitals with different forms. The main thing an orbital tells about an electron sitting in it is the probability of finding the electron at any particular location in space within the molecule or atom.

For several years there was discussion among chemists and physicists as to which method for understanding molecules was more nearly correct. Finally Slater pointed out that both methods in pure form are rather far from being accurate, but that for accuracy something intermediate between them is what is needed. Qualitative discussions by either method are instructive, especially if assisted by numbers from experimental work. Also, calculations can be made by either method, but as it turned out they are much easier to do using the MO method. This method was suited to a fairly good understanding of the structure of most molecules and especially also of their spectra, to which the valence-bond method paid little attention. It is also well suited as a first step in more elaborate calculations which can bring greater accuracy.

Before going home from Zürich, I spent some time in Geneva at the home of a molecular spectroscopist (Henri de Laszlo) whom I had known in London.

After our discussions in the summer of 1927, Hund's thoughts and mine about diatomic molecules continued to develop along somewhat parallel lines. In 1928 I published a paper on the assignment of electronic configurations using MOs to experimentally observed states (*Phys. Rev.* **32**, 186 [1928]). In this paper I said on page 190 "throughout the present paper the essential ideas and methods are those so successfully used by Hund." However, I stated that in this paper I was attempting to assign individual quantum numbers to the electrons in various molecules in various states, as had not been done before. In the paper I showed that the earlier interpretation of the electronic levels of BO, CN, and other isoelectronic molecules as analogous to one-valence-electron atoms needed to be replaced by an analogy to a closed-shell system *lacking* one electron. I sent Hund a copy of my manuscript and he then sent me a copy of a similar paper that he had written, but he said that there was no use in duplication so he would not publish his in full. However, somewhat later he sent me the proof of another paper (*Z. Physik* **51**, 759 [1928]), in which he proposed the now familiar orbital symbols σ, π, δ, etc., and state symbols Σ, Π, Δ, etc., for diatomic molecules. This was a great improvement on Birge's earlier proposal to use atomic state symbols, S, P, D for diatomic molecules which I had at first accepted with qualifications as useful, because Hund's symbols recognized a partial similarity of the molecular to the atomic states, but not an identity. Meanwhile, other important papers relevant to the understanding of band spectra and molecular electronic states were published by Kronig (Groningen, Holland), Van Vleck (USA), von Neumann and Wigner (Germany), and Wigner and Witmer (Germany).

It is convenient here to say something more about the forms of MOs. As Hund proposed, they may be classified as σ, π, δ, etc., according to their angular momentum (0, 1, or 2 quanta for σ, π, δ, respectively) around a line drawn between the nuclei. But there are also other aspects of their forms which are important. As first proposed by Hund, MOs were approximated by united-atom orbitals. However, progress was made, for example in my 1928 paper mentioned above, in interpreting the electronic structures of ground-state and excited diatomic molecules by assigning to them "electron configurations" giving the number of electrons occupying each of the various *experimentally* identified MOs. One does not immediately know the detailed forms of these experimental or "empirical" MOs except as to whether they are of σ, π, or δ type. They can then be tentatively correlated with united-atom forms.

However, at a 1929 meeting in Bristol, England, Professor J.E. Lennard-Jones proposed a different type of description which has proved more useful. This uses the LCAO method, where LCAO is an abbreviation for "linear combination of atomic orbitals." In the LCAO method, an MO is built up, approximately, by adding together with suitable coefficients, some of the atomic orbitals (AOs) of the atoms from which the molecule can be made. Although both this method and the valence-bond method use AOs, they use them in very different ways. The MO and valence-bond methods of describing molecular electronic structure are entirely distinct. Later I shall have more to say about the LCAO method and some refinements of it.

XI

Interpretation of Atmospheric Oxygen Bands, 1928

Of my papers on molecules published in 1928, I was especially proud of two, one being that of the above-mentioned assignment of electron configurations to molecules like BO and CN (done also by Hund). The other was an interpretation of the absorption bands of the oxygen molecule (O_2) which are seen in the red region of the sun's spectrum for sunlight which has passed through the earth's atmosphere. I identified this spectrum as a "forbidden" one, that is, one disobeying certain rules that are obeyed in most molecular spectra. Forbidden spectra, if seen at all, are intrinsically extremely weak, but we can see these "atmospheric oxygen bands" because the sunlight has gone through many miles of atmosphere before reaching us. One important by-product of the analysis was that it showed that the normal state of the oxygen molecule, from which the absorption arises, is a $^3\Sigma_g^-$ state. This is a radical-like triplet state, which makes oxygen magnetic. I saw the latter property demonstrated by the professor in my physics course at MIT. He poured liquid oxygen over a magnet, to which it clung, defying gravity.

My analysis of the spectrum published in *Nature* and the *Physical Review*, gave the ground-state electron configuration of O_2 and also predicted for the molecule three low-energy electronic states. Two of these are the normal state and the $^1\Sigma_g^+$ upper state of the atmospheric bands. The third is a $^1\Delta_g$ state with an energy intermediate between these two. I predicted that there must be a second forbidden system of atmospheric oxygen bands in the near infrared region corresponding to a jump from the normal state up to the $^1\Delta_g$ state. These predicted bands were soon afterward found.

In making my analysis of the atmospheric oxygen bands, I was very much aided by a seemingly small theoretical point which the distinguished physicist H.A. Kramers told me about. It was that if the bands were of the type I suspected, band lines involving a zero change in the rotational quantum number should be absent. And actually they were. I think Professor Kramers told me about this at the University of Michigan in early summer 1928. At that time the University was holding summer sessions to which it attracted a group of scientists for discussions of mutual benefit. I think Kramers and I were among those present in 1928. I have a picture of myself sitting on the grass with Professor David Dennison of the University of Michigan and Dr. F.H. Crawford. We were earnestly discussing symbols for diatomic molecules and their spectra. (Compare p. IX. Ed.) This and other discussions led to an agreement which I published in 1930.

Although I was very pleased with my analysis of the atmospheric oxygen bands and related conclusions about O_2, it did not explain a number of weak band lines which were present, in addition to the stronger lines of the bands which I analyzed. A year or two later Giauque and Johnston in Berkeley showed that these weak bands must be explained by molecules $O^{16}O^{17}$ and $O^{16}O^{18}$ containing the hitherto unknown isotopes O^{17} and O^{18} of the oxygen atom in small amounts. After my earlier work on isotopes in molecular spectra, why did I not make this discovery? Perhaps it was partly because I was beginning to be bored with isotopes or because I was so proud of my difficult and novel analysis of the main atmospheric O_2 bands assuming only O^{16}, that I thought, why bother with those additional weak bands? Really, it would have been relatively easy to identify and analyze them after the main bands had been analyzed. But somehow I had gotten into my head a fixed idea that the oxygen atom is O^{16} only, so that I did not look for anything else. But how did I get this idea? Perhaps it was because Aston with his mass spectrograph saw only O^{16} and did not find the other isotopes because they were present in such small amounts. Even though Urey had found the scarce isotope deuterium of H^2 of hydrogen, and the two isotopes B^{10} and B^{11} of boron were well known, somehow no one, including myself, expected in 1928, to find scarce isotopes of the very familiar atoms carbon, nitrogen, and oxygen (main isotopes C^{12}, N^{14}, and O^{16}). But after the scarce isotopes of oxygen were found, those of carbon (C^{13}) and nitrogen (N^{15}) were found by S.M. Naudé (post-doctoral research associate from South Africa) in my laboratory in Chicago in 1928.

XII

Associate Professor of Physics
at Chicago, 1928

In 1928, A.H. Compton of the University of Chicago had told me that I could have an appointment as Assistant Professor in physics there. About the same time R.W. Wood offered me an appointment at Johns Hopkins University. But at NYU they told me that F.W. Loomis would turn over to me his position as head of the department if I would stay there. I felt entirely unqualified for that but discussed the matter. R.W. Wood offered a full professorship and finally a salary higher than his own. He decried Chicago—where, incidentally, they had once refused to give him a Ph.D. However, I felt a certain perhaps irrational loyalty to Chicago, and accepted an Associate Professorship there. I might perhaps have held out for a full professorship but Dean Gale argued that that would not be fair to Professor A.J. Dempster, who was then an Associate Professor. Afterwards I said to myself: Why couldn't they have promoted him? I finally said: All right, but you must promote me before long. That they did. The initial salary was $6,000, which at that time was very good.

One consideration which favored my decision to go to Chicago was the following. When I went there I was anxious to obtain the best possible facilities for obtaining molecular spectra. Plans for space for physics in Eckhart Hall, built in 1929, were about to be finalized. The head of the Physics Department and Dean of the Graduate School, Professor Henry G. Gale, and the then Assistant Professor George S. Monk, were spectroscopists. In accord with my

66

desires and his own interests, Dr. Monk designed a large spectroscopic laboratory in the basement of Eckhart Hall. The layout included two circles, of 21-foot and 30-foot radius, for the installation of concave grating spectrographs.

A 21-foot, 15,000 line-per-inch grating was available, and Dean Gale, who had inherited A.A. Michelson's ruling engines for making gratings, promised that a good 30-foot, 30,000 line-per-inch grating would be ruled for me on one of the Chicago ruling engines. This promise helped me to decide to accept the post in Chicago. However, once I got there, there was a long delay. The absence of a high-resolution grating then dampened my enthusiasm of molecular spectra, and influenced me thereafter toward more theoretical developments.

Meantime, in the fall of 1928 I had moved to Chicago where I lived for some time in the Quadrangle Club. Before leaving New York, I sold the typewriter I had been using to type my papers. I reasoned that in the great University of Chicago, I would have a secretary or at least a typist to take care of this chore.

After arriving in Chicago I soon had two or three graduate students working on diatomic spectra. Using the 21-foot grating, Sidney Bloomenthal studied and compared the PbO bands obtained using two samples of lead (Pb) of different origin and known to contain different amounts of the lead isotopes Pb^{206} and Pb^{207}. The Pb^{206} was the end product of a series of disintregration steps from the radioactive material from Katanga, in the Belgian Congo, while Pb^{207} is the main isotope in ordinary lead. Bloomenthal found differences in the PbO spectra which agreed with expectation. He also made a vibrational analysis of the bands, and a fine structure analysis with A. Christy of some of the bands. He also analyzed some new CuCl bands excited by active nitrogen. With all this as his research thesis, he received his Ph.D. in 1929.

In 1929–30, S.M. Naudé from South Africa worked at the lab on a postdoctoral appointment. As already mentioned, he discovered the isotope N^{15} in a study of some of the N_2 bands. A major result of his work here was a rotational analysis of the structure of the well-known "first positive" bands of the nitrogen molecule. These correspond to an electronic transition from the excited state $B^3\Pi_g$ down to the $A^3\Sigma_u^+$ state, which is one of the low-energy excited states of N_2 which can be formed from two nitrogen atoms each in its lowest state.

67

In another quite different piece of spectroscopic work, Professor Monk and I collaborated in a study of small splittings in some of the He_2 band lines, also of the Zeeman effect in the He_2 lines. A report on this work was published in *Nature* and in more detail in the *Physical Review* (Vol. 34, p. 1530) in 1929.

XIII

Mary Helen

In the summer of 1929, Hund, Heisenberg, and Dirac were all simultaneously in Chicago. Heisenberg had given a series of lectures in the spring. It was in the summer at a large party in the hospitable house of Professor R.S. Platt of the Geography Department that I first met my future wife, Mary Helen Noé. Heisenberg was also there and contributed much to the joy of the party by playing Christmas songs on the piano. I remember that a lively conversation with Mary Helen ensued from our examination of some Japanese swords which Professor Platt had on exhibit. Meanwhile, the man who had brought Mary Helen to the party, now a well-known expert on our resources of oil, had been helping in the kitchen and had spilled so much grease on his clothes that he was no longer fit to take Mary Helen to her home. So this pleasant duty fell to me.

Thus began a series of visits and other social activities. A letter which I had written to my mother on June 16, and which I now have, contains the following:

> I've been getting frequent exercise, at tennis several times, one morning driving a car, dancing two evenings; one day last week with Mona F. to movies and College Inn—dancing very good—and again last night with Mady Noé. Mady and I first went to the theater, then to the Turkish Village Inn which was very disappointing so that we then went to the College Inn which, although far from perfect, stayed open until 2 a.m., for which I was thankful.

After that I guess Mona F. dropped out of the picture—I don't remember her at all. I was attracted by Mary Helen's tall, slender beauty and by the fact that she had studied at the Art Institute and had much artistic ability (like my mother). Her mother was from Iowa. Her father was an Austrian, Adolf Noé, who, after interesting experiences as a Hungarian Hussar, studied at the University of Göttingen. Some of his fellow students there were Americans. In talking with them, he became interested in America to the extent that he finally emigrated there. In Iowa he met my future mother-in-law and married her. He was now an Associate Professor of Paleobotany at the University and an expert on coal. The underground coal mine at the Museum of Science and Industry in Chicago is a very popular, realistic reproduction of a coal mine which he designed. His father had been in the service of the Austrian emperor and was given a baronet's title as Noé von Archenegg, which his son inherited. It is said that the emperor had asked him what title he wanted and he said, "Give us peace," after which the emperor gave him a lesser title than he otherwise might have had.

I sympathized with Mary Helen when she told me how her mother preferred her younger sister. We saw much of each other during that fall of 1929, and on Christmas Eve we were married. After the wedding at the Episcopal Church there was a reception at the Quadrangle Club with balalaika music. My family members from the East were there. My father and Mary Helen's father, who had both studied in Germany, enjoyed getting acquainted. After a week in a Chicago hotel, Mary Helen and I postponed our real honeymoon until Spring 1930 when we made a trip to Europe whose justification was a Fellowship for me to do scientific work.

XIV

Guggenheim Fellowship, Half 1930, Half 1932

In September 1929 there was a notable meeting of the Faraday Society in Bristol, England to discuss molecular spectra and molecular structure. I did not attend but sent a paper. Also, following the lead of the atomic spectroscopists, who had just agreed on a standard notation, I had been circulating some proposals for a standard diatomic band spectrum notation; O.W. Richardson, who had been doing a great deal of work with the H_2 spectrum, presented these at the meeting. After some further correspondence, I published a report on diatomic notation, in *Physical Review* **36**, 611 (1930). This was based on a rather nearly unanimous agreement which I had obtained from my fellow-workers on band spectra, perhaps most of whom I had met on my trips to Europe in 1925 and 1927. As already mentioned above, some of us were already discussing the question at Ann Arbor in the summer of 1928. Such an agreement is important, since in a new subject it is much easier for people to understand one another if they use the same names or symbols for the same things. It was at the Bristol meeting that Lennard-Jones presented his paper on the use of the LCAO method for diatomic molecules. Among others who presented papers were C.P. Snow (Cambridge), Herzberg (Bristol) about whom more later, and Kondratiev (Leningrad).

C.P. Snow had for some time been an active molecular spectroscopist including work on infrared and optical polyatomic spectra. I had talked with him in Cambridge and later corresponded with him about spectra of certain ethylene derivatives; but before long he turned to writing novels. Somewhat later came his contention that in modern life there are two cultures (scientific and nonscientific), and that something ought to be done to bridge the gap between them.

Some time in 1929 I had been awarded a Guggenheim Fellowship for continuing my research and study for one year at a favorable location. I decided to divide this into two six-month periods, the first one beginning in the Spring of 1930 in Leipzig, where Hund and Heisenberg and other excellent scientists, including the well-known physical chemist Peter Debye, were now located. Among others from the U.S.A., Professor and Mrs. Van Vleck were there.

However, I felt it was justifiable on the way to Leipzig to take a belated honeymoon for Mary Helen and myself, since after reaching Leipzig I was going to (and did) work very hard on my scientific projects. So we went on the steamer *France* on a cruise with brief stops at the Canary Islands, Casablanca and Rabat in Morocco, and in Algiers. From there we went to Naples, Italy from which we took an overnight boat ride so rough that everyone was sick, to Sicily. In Sicily we explored especially Palermo and Agrigento. After returning from Sicily we went to Rome and then on to Florence with pleasant stops at Orvieto and other hill towns. Finally on to Leipzig.

In 1929, in Chicago, I had started a review article on diatomic molecular spectra, including sections on various types of bands and later (perhaps 1932), on the electronic structures of the normal and excited states of molecules. I carried this work on vigorously while at Leipzig and thought it might become a book but never did. I had also become especially interested in 1929 in the structure and spectra of the halogen molecules (fluorine, a very active gas; chlorine, a green gas with well-known uses; bromine, a red-brown liquid; and iodine, a familiar solid). I did not particularly care what these substances might be used for, but was fascinated in trying to understand their constitutions and those of their spectra. So I carried on these two scientific activities day and night during my stay in Leipzig.

At Leipzig, Edward Teller was Heisenberg's assistant and while of course Heisenberg was the champion Tischtennis (pingpong) player, Teller was the runner-up. Tischtennis always followed seminars. During this spring of 1930, Heisenberg received notice that he had been elected to the Saxon Academy of Sciences, a quite unprecedented distinction for one so young. So at the next seminar day, a proper celebration of the event was arranged. Namely, Teller with great difficulty had managed to procure a long gray beard which then Hund, with an appropriate speech and a suitable adhesive, superimposed firmly on Heisenberg's face.

During the Leipzig visit in 1930, I had some good conversations with Teller on molecular problems, to whose solution he made important contributions, long before his later work as "father of the H bomb." During this period we also visited Budapest, meeting Professor B. Pogany and others in physics at the university; one of these was Dr. R. Schmidt who thereafter spent the years 1931–32 at Chicago in my laboratory on a post-doctoral fellowship.

One day we had lunch with the Teller family at their home in Budapest. I learned that they had suffered very much from an earlier communist take-over of Hungary, which before 1930 had come to an end. Teller's very strong anti-communist feelings may be explained by this experience. Also with us in Budapest on this same visit was Yoshio Fujioka, who had been working at Leipzig as a student, with Heisenberg and Teller. Fujioka later became a well-known figure in Japanese university and government science circles.

In Austria we looked up aunts and cousins of my wife in Klagenfurt, Graz, and Vienna, and I visited scientists in Vienna and Graz. In Vienna, we also went to see Carry Hauser, an artist who was a cousin of my wife. He painted a portrait of her which did not greatly resemble her, but was attractive and colorful. In one corner of this picture he placed a little figure to represent me. Then a few days later he decided to do a full-scale protrait of me. This had a broad ribbon of vari-colored background to signalize my activities as a spectroscopist. Both paintings were unusual in having a hand seemingly resting on the border of the picture.

In Graz, we visited the house which had belonged to Mary Helen's Austrian grandfather and in which her father had been brought up. It was a fine house with a big garden. However, at the time of our visit the oil paintings and a chandelier which were formerly in the house had been in storage since the first World War.

Before we went on our European trip, Mary Helen had earned $200 by making the illustrations for a small book by her father entitled "Ferns, Fossils and Fuel." He had visited Russia several years before as a consultant on coal mining. The visit had been arranged by the Allen and Garcia Corporation in Chicago which had interests in coal. After his return, he wrote a small book entitled, "Golden Days in Soviet Russia." This contains observations and amusing picures. It did not imply that he had communist sympathies, although he enjoyed his visit.

Mary Helen and I used the $200 she had earned to pay for the storage and transportation to Chicago of the paintings and other things from the Graz house. Mary Helen's father then gave them to her. The paintings included very fine portraits of the mother and father of Mary Helen's Austrian grandfather, in other words of her Noé great-grandparents. They had been prominent in the life of Vienna in their time. There was also a portrait of the well-liked Austro-Hungarian emperor Joseph II, a brother of Marie Antoinette. And there was a fine floral painting, and another rather gloomy painting which we gave away. Among other papers there was an invitation to Beethoven's funeral.

On the way to Austria we had made a strenuous one day excursion (bus-hike-bus-hike-bus) in the Dolomites. This was in part like the hike I had made with Dr. Mark in 1925. We started from Bozen, or in Italian, Bolzano (12) where we spent a day and a night waiting for the rain to stop. The next day the sun was shining and we climbed up a mountain-slope until we came to a gap or pass in a broad high ridge. We crossed over this Tschagerjochpass, which was covered a foot deep in snow. We picked edelweiss on the way down to a trail which descended to a major highway in a valley between the mountains. After crossing this road we climbed out of the valley on the other side. We followed a trail which finally became lost in barbed wire entanglements and empty helmets left from World War I. We were now on a plateau with no trial in sight. My wife was almost exhausted, but I said we *must* go on, especially as it had begun to rain. With the help of a compass I found the way down to a point on the highway a few miles beyond where we had previously crossed it. Here we caught a bus to a hotel in the Italian city of Cortina d'Ampezzo. After spending the night admiring the sight of a magnificent mountain-side glacier, and buying a native costume for Mary Helen, we made our way back to Austria, and finally then to our pension in Leipzig.

Among the memorable events of our 1930 European visits was attendance at a meeting of the Bunsengesellschaft, a major chemical society, at Heidelberg in June. Many papers were presented in the area of atomic and molecular structure. I gave one in German, in which language I could express only one-half as much in the time allotted as I could have done in English. Evening festivities in connection with the meeting were held in the Heidelberger Schloss. The castle was illuminated as if it were on fire, there was a big dinner, and after the dinner there was dancing in the cellars beyond the famous Heidelberger Thun (this is truly a tremendous cask). The cellars had brick floors and were rather damp but everyone was happy, having been given more than ample supplies of tickets for beer and wine. Typical of the occasion was the young scientist who jovially slapped a General-direktor of the I.G. dye industry on the back.

One day in Leipzig I heard over the radio a screaming roaring speech by Hitler. The billboards and the atmosphere were charged with the scarcely believable premonitions of his coming take-over.

While in Leipzig I was working morning, noon, and night on my scientific writing. This fellowship activity was not interesting for my beautiful young wife. This led her to advise other young women "Never marry a scientist." However, we did go to the movies to see the incomparable performance of Marlene Dietrich in "Der blaue Engel" (The Blue Angel) and with the Van Vlecks to the theater to a horrific Teutonic version of Gilbert and Sullivan's "Mikado." Also, at the pension where we stayed, one of the other boarders, Herr Magat, had a continuous supply of new books in English which he passed on to Mary Helen. They came to him somehow in his business.

The food at the pension must have been extremely meager, since upon reaching Berlin, after leaving Leipzig, we practically fainted. But on Sunday, when we were walking in the park in Dahlem, not far from the Kaiser Wilhelm Institute, we came to a place called Onkel Toms Hütte (Uncle Tom's Cabin) which advertised chicken dinners. We went in and ate and this started our recovery from the Leipzig diet. While in Berlin I of course visited the Kaiser Wilhelm Institute and talked with a number of the scientists there.

On the way home, we visited England, meeting Jevons and Mrs. Jevons in London and others in Oxford and Cambridge. On this and other visits, I have enjoyed many a fine dinner and conversation, with good port to drink after dinner, at various Oxford and Cambridge colleges of which scientists I knew were Fellows. In Cambridge at about that time, C. P. Snow was working enthusiastically and publishing good papers on infrared spectra of NO, CO, and N_2O.

In Bristol I attended the meeting of the British Association for the Advancement of Science. We stayed with the Tyndalls and also saw much of the Lennard-Joneses. Tyndall and Lennard-Jones were, respectively, professors of physics and chemistry at the university.

75

XV

Back to the University of Chicago

Dr. A. Christy came from Berkeley in late 1929 as Instructor in the Physics Department at Chicago and remained until 1931. He supervised the student research during my absence in Europe in 1930 and collaborated with me in a comprehensive paper published in *Physical Review* **38**, 87–119 (1931) on Λ type doubling, a kind of narrow splitting in the rotational levels of diatomic molecules of Π or Δ type, where the electrons have an angular momentum around the molecular axis. In this connection, I had earlier corresponded with Van Vleck and in 1928 we had published a short joint paper (*Phys. Rev.* **32**, 327) in which Van Vleck made important contributions to the theory. I published another paper on Λ type doubling in 1929. This effect gives useful insight into certain intimate relations between different excited states of a molecule.

In 1930 I published two papers on the halogen molecule bands, leading up to my later work on this subject. S.M. Naudé from South Africa was in Chicago in 1929–30 and discovered the nitrogen atom isotope N^{15}. He also carefully measured and analyzed the first positive bands of nitrogen, which are especially conspicuous in the active nitrogen spectrum. Harold T. Byck who studied with me at NYU and later received a Ph.D. at Johns Hopkins was in Chicago in 1930–31 as a National Research Council Fellow. He made valuable progress toward understanding certain interesting and instructive CN bands in which some rotational energy levels of two diffferent electronic states of CN "perturb" each other, causing small shifts in the levels in opposite directions for the two states.

In 1930, James L. Dunham came from Harvard and wrote an important theoretical paper, later often cited, on relations among coefficents which are needed when one is trying to describe the structure of a band by mathematical formulas. He also published a paper on the infrared HCl band intensities. Unfortunately he died as the result of an appendix operation which ordinarily is a safe and routine affair.

As indicated another postdoctoral fellow in 1930 was Walter Weizel whom Mary Helen and I had met earlier in Germany. Before long he returned to Germany to accept a position as Privat Dozent (instructor) at Rostock. We felt that he and his younger colleague W. Finkelnburg were good friends of ours. In 1931 Weizel published a comprehensive and valuable book on band spectra.

Another postdoctoral research worker whom we had met on our visit to Budapest in 1930 was Raoul Schmid. In 1931, I had begun to be actively interested in the structure and spectra of polyatomic molecules, at first relatively simple ones. Our first experimental work in this area was Schmid's on some bands of CO_2 (carbon dioxide); actually, as became clear later, they belonged to the ion CO_2^+. Schmid made progress toward measuring and understanding these, but the bands were too complicated to be properly resolved with the grating we had. Several years later with a new and much better grating, Dr. S. Mrozowski was successful in their analysis.

Another postdoctoral worker was Weldon G. Brown who, after receiving a Ph.D. in Chemistry at the University of California obtained a National Research Fellowship to spend 1931–32 in Chicago with me. He photographed and analyzed some of the absorption bands of the halogen molecules in the visible part of the spectrum, in particular, the long wavelength bands of iodine. He spent a second year of the fellowship in Germany. After returning, he advanced through successive stages to become a professor of organic chemistry at the University of Chicago, where we had many useful scientific discussions. We lived for some years in the same co-operative apartment building. My wife and I and he and his wife Mildred met often.

Regarding graduate students in the period 1929–32, I have already mentioned Sidney Bloomenthal (Ph.D. 1929). Webster Crane worked on the K_2 bands about 1930, but never finished his work for a Ph.D. P.S. Delaup got his Ph.D. in 1930. D.S. Stevens clarified some features of our understanding of certain O_2^+ bands and received a Ph.D. in 1931. P.G. Saper studied the SiO bands and received a Ph.D. in 1932. J.S. Millis made a very thorough study of the Zeeman effect in some of the He_2 bands and obtained his Ph.D. in 1931. Although his work on He_2 indicated that he was well qualified to go on with independent research, he chose instead a successful career as an administrator. Before very long he became President of the University of Vermont (1941–49) and then of Western Reserve University (1949–67).

What I have written so far about life in Chicago has been almost entirely about scientific research and the people taking part in it . Of course I also had the duty of giving academic courses for students, including regular undergraduate courses in physics as well as more specialized courses in spectroscopy and atomic and molecular structure. There were also consultations with students on their Ph.D. research. Further, there were many seminars in physics, and sometimes in other subjects, which I attended. Coffee and tea were served before seminars. There were also various committees of faculty members, assignments to which were changed from year to year. Sometimes I was in charge of the seminar committee and had to find and invite good speakers. One very strenuous committee, of which I was sometimes a member, prepared comprehensive written examinations to be taken by students working for a Ph.D. The results of this "comprehensive" together with those of an oral examination on general knowledge and a thesis decided for each graduate student whether he or she had failed, passed at a low level entitling him or her to a M.S. degree, or had passed at a high enough level to justify a Ph.D. degree.

Besides my educational and research activities, Mary Helen and I had much to do together. After returning from Europe in the early fall of 1930, we remained in Chicago until we left in September 1932 for our second European visit.

In 1930–32 we began setting up housekeeping. Mary Helen's mother and her sister Valerie left to spend two years in Tucson, Arizona. Mary Helen and I then stayed for a while in the Noé apartment with her father; for a time my brother Gyles was a visitor. But before long we rented a delightful furnished penthouse apartment in a building on Dorchester Avenue near the university. It belonged to a member of the university faculty who was then away on a trip. We enjoyed this immensely. I have a photograph of us enjoying the outdoor region at the top of the penthouse. It did not matter that the building seemed to have been somewhat loosely constructed. Every time there was a heavy rain, water seeped through the wall leaving it wet and bright red.

I associate two interesting observations with this building. One day sitting on a couch oriented east to west, I noted that the couch moved a short distance one way, and then back. I thought, we are having a mild earthquake. Confirming this, the newspaper the next morning reported an earthquake in Ohio at the time of my observation. I concluded that the building's rather shaky construction made it a very sensitive detector of a slight shock not noticed by other people.

The other observation was this: one night when we were sleeping near an open window there was a thunderstorm. During the storm, a glowing yellow ball about six or eight inches in diameter meandered in through the open window and poised for a moment beside our bed, then faded away quickly. This I believe was ball lightning. Ball lightning has never been well understood, although there are many reports about its occurrence and somewhat varying behavior. The yellow color of our nocturnal visitor seemed to me the same as that of active nitrogen, with which I was familiar and have written about in earlier paragraphs. As described before, active nitrogen is produced by an elecrical discharge through nitrogen gas. Our ball lightning was no doubt produced by electric discharges in or from thunder clouds, so I think our visitor was a ball of active nitrogen produced in the sky.

After we left the penthouse apartment we moved a number of times to other apartments but I think it was the penthouse we most enjoyed.

As I realized only much later, life at the university was little affected by the 1929 Wall Street crash and the ensuing Great Depression. University salaries and research did not seem to suffer.

During the Depression years, Mary Helen and I visited Colby's household furnishings store to fill some of our needs. There were many massive sideboards and side tables which were beautifully carved and of the very highest quality, from a famous maker who was now bankrupt. Previously selling to people who could afford the best, their prices were now marked down to a small fraction of what they were worth. We bought a few of these treasures together with household linen and other needs. Our wedding gifts had included a complete table setting of silver made by the well-known Towle silversmiths of Newburyport. There were many other fine gifts from wealthy friends of Mary Helen's father. Later we gave the very fine sideboard and side table to our daughter Lucia.

Besides housekeeping needs, Mary Helen and I were very much interested in oriental rugs and Japanese prints and bought some that we especially admired. Later we acquired a very good Japanese print by Hiroshige and a splendid wall hanging in Stockholm in 1932.

Mary Helen was an expert cook, although sometimes the dinner was three hours late. She was also a very good conversationalist, which, though good in itself, considerably inhibited my development in the art of social conversation. She was an excellent party-giver. As an example, when we were in Klagenfurt, Austria in 1930, she arranged a special menu for an excellent dinner at the best hotel, to which we invited all her Austrian relatives who would come.

While in Austria we visited Vienna briefly, admiring the great cathedral and visiting museums. At one museum we found that they possessed what we were told were the original plates prepared by Albrecht for his famous etchings. From these, prints could still be made essentially as good as those issued by Durer long ago. We bought a few of these. Nowadays unfortunately no more can be made because the plates were destroyed in World War II.

In summers, beginning perhaps in 1933, Mary Helen went to the summer school of the Chicago Art Institute in Saugatuck, Michigan. There she did several interesting etchings and water colors. I went along too, although I had little to do except to explore the woods and the St. Joseph River.

After a while I became too bored and asked Mary Helen to show me how to do some watercolors. She refused to give me any instructions whatever, except "Don't be afraid to use plenty of color." I went ahead and somehow created three watercolors including plenty of well-placed color. As I remember them, the first was the best and the others progressively worse, so that after the third I became discouraged. However, more recently when I looked in a drawer where we kept a number of Japanese prints which I bought in Kyoto in 1953, I found four good watercolors which I must have done at Saugatuck, presumably later than the three which seem to have disappeared. In spite of my complete lack of formal training, when I look at these four now as an amateur art critic, I think they are definitely good. Others to whom I have shown them seem to agree. Their subjects are mostly nature along the river. One picture is of a house high up with stairs leading up to it. Mary Helen also did a watercolor of this house in a style very different from mine.

Another pleasurable activity in which Mary Helen and I participated was to take our handsome black cocker spaniel Carlos to a dog show at some country town. He and his amiable but less handsome black brother George were brought as puppies from California when Mary Helen visited her sister Valerie and her husband there in 1957. As puppies they once went with me and Valerie to one of the numerous scientific Gordon conferences which take place every summer in New Hampshire using dormitories belonging to some of the numerous boy's schools located there. Our Carlos, sometimes in the hands of a trainer, won a number of ribbons. But one time when we had brought along some friends to a show to see him, he made the unfortunate mistake of biting the judge.

I had originally been a cat man. At my grandmother's house my Aunt Sarah always had a cat, one of which , "Tammy Lumpkins,"I rememember vividly. There usually were birds at our house too. It was Mary Helen who converted me into a dog man.

I usually went to one or two of the Gordon Conferences each summer, most often to one on molecular electronic spectra or one on molecular complexes. With talks and discussions, such a conference was very valuable to the participants in keeping up to date and getting new ideas. But afternoons were also available for climbing mountains or visiting attractive scenery.

I must now record two family events of the Depression years. On July 15, 1934 our first child, Lucia, was born. The name Lucia descended from aunt to niece for several generations in the Mulliken family. As a middle name, Maria was chosen after an Austrian ancestor. My father's favorite sister was named Lucia; she taught school in a country town but to everyone's sorrow succumbed to tuberculosis. This happened when my father was a student in Germany and he was very depressed. Our Lucia's birth made my father happy, but in the fall his health declined and he died before his 70th birthday. I think he was expecting this to happen when he made one last trip with my mother, while he was still able, to Nova Scotia.

XVI

Guggenheim II.
Europe Again in 1932–1933

In the fall and winter of 1932–33, I went with Mary Helen to
Europe for the second half of the Guggenheim Fellowship. I had
planned at first to attend a meeting of the German Physical Society
in Hamburg in September. To reach there, we might have gone
directly on a Hamburg–America line steamship. However, the
Canadian Pacific Line offered at the same cost an alternative
routing which appealed to us; namely, first to Glasgow, Scotland,
where we had a few days to see some of Edinburgh and also Loch
Lommond and the west; then to Newcastle, England. While in
Newcastle I talked to W.E. Curtis at the University of Durham on
molecular helium (He_2) bands.

From Newcastle we embarked on a small vessel that bounced
over the waves to Bergen, Norway. From there we went to
Göteborg, Sweden, where we decided on a brief detour to
Stockholm. We went there for three days but stayed two weeks. My
good friend Erik Hulthén, whom I had first met in Lund in 1925,
was now professor of physics at Stockholm University. He and his
wife took care that we enjoyed the fascinating city of Stockholm.
One day he and I made a trip to Uppsala to call on the famous
Professor Manne Siegbahn. In Stockholm I visited the Institute of
Technology where Professor Alvin Lagerqvist had a fine spectroscopic laboratory. I also became acquainted with Inga Fischer, later
Professor Fischer-Hjalmers, who was working on molecular quantum theory. In 1932, Erik Hulthén was a member of the committee

which decided on the award of the Nobel Prize in physics. One day he told me he was sorry to say they couldn't give me the prize that year. I certainly didn't think I deserved it, but his comment suggested that I must have been one of those who was considered. I wondered for what, but surmise it must have been for experimentally discovering half-integral vibrational quanta in BO as described earlier. The theoretical necessity for the half-integers very soon appeared as a consequence of quantum mechanics. Anyway, my contribution didn't deserve a Nobel Prize.

Besides my science, Mary Helen and I together found much of interest in the then very modern things the Swedes were doing. We especially enjoyed visiting a store called Vackrare Vardagsvarer which sold beautiful everyday ware. Also there were some beautiful wall hangings in which Marta Maas-Fjetterstrom had combined esthetic elements from Persian rugs harmoniously with some fine ideas of her own. We were very tempted to buy one of these, but we did not have much money to spare. Nevertheless, finally at the last moment before the bank closed we went in and got the necessary $90 for one of the wall hangings. Our choice was called Röda Hästerna (Red Horses), a synthesis of a Persian garden carpet and striking Swedish horses. Many years later I gave the Red Horses to the University of Chicago where it hangs on the wall in the dining room of the Quadrangle Club.

Another acquisition in Stockholm (for $2) was an original Japanese wood-block print. This was one of a series by the famous Hiroshige, which showed scenes on the old road from Tokyo to Kyoto. It was called "crying stone on the Tokaido Road."

From Stockholm we went next to Copenhagen where we had lunch with Professor and Mrs. Bohr at the marble palace in the Carlsberg brewery grounds which had been left by the former owner as a residence for the "the first citizen of Denmark." The brewery provided some extraordinary potions which are not on the market. Several other scientists were there, among them Franck. Mrs. Bohr tried patiently, but in vain, to stop the men from talking about science (or perhaps it was politics) before the coffee got cold.

We went on as previously planned for a six-week stay in Utrecht, where I had the opportunity to talk with Kramers and other Dutch scientists. Pan Jenkins was also spending a fellowship period at Utrecht at this time. During our Utrecht visit we made a trip to Groningen in northern Holland, where I had discussions with several scientists. Kronig was then a professor there. He had earlier had a faculty position at Columbia for a few years, but then returned to Holland.

After Utrecht, we made a short visit to Leipzig, where Heisenberg, Teller, and Hund were still located. Hund was now married; his wife was a mathematician. He was very proud of the new house, not yet quite finished, which he was having built. In the hotel lobby he talked quite freely with us about the ominous approach of Hitler's take-over which he then forecast as inevitable. That night at 2 a.m. there was a knock on the door. It was the police. They said "Ihren Pass, bitte." I showed them our passport, and they went away.

From Leipzig we went to Göttingen and then to Berlin. On the way to Göttingen, we visited Weizel in Karlsruhe, where he was now a very young professor, with Finkelnburg as his Assistant. Weizel was very much annoyed by the formality and dignity which were required of a professor. In Karlsruhe I also met Professor A. Stock, the great pioneer of boron chemistry.

In Göttingen, Franck and others were very upset about coming events. We did not stay long in Göttingen, but I believe I talked to Franck's seminar about ideas which later gave rise to molecular orbital structures of water and other simple molecules. My wife had some appendix trouble and stayed in the hospital for several days, and by special permission, I stayed there too for a few days to keep her company. However, the experience was extremely tiring, since the nurses wakened us every morning at about 4.

Fortunately I escaped briefly for a visit to Darmstadt to see Gerhard Herzberg. At that time he had built a long-path absorption cell using mirrors at the ends to increase the path length, and also a vacuum spectrograph. He also was looking for the Vegard–Kaplan bands of nitrogen in absorption; these are well known as emission but not as absorption bands. He did not find them; they were first found in absorption by P.G. Wilkinson in Chicago in 1958.

Being eight years younger than I, at the time of my 1925 visit to Germany, Herzerg was only in the second year of his undergraduate studies in Darmstadt. By 1929 or 1930 he had progressed so far in research that I was eagerly awaiting his publications as they appeared. Herzberg married in 1929. His wife had also obtained a Ph.D. in spectroscopy, and collaborated with him subsequently in many important papers. By the time I visited him in 1932, he was well known internationally, and his current work was of great interest and value. At that time it was mainly on diatomic spectra, where he put foward some important ideas on the electronic structures of diatomic molecules. He also wrote, in collaboration with Edward Teller, on some other aspects of molecular spectroscopy. Further, at about this time, he wrote a book on atomic spectra and published some good ideas on a phenomenon called predissociation which occurred in diatomic molecules. Because I felt pretty ignorant on the subject, which seemed rather important, I gave up my above-mentioned plans to publish a book on diatomic spectra. However, my articles, written largely in Leipzig in 1930 and in Chicago in 1931 and published in *Reviews of Modern Physics* (1930–32), covered the subject rather thoroughly except for my inhibitions about predissociation. Soon after, Herzberg came out with an excellent book on diatomic spectra. This was followed by other always excellent books on infrared and Raman spectra, and later on polyatomic and on radical spectra.

Beginning in his student days, Herzberg was always very interested in astrophysics. He found and identified the spectra of several radicals which could be seen both on earth and in comets or other astronomical sources. He recently co-authored a book bringing up to date his very extensive tabulated compilation of existing information on diatomic spectra. I had earlier published a similar but much smaller set of tables in my *Reviews of Modern Physics* survey. However, meantime I had turned my attention to a long series of articles on the structure and spectra of polyatomic molecules, published in 1932–35. A belated recognition of the value of these articles was, I think, mainly responsible for the Nobel prize I received in 1966.

In 1971, Herzberg also received a Nobel prize for his work on molecular spectra. His several excellent books, making knowledge and understanding of molecular structure and molecular spectra much more accessible than before, would in my opinion almost have deserved a second Nobel prize. It is very important for every scientific (or other) subject to have good books which clearly and comprehensively survey it. Herzberg's books, although they do not go into some of the more sophisticated aspects of quantum-mechanical theory, give a clear understanding of its essential results.

Although Herzberg was trained as a physicist and I was trained in physical chemistry, but held university appointments in physics, we both received a Nobel Prize in chemistry. This recognized the fact that, although molecular spectroscopy was at first developed by physicists, it is now mainly chemists who are interested in molecules and spectra. (See my article in *Physics Today*, **81**, 52 [1968].)

Returning now to our trip from Göttingen, we went to Berlin where we stayed at the Pension Fritz on Unter den Linden. Every morning early, looking out the window, we could see and hear the Nazi storm troopers marching in the street below, and then alternately the Communist storm troopers. Christmas dinner at the pension was featured by carp with raisin sauce.

In January of 1933, my wife's appendix demanded attention. In Göttingen, Herr Professor Dr. Stich, belying his name (embroidery in English, I believe) had decided not to operate. However, wishing to take no chances, I obtained the names of the best and second best surgeon in Germany, in case trouble should develop while we were in Berlin. The first of these, Professor Sauerbruch, as it turned out subsequently, became Hitler's physician. However, we chose the second, Dr. Nordmann, to operate. He did an extraordinarily fine cosmetic job, leaving a scar only a half inch long. As we found out later, he had done the same for Marlene Dietrich.

In visiting the Kaiser-Wilhelm Institute in Dahlem, I was much impressed with the work that Hans Beutler had been doing on inner shell excitations of atomic spectra. Later, after I had proposed it, he came to Chicago. Among fellow Americans in Berlin that winter were Weldon and Mildred Brown. After his work with me in Chicago in 1931, he had continued his National Research Fellowship in Germany in 1932–33.

After leaving Berlin we visited Switzerland to recuperate at an economical winter spot, but it rained, so we went on to St. Moritz, where the snow was excellent. While there we saw a horse race on ice. I recalled the story of how R.W. Wood had once attended a ball there dressed as the devil. For this purpose he attached an umbrella casing to his rear in which he enclosed a live eel. This provided him with a very lively wriggling tail.

Next we went to Holland and from Amsterdam we went to England. Jevons had meantime written an excellent book on band spectra. In Cambridge we stayed with the Lennard-Joneses. He had recently been appointed to the J.H. Plummer professorship there. At his invitation I gave a lecture on the structure and spectra of simple polyatomic molecules. Charles Coulson, who was now in Cambridge, had been a student of Lennard-Jones at London University. He recalled later that I spoke about the double bond, although I remember talking only of molecules like water and ammonia. I remember being somewhat surprised but pleased that Dirac, who appeared in the front row, thought it worthwhile to attend.

Among others at Cambridge were Hartree, Norrish, Emeleus, and Todd, all doing novel, exciting and valuable work in their respective fields of chemistry. Hartree was using his "self-consistent field" theory in understanding atoms. Norrish used flashes of light to break molecules into radicals, whose absorption spectrum he could then obtain using a second light flash. Todd was extracting bright pigments from various insects. Coulson was contributing to the development of molecular theory and was writing a small but very readable book on valence theory.

XVII

Chicago Again, 1933

Back in Chicago in 1933 two graduate students were doing research. One was John Clements who, using a temperature-variation method, made good progress in the classification of vibrational bands in the visible and ultraviolet absorption spectrum of sulfur dioxide, a molecule which greatly interested me. He received a Ph.D. in physics in 1935. The other, S.H. Chao from China, was working on the ultraviolet NH_3 (ammonia) bands, and received a physics Ph.D. in 1936. Because we had as yet only the 21-foot radius, 21,000 line per inch grating for the work on SO_2 and NH_3, the results were little more than preliminary. In 1937 Dean Gale finally gave us the long-desired 30-foot, 30,000 line grating and from that time on we got some rather good spectra of polyatomic molecules. H.J. Plumley, an excellent student, did very good work with the electronic absorption bands of bromine (Br_2) and received a Ph.D. in 1937. We had hoped he would go on in academic research, but he disappeared into an industrial job.

My own most intense interests centered mainly on writing a long series of fourteen papers under the heading "Electronic Structures of Polyatomic Molecules and Valence" with various sub-headings. The work on this series was begun in Chicago in 1931, was carried on vigorously in Europe in 1932–33, and finished in Chicago in 1935. The series discussed spectra as well as electronic structure for a number of major types of molecules.

When I sent these papers to the journals I felt that the series was very important and a good piece of work. For some time I wondered why other people did not pay more attention to it. But finally in 1966 when I received the Nobel Prize in Chemistry, I think it was largely because of a belated recognition of the value of this series. However, even before 1966, recognition had already been growing for a few years, during which I received several awards and medals.

The first four papers of this series were published in the *Physical Review;* all the later ones in the then newly established *Journal of Chemical Physics.* This latter journal was established largely on the initiative of Harold Urey, who argued strongly that a considerable part of the current research being published in the *Physical Review* was largely of chemical interest. I was not at first convinced that a new journal was needed. However, by 1934, I had largely shifted over to the *Journal of Chemical Physics* for the publication of my papers.

The polyatomic series had been preceded by a long paper on "Bonding Power of Electrons and Theory of Valence," already briefly reviewed. The problem of valence, primarily how many and what kind of atoms can attach themselves to a given atom to form a molecule, had long been a central problem of chemistry. Of course there was the question of what sort of forces hold the atoms together in a molecule. In the years following 1926 this question was beginning to be answered for the first time by the new quantum mechanics. As I have mentioned previously, two considerably different ways of applying quantum mechanics had been advocated, namely, the exchange theory of Heitler and London, further developed by Pauling and Slater as valence-bond theory, and the molecular orbital theory which Hund and I initiated, but to which Lennard-Jones, Herzberg and others also made important contributions. Slater soon showed that something between the two theories was needed for accuracy. However, for the most part it has turned out that for practical calculations on the structure of normal molecules as well as for understanding their excited and ionized states and their spectra, it is probably best to start with molecular orbital theory and then if one wishes high accuracy to introduce improvements to realize "electron correlation."

In molecular orbital theory, each state of the molecule and of its ions is characterized by an electron configuration giving the number and kinds of MOs and how many electrons are present in each. Most important of course is the "ground" or normal state of the molecule. The number of electrons in any one molecular orbital in the ground state of a stable molecule is most often 1, 2, 3 or 4, namely 1 or 2 for any σ type of MO, 1, 2, 3 or 4 in any of π type. The number is limited by the Pauli principle which permits the presence in any one molecule of at most two electrons in MOs of identical form. However, "degenerate," e.g. π, MOs comprise two or more otherwise alike but differently oriented forms which the Pauli principle counts as different and so permits to be simultaneously occupied. In an electron configuration, degenerate MOs often contain up to 4 or sometimes 6 electrons depending on the symmetry of the molecule.

Most stable molecules contain an even number of electrons, with 2 or 4 or sometimes 6 in each MO, but in radicals or especially singly ionized molecules, the electron content of one of the MOs can be reduced to 1 or 3 or sometimes 5.

In the first paper of my 1932–5 series, I briefly characterized the structures of molecules of a number of types, using descriptive symbols to specify electron configurations. In the second paper, I introduced the noun "orbital" and defined atomic orbitals (AOs) and molecular orbitals (MOs) as *something like* the orbits of Bohr's theory, but very different in some ways because of the radically new viewpoint of quantum mechanics. One feature is that the form of an orbital (when squared) tells only the probability of finding an electron in any particular position in space. Each AO or MO has a particular mathematical form. I soon realized that the forms of MOs can be classified in simple ways depending on the symmetry of the molecule.

The possible types of MO for each type of symmetry of a polyatomic molecule are described and labelled in the fourth paper using the mathematical methods of group theory, as Van Vleck suggested I do when I told him about how I was classifying MOs by symmetry. Each type or species is one of several "irreducible representations" of the symmetry group of the molecular skeleton, and is indicated for most polyatomic molecules by a symbol such as a, b, e, or a_1, b_1, etc. There can often be more than one MO of a given species in the electron configuration of a molecule; when this happens, some sort of individual label must be added to the group-theory symbol.

In one particular case however, that of linear molecules like CO_2 and C_2H_2, I used diatomic symbols, namely σ (or σ_g or σ_μ) for MOs of cylindrical symmetry; π for MOs having one nodal plane through the molecular axis, or if there are two such planes, δ, δ_g, δ_μ, and so forth.

I adopted the other polyatomic symbols a_1, a_2, e, etc., from a system used by Placzek for classifying molecular vibrations. Besides introducing the group-theory symbols, the fourth paper covers several points about their use, especially in connection with electronic spectra. These are characterized as allowed or forbidden by certain "selection rules", if allowed by their type of polarization. Forbidden spectra disobey the rules and are seldom seen or are very weak, except under special circumstances.

The fourth paper also deals with the quantum theory of double bonds, where two atoms in a molecule are joined by a pair of π electrons in addition to the usual pair of σ electrons found in molecules with single bonds. Ethylene has a planar structure $\underset{H}{\overset{H}{\diagdown}} C = C \underset{\diagdown H}{\overset{\diagup H}{}}$ of group theory species D_{2h}. It is the prototype or simplest example of molecules containing a double bond. Such molecules belong to the important class of "unsaturated" molecules. Polymers (built from two or more like molecules) of ethylene (polyethylene) or propylene are especially familiar as wrapping material for food packages and other similar uses.

Papers V and also VII are devoted to molecules of type RX_n, including water (H_2O), ammonia (NH_3), and methane (CH_4), as well as the important radicals CH_2 and NH_2. All these are prototypes of many other bigger molecules. They belong to several different group theory species. Thus H_2O, also CH_2 and NH_2, belong to the C_{2v} species, NH_3 to the C_{3v} or trigonal (umbrella-shaped or pyramidal) species, while CH_4 belongs to the T_d (tetrahedral) species. Of interest is a rule given by Zachariasen which says that RX_n molecules (a) are planar (D_{3h} species) or (b) pyramidal (C_{3v}) depending on the number of valence electrons present. Electron configurations and ionization potential data are given in these papers and spectra are discussed.

One intriguing situation is the fact that although NH_3 is pyramidal in its normal state, in its first excited state or when ionized it becomes planar, with D_{3h} symmetry. This is an example of a general rule that the excited states of molecules often have different symmetries than the ground state. Good examples are found in many of the linear triatomic molecules discussed in Paper XIV.

A notable feature of NH_3 is the low value of its ionization potential, I, for the most easily ionized electron. This occupies a non-bonding MO of a_2 type. It is responsible for the fact that NH_3 is an electron donor molecule, forming rather stable compounds or complexes with electron acceptor molecules, e.g. BCl_3. In the wave function of such a complex, an electron from the donor is partially transferred to the acceptor.

Paper VI is devoted to a general discussion of the MO method. A paper published in 1925 entitled "Structure, Ionization, and Ultraviolet Spectra of Methyl Iodide and Other Molecules" but not included in the long 1932–5 series deserves mention here. Electron configurations are given for CH_3I in its ground and some of its low excited states, with a discussion of the nature of the MOs occupied.

Except for the altered symmetry and the greater complexity in CH_3 than in Cl, CH_3 and its spectrum are similar to those of ClI, discussed in an earlier paper. Omitting inner electrons, the latter's electron configuration may be written $(3s_{Cl}\sigma)^2(5s_I\sigma)^2(B\sigma)^2(3p\pi_{Cl})^4(5p\Pi_I)^4$. The MOs are all of σ or π type. All of the MOs except $B\sigma$ can be approximated in LCAO form by the Cl or I atomic orbitals which are indicated. The $B\sigma$ MO is a bonding MO linking the Cl and I atoms. The MOs of the electron configuration are here written as usual in the order of decreasing ionization energy, i.e., ease of removal. Most easily ionized is an electron from an iodine $5p\pi$ orbital. (CH_3 is similar, but with the symbols a_1 and e instead of σ and π.) Omitting iodine inner electrons, the electron configuration is $(1s_C)^2$ $[sa_1]^2 (5s_Ia_1)^2 [\pi e]^4 [\sigma a_1]^2 (5p\pi_I e)^4$. The bonding C–I MO is $[\sigma a_1]$.

The brief paper VIII on "Ionization Potentials" compares some observed (I_{obs}) with predicted (I_{pred}) values. Molecules of types HA, CH_3A, and C_2H_5A are discussed. In these, $I_{pred} - I_{obs}$ for the non-bonding electron A atom ionization potential (I) are not zero, but positive, and increasingly so, as we go to more electronegative A atoms (mostly halogens) (13). This is explainable by charge transfer i.e., partial electron transfer, from the rest of the molecule to the A atom. The charge-transfer effects also often have some influence on the ionization potentials (I^0s) of bonding and antibonding MOs.

Paper IX deals with methane, ethane, ethylene (already extensively considered in III and IV), and acetylene. Electron configurations are given and used in interpreting the Is. Excited MOs are discussed in connection with tentative interpretations of ultraviolet spectra.

Paper X is devoted to aldehydes, ketones, and related molecules. The most familiar aldehyde is formaldehyde H_2C—C=O. It has various practical uses. Its spectrum is particularly interesting, and has been studied very thoroughly. The related molecule acetone is a well-known solvent. This paper deals with molecules discussed by me and especially by H.L. McMurry in his work for the Ph.D. in physics in 1941.

Paper XI and XII deal in some detail with various applications of the idea of electronegativity to understanding molecules.

Paper XIII is an interesting example of the uselessness of theory when it is applied in trying to interpret an erroneous experimental model for a molecule, in this case the boron hydride (B_2H_6) molecule. It was natural to think that this molecule would have the same geometrical form as the familiar ethane molecule C_2H_6, which has trigonal symmetry. Early experiments by the method of electron diffraction seemed to confirm this idea, but later it was found to be wrong. The correct symmetry and form were first definitely established in 1946 by the well-known English spectroscopist W.C. Price during a year which he spent working in my laboratory. It turned out that B_2H_6 and many other more complicated boron-hydrogen compounds have anomalous structures which do not obey the ordinary rules of chemical valence. Hence my paper XIII, which made various predictions about the structural properties of B_2H_6 was simply nonsense. However, the other papers in the series were soundly based with respect to experimental evidence, and my pride in them was for the most part well justified.

The last paper of the series (XIV) deals with a considerable number of linear molecules, that is, molecules in which all the atoms lie on a straight line. These include carbon dioxide (O=C=O), acetylene (H—C≡C—H), carbon disulfide (S=C=S) and many others. This property makes it possible to classify the MOs and the electronic states of these molecules with the diatomic type of symbols (σ, π, δ, etc. for orbitals; Σ, Π, Δ for states). Each is linear in its ground state, but becomes bent (C_{2v} or other symmetry) in most of the excited states. However, when one electron is removed to form an ionized state, the ionized molecule retains the linear symmetry of the ground state.

For example, the carbon dioxide molecule, which is linear (O=C=O) in its ground state becomes bent (symmetry C_{2v} like H_2O) in its interesting, but not yet well-understood, excited states. On the other hand, when an electron is removed to form the ion CO_2^+, the latter is linear in its excited states as well as in its ground state.

Simultaneously with the polyatomic series, I published several other papers. Jointly with my student D.S. Stevens in 1933 I published in the *Physical Review* a paper on some new O_2^+ bands and on the dissociation energy and the ionization potential of O_2.

In 1934 I wrote about certain spectra and other features of N_2. Also in 1934 I discussed the bearing of electric dipole moments and infrared spectra on the structure of CO. Electric dipole moments are an important characteristic of polar molecules but are zero for symmetrical molecules like O_2, N_2, and H_2. Polar molecules have an unsymmetrical distribution of positive and negative charges, which produces an electric dipole moment.

For diatomic molecules using spectroscopic information, a "potential curve" can be constructed showing how the energy of the molecule would be increased or decreased as a function of the distance between the two nuclei (R) by stretching or squeezing. In a somewhat similar way, one can obtain a curve showing how the dipole moment changes with R. In CO this shows that the dipole moment reverses its direction as the distance between the C and O nuclei is increased or decreased.

One of the most familiar and useful concepts in chemistry is that of the relative electronegativity of different atoms. The more electronegative an atom, the stronger its tendency to acquire an electron and thus a negative charge. The physical basis of this concept long remained obscure, although it appears that the electronegativity of an atom must be related somehow to its electron affinity, the energy gained if it catches an electron; or to its ionization energy, i.e., the energy required to remove an electron; or to both.

Pauling in 1932 proposed an approximate scale of relative electronegativities of atoms based on information on the energies of formation of various compounds. This scale proved rather successful, although one cannot expect to obtain an exact scale for the rather fuzzy concept of electronegativity.

Pauling's scale was one of *relative* electronegativities. In 1934 I published a scale of "absolute" electronegativities, obtained in a different way than Pauling's scale. In my scale the absolute electronegativity of an atom is equal to the average of its ionization potential and electron affinity. However, these quantities must be calculated for suitable *valence states* of the positive and negative ions, and since many atoms have more than one valence state, they may have somewhat different electronegativities for different valence states.

However, for the most usual valence states, the *differences* in electronegativity of any two atoms on my scale agree pretty well with the *relative* electronegativities as given by Pauling's scale. My paper explained and showed how to calculate the needed valence states, and gave tables of these for a number of atoms. The concept of valence states was also proposed independently in a paper by Van Vleck. Both Pauling's and my scales have been much used, and extended to atoms not considered in the original tables.

Another paper which I published in the *Physical Review* Volume 46, in 1934, was entitled "The Halogen Molecules and Their Spectra, J-J-like Coupling, and Molecular Ionization Potentials." The three topics in the title are distinct but interconnected. The halogen molecule discussions begun at Leipzig in 1930 and Chicago in 1931–2 were here refined and extended. Writing MOs in LCAO form, one has for the electron configuration of iodine (I_2) . . . . . ($p\sigma_I$ + $p\sigma_I$, σ_g)^2 (π_I + π_I, π_u)^4(π_I − π_I, π_g)^4, where the dots refer to inner shells. Many excited states can be predicted in which an electron is excited from one of the two π MOs into an MO of higher energy (e.g., $p\sigma_I$ − $p\sigma_I$, σ_u); or at the same time the numbers of electrons in the several lower MOs may be permitted to vary. When an excited electron is only loosely attached, its interaction with the other electrons, which may include, for example, incomplete shells now containing just three π electrons may be of a special type called Ω-s coupling. This resembles what in atoms is called J-J coupling. A full explanation would be complicated, so I omit it.

The discussion of ionization potentials given in this paper is especially useful since the same ideas are used in all my papers on both diatomic and polyatomic molecules. As has been mentioned before, every molecular state can be described by an electron configuration in which brief designations are given for a series of MOs, with a superscript index to tell for each MO how many electrons are present in it. An important characteristic of each MO is its ionization potential, which means the energy required to remove one electron from it. In writing the electron configuration, the innermost MO, of highest ionization potential, is written first, the MO of next largest ionization potential next, and so on.

When any electron is pulled out of a molecule, there is very often a readjustment in the distance between atoms in the molecule and sometimes also in the shape of the molecule if it is polyatomic. Unless otherwise stated, it is understood that the ionization process allows for these changes, in which case one speaks of the "adiabatic" or "true" ionization potential.

But sometimes one is interested in the ionization energy which would be needed to remove the electron without any changes in the shape or dimensions of the molecule. For this situation, I introduced the term "vertical ionization potential." In theoretical calculations or estimates of ionization potentials, it is much easier to obtain vertical than adiabatic ionization potentials. For simplicity, I use the symbol I to denote ionization potential.

There are important empirical relations between the ionization potentials of molecules and those of the atoms from which the molecule is built. For these no strictly theoretical explanations have yet been found. MOs fall into three main classes; bonding, nonbonding, and antibonding. In homopolar (symmetrical) diatomic molecules, bonding MOs have LCAO forms, $(a + a)$; antibonding MOs, $(a - a)$, approximately, where a stands for an approximate AO. Nonbonding MOs are of form a, that is, they are just AOs. In polar molecules with atoms a and b, LCAO forms become $(\alpha a + \beta b$, with $\alpha > \beta)$ for bonding MOs; $(\alpha a - \beta b$, with $\beta > \alpha)$ for antibonding MOs.

Since bonding increases and antibonding decreases molecular stability, it is immediately plausible for a bonding MO of form $(a + a)$ to have $I_{a+a} > I_a$. For a nonbonding MO, one might expect I to be about the same as for the atom, I_a. For an antibonding MO of form $(a - a)$, one expects $I_{a-a} < I_a$. In a bonding heteropolar MO, I is some weighted average of I_a and I_b, and is certainly $> I_b$; and so on. However, as we learned later, the Is of nonbonding MOs in heteropolar molecules are often somewhat increased or decreased by partial transfer of an electron to the atomic type MO under consideration.

In the paper under discussion, observed vertical I values and corresponding predictions are listed for several MOs of N_2 and CO, and predicted relations of molecular to atomic I values are given for several halogens X_2 and XY, and for HX (hydride) molecules. In the discussion of the relation of atomic and molecular Is in the paper it was pointed out that the atomic Is used in comparisons must be valence-state Is. (See above, in the discussion of electronegativity.) These are of two kinds: one which I called I*, for removal of a nonbonding electron from the molecule; the other which I often called I° for removal of the electron from a bonding or antibonding MO.

On the preceding pages I have reviewed some of my long series of papers on polyatomic molecules and related matters published in 1932–35. These papers, and a few others published in the same time period, particularly those on electronegativity and on ionization potentials, may be classified as theoretical. However, many, perhaps most, of the papers in the long series itself might more properly be called interpretive rather than theoretical, because they were devoted not to introducing new theory but to *applying* old and new theory, and *in interpreting* or explaining known facts about a considerable variety of molecules and of types of molecules.

The first paper (I) of the long series was primarily a survey of what was to follow, but was expressed in terms of relatively primitive ideas about molecular symmetries. These ideas were clarified by Paper IV. The last paragraph of Paper I promised a later discussion of transition metal compounds (molecules containing d electrons). But I never got around to doing this, even though when Paper I was proposed I had some good ideas and was very enthusiastic about developing them. I might have done this after XIV was finished, but somehow had lost my motivation, or perhaps felt that fourteen related papers was enough for now. Yet I have always remembered my early enthusiasm for these unwritten papers, and felt convinced that they would have been good.

In any event, after the long series was finished and sent off for publication, I went in the fall of 1935 with my wife and our year-old daughter Lucia to California for visits in Berkeley and Pasadena.

Science at Berkeley was very lively, and I had good talks on band spectra with Birge and Jenkins, and with Joel Hildebrand,

Latimer, Giaque, and others on various topics. Ernest Lawrence was going strong with his cyclotron. I had first met him in the east when we were both National Research Council Fellows. My wife and I once had tea (or perhaps it was cocktails) at Oppenheimer's elegant apartment. His style seemed to me effete, esoteric, but his heart was also very much in physics. This was of course long before the atomic bomb development at Los Alamos.

I was especially glad to meet G.N. Lewis, whose papers on valence theory I had studied with great enthusiasm when I was a graduate student at Chicago. He asked me to talk to his seminar, and I discussed my ideas of the MO structures of some typical simple molecules, including I believe, ethylene. I pointed out that the lowest excited state of almost *any* molecule *must* be a triplet state, in which the spins of two electrons (namely the excited one and its former partner now left behind) must be parallel. At that time most chemists had different and erroneous ideas about the nature of the lowest excited states of molecules, yet the correct answer was perfectly clear from MO theory, which however was not yet generally disseminated or popular. I think this seminar talk first introduced Lewis to his later strong interest in triplet states.

Pasadena at that time seemed an earthly paradise, with good science too. We had a dip in the Pacific Ocean at Christmas. Although Pauling and I were at that time rivals on the subject of valence bond theory, we had friendly relations with the Pauling family: Linus and Ava Helen one day took us for a memorable expedition into the desert.

As I remember it, I learned to drive while in Pasadena, using a car lent to me by a kind friend, Andy Neff. With this car I drove successfully through some shallow rivers and up the then dirt road to the top of Mt. Wilson, the site of a well-known astronomical observatory, and down again. There was a rule that if going down you met anyone coming up you had to back out of his way. Anyway, I became a successful driver, sometimes later reported to be rather a dare-devil; I never understood why. My memory of learning to drive in California seems however to conflict with a letter I wrote to my mother in 1929 (see Chapter XIII) where I said I had been driving. Somewhat later I bought a Ford.

I seem to recall 1936, going on to 1937, as a period of letdown, although I did produce three worthwhile papers. These concerned low electronic states of simple heteropolar diatomic molecules and were published in the *Physical Review*.

These three papers discuss four types of commonly occurring states which I called N (normal or ground state), T (triplet), V, and Q. Such states occur for homopolar molecules like H_2 or Cl_2 as well as for the heteropolar molecules discussed in these papers. V states are particularly interesting. They have fairly high energy, relatively large distances between the atoms, and low vibration frequencies, yet require relatively large energies to dissociate them. In the valence-bond or AO type of approximate description, V states are ion-pair states, even in homopolar molecules. In the MO type of description, in a V state relative to state N, one electron has been excited from a bonding MO to the corresponding antibonding MO. Another feature to be discussed a little later, is that the spectra of N $\rightarrow$ V transitions are of exceptionally high intensity. Although this fact is not discussed in these three papers, V states and N $\rightarrow$ V transitions are well known for polyatomic as well as for diatomic molecules.

As I showed later, molecules with double bonds have two kinds of N $\rightarrow$ V transitions which I have called N $\rightarrow$ V$_\sigma$ and N $\rightarrow$ V$_\pi$ depending on whether in the AO description the charge transferred to a neighboring atom is a σ or a π electron.

For nearly every molecule, as I have already mentioned, MO theory shows that the lowest excited state must be a triplet state. In this, one electron of the normal state is excited to the lowest-energy excited MO in a special way. The electron which is excited was previously paired with a second electron occupying the same MO but with its spin pointed in the opposite direction. In the triplet state, the spin of this remaining normal-state electron now points in the *same* direction as that of the electron in the excited MO, so the angular momenta of the two spins are parallel. This gives T states certain properties: (a) the state is magnetic; (b) the spectroscopic transition N $\rightarrow$ T is usually very weak (nearly forbidden). However, exceptions occur and N $\rightarrow$ T can be stronger if the molecule contains atoms of high atomic weight, for example iodine.

N, T, V, Q are *informal* symbols for certain especially important types of states. Instead of N, Herzberg in his books and papers uses X, but I prefer N. Q states are states where the excited electron is of π type, and there are N $\rightarrow$ Q spectroscopic transitions. However, the symbol Q is little used, while spectroscopists do refer very often to V states. These and other informal symbols are commonly used to label individual states, expecially when a new state state is discovered but its formal classification is not yet known. Even when the correct systematic formal symbols of diatomic type for diatomic or linear molecules or of group-theoretical type for polyatomic molecules have been determined, it is necessary in addition to have an informal symbol or name to identify each particular individual state of a molecule.

Although I was not quite as enthusiastic as usual about the papers I was writing in 1936, I was cheered by two events. For two or three years I had wondered why I had not been elected to the National Academy of Sciences, the organization which aims to include the best scientists of the United States. I had been feeling that I was qualified, but no doubt I was too impatient; the election procedures take time. However, in the spring of 1936, when as it happened I was in Washington during a meeting of the Academy, I learned that I had been elected to membership. Professor A.H. Compton, who was there, first told me. Most new members are not present but learn of their election from congratulatory telegrams. I was pleased also that Ava Helen Pauling greeted me affectionately, even though Linus, who was already a member, and I were rivals in our ideas about molecular structure.

The second encouraging event was the annual tradition of many years at the University of Chicago called the Trustees' Dinner in which the University trustees, mostly businessmen, invited all the faculty to dinner at a downtown hotel, preceded by cocktails and followed by cigars for those who wished them.

After dinner there were three speeches. One was given by the president, who was then the relatively young Robert M. Hutchins, with his rather novel ideas about education. Another spoke for the trustees and a third spoke for the faculty. Each speaker talked on things related to his field of activity, especially things relevant to the university. In 1937 President Hutchins invited me to speak for the faculty. In the meantime I had had two or three pleasant conversations with him about university and human affairs. In one of these, he expressed the view that every human being is a mixture, in proportions varying from one to another, of the gold (the finer or nobler qualities) and the brass (the mediocre and/or ignoble qualities). More recently I have been told that this idea was first held by the early Greeks.

Earlier Hutchins had accused the faculty, or some of them, of "pebble picking," which I interpreted to mean working on things of minor or trivial importance. This naturally offended the faculty. However in talking with him I saw that his criticism was intended for the social scientists and not for others such as the physical scientists. In fact, in terms of financing, Hutchins showed his approval of these.

My speech was entitled "Science and the Scientific Attitude." It was a plea for everyone so far as possible to deal with his and the world's problems in the way that a scientist does. Of course, to do so would involve some knowledge of the facts and methods of science, an educational area which scientists felt had been too much neglected in this country, especially in recent years, whereas, in contrast, many scientists are interested and active in areas outside of science.

However, there is a great difference here between the physical and the social sciences. In the former, we can usually make exact measurements or observations and predictions, with relatively small margins of error. But in the social sciences, the margin of error often becomes larger than the question which is to be decided. In other words, the degree of uncertainty about the (or a) correct answer to a question is often greater than what is considered certain. A similar uncertainty may also exist even about what is the right *method* to solve the problem. Such difficulties it seems to me are conspicuous today in the greatly differing conclusions and advice which even the best economists offer us. It is inevitable that we all experience dilemmas in life about what is the right or best thing to do. My talk at the trustees' dinner advocated using a scientific approach whenever possible. In many cases this means no more than being rational. But perhaps, in some situations, instinct or intuition or even poetic feeling may be better.

On rereading my speech (14) I now think much of it is sophomoric, but that it contains a few gems. I will quote three of these:

"I think it was in a course on quantitative chemical analysis that an appreciation of the scientific method and its rigors began really to take hold of me. Before that, I had been interested in the wonders of science in an irresponsible and second-hand sort of way. But in quantitative analysis, which, by the way, I detested, I was brought face to face with the unpitying relentlessness of nature, in the form of some brute facts of chemical technique."

"The primary objective of science, of course, is to try to find out what *Nature* is really like: that is, to distinguish the *actual* universe, including mankind, from all the numberless forms the universe might conceivably have taken."

"The scientist trying to discover nature's secrets soon finds that only the most persistent, rigorously honest and boldly imaginative effort can win. Nature plays the perfect Sphinx and is completely adamant to every clumsy attempt to force the locks that guard her secrets. Yet to the man who finds the correct combination for one of these, i.e., the truth, she yields without the slightest resistance. Further, the devotee of science, that is, the man who woos nature for her secrets, must develop enormous *tolerance* in seeking for ideas which may *please* nature and enormous patience, self-restraint and humility when his ideas over and over again are rejected by nature before he arrives at one to please her. When the scientist does finally find such an idea, there is often something very intimate in his feeling of communion with nature."

I arrived at the ideas and feelings expressed in this last quotation during several hard-fought struggles to find answers to scientific problems. I do not now remember just which problems so strongly affected me. In the total field of science, these were not among the largest problems, but nevertheless I always experienced an extraordinary thrill when I felt I had really come in touch with even a small part of *Nature*. Besides these major thrills, there is every day in doing basic research the feeling like that of the early explorers, that one is doing or finding something that no one has ever done or seen before.

After we returned from Europe in 1933 just after Hitler took power, I was worried about what his actions would lead to. Many of the best German scientists migrated to England and America, James Franck and others left Göttingen. After some time in England and at Johns Hopkins University, Franck came to the University of Chicago as a professor in chemistry. We kept in touch but did not undertake any joint programs. Hertha Sponer became a professor at Duke University, where she continued her work in spectroscopy. Heinrich Kuhn became established as an atomic spectroscopist at Oxford. Gerhard Herzberg obtained a position in Saskatchewan in 1935, on the initiative of his former student, John Spinks; he remained there until 1945.

Meantime the British and French were appeasing Hitler. If they had taken firm action soon enough, they could have stopped him, but they did not. It was my opinion at this time that he was gaining so rapidly, he could not have been stopped without major warfare after about 1936. The appeasement was in vain, and World War II began in 1939.

At about that time, Heisenberg was visiting in Chicago. As an Aryan, he was not subject to persecution by the Nazis, who perhaps hoped instead to find his scientific ability useful. Once when I

101

talked with him briefly, he told me that as a German he felt loyalty to his country and was returning there with the hope that he could do some good there. Perhaps, I surmised, in alleviating some of the harm done by Hitler.

When Hitler took over Czechoslovakia, Chicago became the capital of the government in exile, in the person of Edward Benes as president. At luncheon in the Quadrangle Club, I had a number of interesting talks with him about the future of his country. In 1939 we shared the experience of being given an honorary degree by Columbia University. Some time later when the war was over and he was about to return to Czechoslovakia to take things in hand, I discussed with him the problem of dealing with the Russians. He thought he could manage it, but as it turned out he couldn't. At the time I was doubtful.

In 1939–42 a new group of students at Chicago was doing Ph.D. theses on polyatomic spectra, with considerable success after we had the new grating. Financially we had been materially assisted by a grant from the Rockefeller Foundation for "Molecular Spectra Research."

The experimental work was supervised by Dr. Hans G. Beutler, who had left Germany in 1939 after a notably successful research career at the Kaiser Wilhelm Institut in Berlin where I first met him and was impressed by his work. Following a year at Ann Arbor, Beutler came to Chicago in 1937 where he remained until his tragic death in 1942. After the war, Professor George R. Harrison of MIT gave us a vacuum spectrograph which he had built; later we put this to good use. In exchange, we sent him one of the two Chicago engines for ruling gratings.

During his stay in Chicago, Beutler made an extensive study of the theory of the grating spectrograph. He left an unfinished manuscript which Ralph Sawyer of the University of Michigan edited and published. Edson R. Peck made some valuable contributions in instrument development, for which he was awarded his Ph.D. in 1945 after the war.

In 1940, the excellent Polish spectroscopist, Dr. Stanislaus Smrozowski joined the group as a Research Associate and remained until 1945. Luckily for him he had come to Berkeley on a fellowship in 1939, just before the outbreak of World War II. While in Chicago he concentrated largely on a detailed analysis of the CO_2^+ spectrum, following up the earlier work of Schmid and coordinating with the work of F. Bueso-Sanllehi (Ph.D. in Physics 1941) on one especially continuous and important band of CO_2^+. Smrozowski published four excellent papers on this work on CO_2^+.

I wrote two papers on theoretical aspects of the spectra and structure of triatomic molecules, correlating with the Ph.D. work on N.C. Metropolis (SO_2) and L.N. Liebermann (CS_2).

In the fall of 1940, I sent off for publication an article by myself, Carol A. Rieke, and Professor W.G. Brown, on "hyperconjugation." Just after we had sent the manuscript off to the editor of the *Journal of the American chemical Society,* I celebrated the occasion by enlisting one of my graduate students, F. Bueso-Sanllehi, to drive west with me in my Ford. Bueso had been working on part of the CO_2^+ spectrum. Later, after he got his Ph.D., he became a professor and later dean at the University of Puerto Rico but finally died in a drowning accident.

Starting from Chicago at 11:00 a.m., we reached Cheyenne, Wyoming, by the second night. At nightfall of the third day we drove up to the Jemez Mountain Inn, in New Mexico, near the present Los Alamos. They told us it was closed for the season, but they let us have dinner and then sleep upstairs with the kitchen workers.

Next day we crossed New Mexico to the Carlsbad Caverns, where we went in to look around. Very many bats were there. Emerging afterwards from the darkness of the caverns into the bright sunlight outside, I suddenly smelled ozone, but only for a moment. The explanation must be that the sunlight produces a very small amount of ozone from the oxygen of the air, not enough to be perceptible except to a nose which had become hypersensitive to ozone through its complete absence in the caverns.

Thereafter we made the lengthy trip across Texas and back home, wearing out two or three tires. I thought this trip a worthy celebration of the paper on hyperconjugation, about which I will say more later.

Belonging to the University of Chicago is the Yerkes Observatory at Williams Bay, Wisconsin, on Lake Geneva. Here various observations by astronomers on stars and planets are made, recorded, and analyzed. Among other records are photographs of spectra. Professor Harvey Lemon of the Physics Department introduced me and my group to the custom of visiting Yerkes for small seminars to discuss recent developments in their and our research. The seminars were mainly about conclusions based on spectroscopy, because not only we but also the astronomers used it; they mainly to learn about stars. The Chicago contingent also learned something about telescopes and astronomy. Between discussions there were some picnic lunches and swimming and sailing on the lake. Also the observatory director, Professor Otto Struve, one of a famous family of astronomers, and his wife, helped to make us welcome. Among others who lived at Yerkes were the world-famous astrophysicist Professor S. Chandrasekhar and his wife. They had come from India, first to England, then to Yerkes. Afterward, Chandrasekhar began driving his car to Chicago for lectures. At such times, he drove rather rapidly. Finally, he and part of the astronomy work moved permanently to Chicago.

H.L. McMurry, as a graduate student with me first tried experimental work, but soon concluded that he was not very efficient in the laboratory. He then worked successfully in the theoretical interpretations of aldehyde, ketone, and carboxy-group spectra and published several papers which built on the ideas proposed in paper X of my long series on polyatomic molecules, and also used some ideas from my 1939–40 series on intensities, which I will discuss shortly.

McMurry, Metropolis, and Liebermann received their Physics Ph.D.s in 1941. Liebermann's daughter, Mary Kathryn Levin, about 1980, became an Associate Professor and later a Full Professor in our Physics Department at the University of Chicago. I feel that I can claim to being her scientific grandfather.

J.B. Coon (Ph.D. in Physics, 1946) worked on the ClO_2 (chlorine dioxide) spectrum, whose bands have intriguing structure because of the spin of the odd electron in the molecule, and also have characteristics which show that this triangular molecule unexpectedly has two unequal legs. Anthony Turkevich, now a Professor of Chemistry at Chicago, was here in 1940–41 as research assistant, and obtained a high dispersion (very detailed) photograph of the benzene (C_6H_6) absorption spectrum. As I have previously mentioned, our spectroscopic group often met with the astronomers at Yerkes Observatory, Williams Bay, Wisconsin. In June, 1938, Professor Struve at Yerkes and I arranged a four-day astronomy-physics symposium there.

One graduate student during this pre-war period was Leona Woods, who analyzed some CuF (copper fluoride) bands and received a chemistry Ph.D. in 1943. Later she worked on nuclear physics problems with Enrico Fermi. She married a nuclear physicist, John Marshall, and they had two children, but later they were separated. A second marriage was to the late Professor W.F. Libby.

Another student who received a Ph.D. in physics in 1939 was O.G. Landsverk. He investigated the spectrum of carbon as given out using a graphite electrode in a large bulb. He found an interesting new band which clearly belonged to C_2 (diatomic carbon). This belonged to a new electronic state. The band or bands are now known as the Mulliken bands, the only bands to which my name has been attached. In a paper published in the *Physical Review* **56**, 778 (1939), I assigned an MO transition for this band and discussed it in relation to the other known states of the C_2 molecule.

XVIII

World War II, 1942

In 1942 World War II was upon us. However with the cooperation of Otto Struve, James Franck, and Weldon Brown, I arranged a conference on spectroscopy in June which ranged from wavelength standards and atomic spectra of crystals, of planets and comets, to spectra of simple molecules, organic molecules, and dyes. I have since felt that this conference set a pattern which has been taken up after the war in the very successful annual conferences on spectroscopy at Ohio State University.

At our 1942 conference, I presented two papers. One of them was entitled, "Structure and Ultraviolet Spectra of Ethylene, Butadiene, and their Alkyl Derivatives." I had already had something to say about ethylene and butadiene, but Professor Emma P. Carr of Mount Holyoke reported some new information on these at the conference, so I took the occasion to give an up-to-date review of what we all had learned about these molecules. I also included something about some of their derivatives, that is to say, about related bigger molecules in which some of their hydrogen atoms had been replaced by alkyl groups. These are groups like CH_3 and C_2H_5 and other similar larger groups containing C and H atoms.

My other paper at the 1942 conference was entitled "Electronic Structures and Spectra of Triatomic Oxide Molecules." This, I think I can say now, was an important paper. It was published in 1942 along with the other conference papers in the *Reviews of Modern Physics*.

106

In it I introduced a new diagram showing the known ionization energies of normal-state and excited-state MOs of a number of triatomic oxide molecules of the type AO_2 as a function of the ground-state apex angle θ (the angle OAO), over a range of θ from 120° to 60°. Starting from CO_2, which is linear so that θ is 180°, I noticed that the ionization energies are also related to the number of outer electrons, counting all s and p electrons of the outermost shell of each atom in the molecule.

With 16 outer electrons as in CO_2, or less (as e.g. in $CO_2{}^+$), θ is 180°. When more outer electrons are added, θ decreases steadily, NO_2, O_3 or SO_2, and ClO_2 have 17, 18, and 19 outer electrons respectively in their ground states, and θ decreases steadily. My diagram shows how the ionization energies of each of the occupied and some of the unoccupied MOs vary with θ and simultaneously with the numbers of outer electrons for a roughly defined "average" AO_2 molecule. The diagram is based on a combination of theoretical considerations and empirical evidence. Although θ and the number of electrons of course change discontinuously from molecule to molecule, the curves in the diagram are continuous. But of course they have meaning only at points which correspond to discrete numbers of outer electrons and of θ. In the same paper, I interpreted the spectra of various AO_2 molecules with the help of the diagram.

Some time later the English spectroscopist A.D. Walsh made one or two improvements in my AO_2 diagram and also generalized it to cover a wide range of polyatomic molecules of various shapes, formulating rules and showing diagrams for the ionization energies of their MOs. Since then, many chemists refer to all these as the Walsh diagrams or rules, but some call them the Walsh–Mulliken or Mulliken–Walsh rules in view of the fact that my AO_2 paper initiated the main ideas which started the ball rolling.

In 1938 I began work on a series of ten papers entitled "Intensities of Electronic Transitions in Molecular Spectra," with various subtitles. These were published in 1939–40, mostly in 1939. The reason for my strong interest in this subject is explained in the beginning of Paper No. I of the series where I said "The problems of the relative intensities of band lines in a band, and of bands in a band-system, have received a considerable amount of attention, both experimental and theoretical. The problem of the absolute strengths of electronic transitions in molecules, on the other hand, has been studied hardly at all except experimentally . . . A systematic development of the theory and its systematic application to existing and new data seems to have fruitful possibilities . . . The theoretical interpretation of absolute intensity data should be especially useful in the case of continuous spectra," where there are no band lines which could be analyzed to obtain information about electronic states. A similar remark applies to absorption spectra of substances dissolved in a liquid. In that case individual band lines are blocked out and only broad continuous bands can be seen. And even for vapor spectra, where bands divided into fine lines do occur for many electronic transitions, some transitions, or parts of them, occur only in the form of broad continuous bands.

My interest in absolute intensities was probably excited by the fact that the $N \to V$ transitions discussed in my three 1936–37 papers show, among other special characteristics, usually high intensities. For diatomic molecules, $N \to V$ transitions show bands with sharp lines. Paper No. I of the Intensities series is mainly devoted to obtaining convenient formulas for various ways of describing the strengths of spectroscopic transitions of all kinds. Paper No. II, with the sub-title "Charge-Transfer Spectra," deals with $N \to V$ and other somewhat similar kinds of transitions. Several special characteristics of $N \to V$ transitions have been mentioned previously. Another feature is that in the AO approximation an $N \to V$ transition involves the transfer of an electron from one atom to an adjacent one; hence the designation "charge-transfer spectrum." But in the MO approximation, it involves transfer of an electron from a bonding to the corresponding antibonding MO. Simple formulas are discussed in II for calculating the intensity of an $N \to V$ transition by each of the two approximations, and the results are compared for H_2, O_2, and I_2 and other diatomic molecules with those of experimental measurements. Rough agreements are obtained on both approximations. That is all that can be expected, since the calculated AO and MO results both differ considerably from those of exact calculations. $N \to V$ transitions are known also for ethylene (C_2H_4) and other polyatomic molecules.

$N \to V$ transitions in AO approximation involve charge transfer only between atoms within a molecule: intramolecular charge transfer. Later (about 1952) I identified a very different type of charge-transfer spectra, this time with transfer from one molecule to another, i.e., intermolecular charge transfer spectra.

Succeeding members of the Intensities series dealt with a variety of molecules. Nos. III–VIIIa are concerned with spectra and related properties of organic compounds, as are also some later papers. Before I wrote these papers, I had greatly increased my knowledge about these compounds in mild orgies of conversation with two organic chemistry colleagues, Professors G.W. Wheland and W.G. Brown. Eagerly I learned of various facts and emperical relationships and sought to explain them.

No. IX and part of XI of the Intensities series dealt with calculations on some of the halogen molecular spectra, increasing my understanding of them which began in Chicago and Leipzig, as earlier described. The halogens have since continued to be among my favorite molecules. Paper X also considered intensities in the spectra of the hydroxyl (OH) radical, a well-known fragment of the water molecule. It also dealt with some halogen atom compounds, namely hydrogen and alkyl halides.

Returning to Nos. III–VIIIa, the sub-title for III was "Organic Molecules with Double Bonds; Conjugated Dienes," and for IV it was "Cyclic Dienes and Hyperconjugation." A diene is an organic molecule with two double bonds. If they are next to each other they are called "conjugated." They then show slightly different bond lengths and chemical behavior than for double bonds which are not conjugated.

The simplest molecule with conjugated double bonds is butadiene, with formula $H_2C\!\!=\!\!CH\!-\!CH\!\!=\!\!CH_2$. Actually, the carbon atoms are not on a straight line, but one expects either or both of two geometric forms, *trans* and *cis*, as given by Fig. 6.

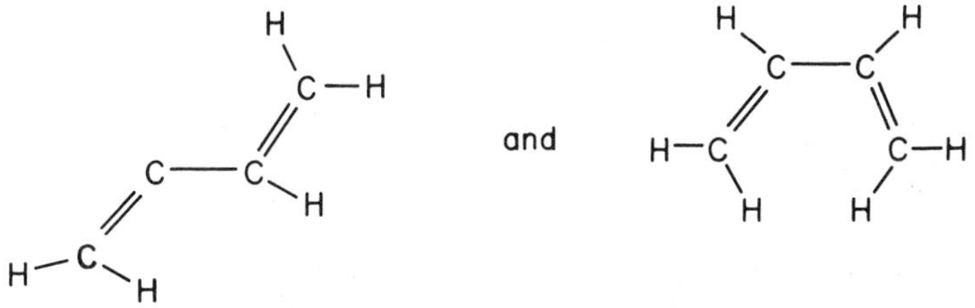

Fig. 6. Trans and cis forms of butadiene.

The *trans* form has symmetry C_{2h}, the *cis* form C_{2v}. Experimental evidence indicates that butadiene exists mainly in the *trans* form, with probably a few molecules in a slightly twisted version of the *cis* form.

MO theory makes interesting predictions about the structure and spectra of *cis* and *trans* butadiene. Note that in either form the central C–C bond is a single bond. Single bonds in general are longer than double bonds. Recall also that a double bond is made up of a σ and a π bond. The π bonds in butadiene (as also in unconjugated double-bonded molecules, for example ethylene) are mainly responsible for the longest wavelength and best known parts of the absorption spectrum, lying in the ultraviolet region. A single π bond would produce one $N \rightarrow V$ transition, but MO theory shows that two π bonds in a conjugated system must produce four $N \rightarrow V$ transitions, whose intensities can be calculated approximately from the theory. It is of special interest that the $N \rightarrow V$ transition of longest wavelength is the strongest, especially for the *trans* form. MO calculations indicate that the relative intensities of the several N → V transitions are very different for *cis*- and *trans*-butadienes.

In VII on "Conjugated Polyenes and Carotenoids," molecules with a considerable number of consecutive conjugated double bonds are considered. Here there are many N → V transitions, but just as in butadiene, the one of longest wavelength is the strongest. With increasing length of the polyene chain, the strength of this N → V transition increases. At the same time it shifts to longer wavelengths, finally giving visible color. Many familiar colored substances are polyenes or related compounds containing long conjugated polyene chains. Carrots owe their color to such a compound, called carotene, and other colored substances, e.g., butter, often contain molecules containing conjugated polyene chains.

All this is in agreement with the results of MO calculations. One result of these calculations is that the relative intensities of different N → V transitions depend very much on molecular geometry, as illustrated by butadiene. Many of the conjugated polyenes and related compounds are not entirely strung out in long chains, but have kinks of *cis* form. The intensities are then greatly affected.

In IV, whose title is "Cyclic Dienes and Hyperconjugation," conjugated dienes are considered in which the two double bonds are hooked together by single bonds to form a ring. (See Fig. 7.)

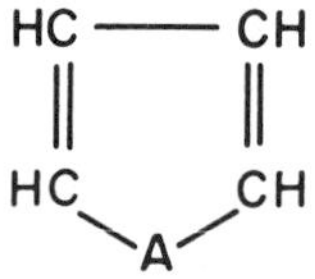

Fig. 7. Cyclic diene.

Here A may be an atom or a simple radical. It provides two single bonds which form links to the end atoms of the butadiene-like conjugated double bond structure, creating a ring of atoms.

Following are some examples. In thiophene, A is an S (sulfur) atom. In furan it is an O (oxygen) atom. In pyrrole, A is NH, where the N atom has three single bonds, two to close the ring and a third to hold an attached H atom. In cyclopentadiene, A is CH_2, like NH, but with two attached H atoms.

In these cyclic dienes, the geometrical arrangement of the conjugated double bonds is evidently of the *cis* type as in *cis*-butadiene and MO theory predicts relationships similar to those in *cis*-butadiene for the intensities of the expected N → V transitions. These predictions are confirmed by the observed spectra, so far as is known. Another cyclic diene is cyclohexadiene, which is like cyclopentadiene except that there are two CH_2 groups side by side instead of one such group. The cyclic dienes are interesting in that, because of differences in the inner angles in the ring, they are observed to differ markedly with respect to the relative intensities of different $N \rightarrow V$ transitions in ways which agree rather well with calculations by MO theory. I was very pleased to find that MO theory can give an understanding of the dependence of the strengths of $N \rightarrow V$ transitions on molecular geometry in conjugated dienes and polyenes.

In the cyclic dienes, there is a weak interaction between the A atom or group and the conjugated diene system that can be understood as an extension of the conjugation. This occurs because there is a pair of p electrons on A which function essentially as π electrons and which join weakly with the π electrons of the double bonds to form a larger conjugated system. In cyclopentadiene, the two bonds from C to 2H in the CH_2 group function rather as if there were a very weak double bond from the C to the H_2 group, and one can think of the CH_2 group as functioning, though weakly, conjugatively, like the π-behaving p electrons in the other cases. Because of this similarity, the name hyperconjugation was invented to describe this and similar situations; there will be more about hyperconjugation later. At first I called it superconjugation, but W.G. Brown proposed hyperconjugation as a better name. The idea was to designate a special, usually very weak effect somewhat resembling conjugation. At any rate, the name refers to cases where a grouping like $-CH_2$ or $-CH_3$ has weak conjugative quasi-π group properties like those in multiple bonds. To indicate this, one can write the groups as $-C=H_2$ and $-C\equiv H_3$.

Paper V discusses the spectrum of benzene, which has one strong $N \rightarrow V$ transition rather far in the ultraviolet (near wavelength 2000 Ångstrom units). Paper VIIIa, has a sub-title "Odd-numbered Conjugated Polyene Chain Molecules and Organic Dyes." In conjugated polyenes of the kind discussed in VI, the number of atoms in the conjugated chain is *even*. In VIIIa it is shown that conjugated polyenes also exist with an *odd* number of atoms in the polyene chain. In the commonest examples the chain forms a positive ion such as $NH_2 \cdots CH \cdots CH \cdots Ch \cdots NH_2^+$, where the dots indicate a bond structure which is most simply described as a quantum-mechanical mixture of two forms: $NH_2^+=CH-CH=CH-NH_2$ and $NH_2-CH=CH-CH=NH_2^+$. $N \rightarrow V$ transitions occur as in the even polyenes, and I found by very simple calculations that the intensity relations among the various $N \rightarrow V$ transitions are very similar to those in the even conjugated polyenes. Many dye molecules are salts whose positive ion is built on an odd-numbered polyene chain with nitrogen at each end as in the example above.

Paper VI, with subtitle "Molecular Refractivities of Organic Compounds" is concerned with a molecular property which is defined in terms of the index of refraction and the strengths of the various electronic transitions in the absorption spectrum. The property is defined for a frequency at which there is no absorption, commonly for the frequency of the yellow lines (D lines) of sodium. Existing experimental data on molecular refractivities can be expressed by an equation given in VI, which represents the *average* behavior for hydrocarbon molecules containing single and double bonds, *plus* an extra term varying from case to case called the "exaltation." The exaltation shows particularly large positive values for compounds containing conjugated double bonds, also distinct but small effects if hyperconjugation is present. With the aid of calculations making some reasonable assumptions, I showed in VI that a large part of any observed exaltation can be explained as a consequence of relatively high intensities in the $N \rightarrow V$ transitions of these compounds.

The name and the concept of hyperconjugation were briefly presented in paper IV of the Intensities series. A much more extensive paper by myself, Carol Rieke, and W.G. Brown was published in the *Journal of the American Chemical Society* in 1941, making use of rather extensive theoretical calculations. Mrs. Rieke, wife of a physicist working nearby, had cooperated with me for some time in many computations on molecules. We thought our paper was a pretty good one on a rather new idea.

I should, however, mention that other chemists (Pauling, Wheland, and Hückel) had already noticed some abnormally small but distinct shortenings of single bonds when next to double or triple bonds, for example, shortening of the C—C single bond in methylacetylene (H_3C—C≡CH). They realized that this effect might be attributed to something like conjugation, but they did not give a name to it, or make any calculations or give it extensive consideration. Besides producing shortened bond lengths, hyperconjugation causes small energy changes. A number of other interesting features are considered in our paper.

Since the time our paper was published, the idea of hyperconjugation has often been used by organic chemists. Also in considering later papers (see below) I shall discuss some special cases of hyperconjugation where because of polar effects the energy effects are much larger than in our 1941 paper.

I will now turn to two papers, published in 1941 in the *Physical Review*, which, as I have already mentioned, I wrote to coordinate closely with the work of my students Metropolis and Liebermann. Unlike most of my papers, which have dealt with electronic spectra and structures in terms of electron configurations and MOs, these two papers deal with the description and detailed classification of the rotational energy levels of triatomic molecules.

The papers are entitled "Species Classification and Rotational Energy Level Patterns of Non-Linear Triatomic Molecules," and "Correlation of Energy Levels of Linear and Bent Triatomic Molecules and the Ultraviolet CS_2 (Carbon Disulphide) Absorption Spectrum." In two papers related to the first of these, Metropolis discussed the structures of the electronic bands of SO_2 (sulfur dioxide) and similar molecules, as a function of the shape of the molecule in its upper and its lower electronic states. The second was especially relevant to the work of Liebermann on the CS_2 spectrum.

In IV of the long series of papers on polyatomic molecules which I published in 1932–35, molecular orbital and electronic states of these molecules were classified under species designations based on molecular symmetry, using group theory methods. Vibrational and vibronic (combined electronic and vibrational) states were similarly classified. It then remained to classify the finer-scale energy levels or sub-levels which result from molecular rotations. In the two papers on triatomic molecules now being discussed, I again used group theory methods. Every non-linear polyatomic molecule has rotational wave functions based on its behavior as a top. Every such molecule has three moments of inertia. If two of these are equal, it behaves as a symmetrical top, which may be either prolate like a carrot, or oblate, like perhaps a half-grapefruit. Examples of the oblate type are BCl_3, which is planar, and NH_3 which has a low-pyramical geometry. If all three moments of inertia are equal, it is a spherical top molecule. For each of these cases, the rotational wave functions have characteristic forms. Asymmetric-top molecules (i.e., with all moments of inertia unequal) have more complicated rotational wave functions. Each of these types has characteristic types of patterns of rotational or top energy levels. The foregoing discussion applies to non-linear polyatomic molecules of any size.

In the first of the two above-mentioned papers, I presented a diagram which Metropolis calculated for me, for a hypothetical asymmetric-top molecule like SO_2 but covering a broad range of apex angles α from a near-prolate case with a $\alpha = 120°$ near through the near-oblate case ($\alpha = 70° 32'$) to a second near-prolate case with $\alpha = 40°$. The diagram shows how the rotational energy would change with α for each of the occupied and a few unoccupied MOs. Metropolis in his two papers used this diagram in discussing the SO_2 molecule and its spectrum; in the ground state of SO_2, α is near 120°.

Each curve in the diagram has a label A, B_a, B_b, or B_c which refers to a group-theory species classification, of which there are four different kinds or species for asymmetric-top levels. These are

113

explained in the paper. Besides the top-species classification, one can combine this with the vibronic species classification, giving what I called a gyrovibronic species classification. There is also an "over-all" species classification, which takes account of all types of symmetry, including nuclear behavior. Finally, there is an over-all rotational quantum number J which measures the total angular momentum.

In the second of the above-mentioned papers, I showed a set of vibronic levels of a $^1\Sigma_g^+$ and a $^1\Pi_g$ electronic state of a linear triatomic molecule AB_2 together with gyrovibronic levels of the corresponding electronic states of bent AB_2. A correlation is set up between the sets of gyrovibronic levels of the two cases. In the diagram, curves are drawn connecting the two sets of levels. Liebermann in his Ph.D. thesis used the diagram in discussing the ultraviolet absorption bands of carbon disulfide (CS_2), whose ground state is linear. It is concluded that the longest-wave part of the spectrum represents an allowed electronic transition to a $^1B_2$ bent molecule upper state related to a $^1\Pi_g$ linear molecular state.

In the latter part of 1942, the headquarters of the atomic bomb project ("The Manhattan Project") became centered at the University of Chicago, with A.H. Compton as director, and Norman Hilberry as associate director. To try to disguise the nature of our activity, it was called "The Metallurgical Laboratory." Leading the research toward a self-sustaining fission reaction was Enrico Fermi.

I now envisaged the physics building in its war-time activity as a totally different place than before; all its objectives and functions had been transformed and familiar things appeared in a wholly new light. At meetings in what used to be the seminar room in Eckhart Hall, I had the feeling that at any time the Germans, who we thought could be ahead of us, might drop an atomic bomb on us. Actually, they were far behind us.

The project had several divisions. I think perhaps I was considered for awhile as Director of the Chemistry Division, but finally I was given the job of Director of the Information Division. Its main function was to supervise the production and distribution of classified reports within the local project and to and from related projects in other locations. Later I learned that my father, as a major in the Chemical Warfare Service, had a similar position as information officer in that organization.

As Information Director, I was, among other things, in charge of a large stenographic pool. I forget how many, perhaps 20 or 30

114

girls. But this did not bother me, since I was assisted by a capable older woman who took care of the pool. In dealing with the reports, Herman Fussler, later director of the university library, also assisted me. On the scientific side, beginning in 1943, I was assisted by Eugene Rabinowitch, the well-known chemical physicist who had written a book on uranium chemistry and many research papers. Another scientist cooperating with Rabinowitz in the Information Division was H.H. Goldsmith.

One troublesome problem was the budget. Most people needed or wanted a salary increase. My own university salary of $8,000 couldn't be changed, but was proving inadequate, so that I had to sell some stocks which I had inherited. When I first joined the physics faculty in 1928, my salary of $6,000 had seemed very ample, but times had changed.

During my time on the project I learned how to go home at the end of the day and forget the day's problems, and go to sleep promptly. This was a great change from previous times when my sleep had been interlaced with thinking about research problems.

In 1944 I organized material from project members into a Report on Nucleonics, a preview of the nuclear future initiated by Dr. Zay Jeffries. Rabinowitch and I collaborated in a chapter on "The Impact of Nucleonics on International Relations and the Social Order." During the first half of 1945 the scientists in the Project had many very serious discussions and sought to influence the way in which the atomic bomb would first be shown to the world. One result was the Franck report.

In an activity not officially recognized as a function of the Information Division, Rabinowitch and Goldsmith began to issue mimeographed sheets reviewing the discussions on the future among project members. Finally these took on printed form as the *Bulletin of the Atomic Scientists*, which has been and still is a very active publication (15).

As The Manhattan Project drew to a close, planning began for the publication of a series of volumes as a permanent record of scientific work of the Manhattan Project. I was Editor-in-Chief of the resulting Plutonium Project Record (16). (The Plutonium Project was the name finally adopted for the laboratories and installations associated with the work begun in the Metallurgical Project at Chicago.) The chemistry section of the Plutonium Project Record (PPR) through the efforts of J.C. Warner is especially complete. Many of the other sections, for example physics, are very incomplete because the potential authors wanted to get back to their own peace-time research. Hoylande D. Young entered the PPR program in 1945 as Technical Editor and carried on after the war as General Editor.

During 1944 and 1945 I was chairman of a committee to organize a Division of Spectroscopy in the American Physical Society, but the plans became dormant until after the war. They were then broadened with the result that the present Division of Chemical Physics was organized. Its first meeting took place in March 1951, with myself as chairman.

In June of 1945 A.H. Compton resigned as Dean of Physical Sciences and Chairman of the Physics Department at the University of Chicago. W. Bartky became Dean, and W.H. Zachariasen took over as the dynamic new chairman of physics. At a memorable meeting, several personnel changes were made, including recommendation to the administration for the appointment of Fermi and Teller as Professors, and Simpson as instructor.

In August, 1945, after the bomb had been dropped, people began to think about their post-war plans. I at first wondered whether I should continue in the pursuit of molecular spectra and structure or perhaps shift to nuclear or other problems, but finally concluded that what I had been doing was well worth continuing. At this time two new Research Institutes, now the Fermi Institute and Franck Institute, were being organized at the university. There was some encouragement, especially by the then Vice-President Reuben Gustavson, toward my establishing an Institute of Molecular Structure and Spectra, or perhaps of Molecular Physics, but finally that idea was dropped.

Meanwhile Gerhard Herzberg had joined the Astronomy Department and proceeded to build a very fine spectroscopic laboratory at the University's Yerkes Observatory at Williams Bay, Wisconsin. Two or three years later I tried to persuade the Physics Department to offer a joint appointment to Herzberg, but a colleague adamantly opposed this proposal with the argument that we already were adequately represented in the field of spectroscopy. Hindsight shows that he was right. Herzberg was soon called to Ottawa, where he brilliantly developed a world-famous institute of spectroscopy, with emphasis on applications to astrophysics. This led later to a Nobel Prize in chemistry for Herzberg.

XIX

After the War: The Laboratory of Molecular Structure and Spectra

After the war-time interruption, the work of our laboratory was resumed. John R. Platt came as Assistant Professor of Physics and was soon active in work on molecular spectroscopy. He and I also had some lively discussions on things in general. Students and postdoctoral associates were also soon at work.

For a while we were assisted by remaining funds from the Rockefeller Foundation grant. Then on September 1, 1946, we began to have support from a contract with the Office of Naval Research (ONR) with its new and very liberal policies. We were free to do basic research in applications of spectroscopy, with the justification that in the long run they should have value to the Navy. The ONR support was continued for a number of years. We received additional support at various times from contracts with the Army Research Office (Office of Ordnance Research, at first), and the Air Force Cambridge Research Center, and also from grants from the National Science Foundation (NSF).

Beginning in 1947, we issued a red-covered report about once a year, sometimes in two sections, including preprints or reprints of all papers on research which had been done under the ONR or the other research contracts. All but the earliest reports have been under the name of The Laboratory of Molecular Structure and Spectra (LMSS for short), a name which we adopted in 1952. It meant that emphasis in our laboratory was about equally divided between experimental and theoretical work on molecules. Our secretary-typist at the time was a philosophy student, Mr. H.H.

117

Brimmer, II. Our Red Reports were at first issued as of the Physics Department, Spectroscopy Laboratory, University of Chicago, but soon were issued under the LMSS logo. The last Red Report was issued in 1970.

In the absence of a formal institute, the LMSS had first developed as an informal group. For its activities and the Red Reports I was responsible, at first with the cooperation of Professor Platt and of C.C.J. Roothaan after he had become a member of the Physics Department staff. Besides these relatively permanent members, the LMSS included postdoctoral research associates and graduate students with a B.S. mostly from the University of Chicago or sometimes from another university. These graduate students came to us through the usual departmental channels and carried on Ph.D. work with Platt, Roothaan, or myself.

Most of the students worked for a physics Ph.D., but some for a Ph.D. in chemistry. This was because the LMSS was in the research field of Chemical Physics with some projects of more interest to physicists and others to chemists.

Each Red Report was really a joint report to all the agencies with which we had contracts. This arrangement was convenient for us in preparing and distributing the reports, and later in making reference to them.

In each report, we listed the time period covered for the whole report and for each person, scientific or non-scientific, who had participated in the work.

The personnel list included the names of all the people working with the LMSS, with the dates during which they were here and the contracts or grants which supported their work. First listed were the university faculty members, mostly Physics Department Professors and occasionally visiting Professors. Most of the time I was in this group, together with John R. Platt for some years, and later Clemens C. J. Roothaan who first came as a student with me, but soon had a physics Ph.D. and joined the faculty. Next were listed research associates, supported by contracts or grants.

Besides the student research, much of the work of LMSS was carried on by postdoctoral people working either more or less independently or in cooperation with one of us. Some of them came to us on fellowships from other institutions in this country, or often from abroad. Some were visiting Professors on leave of absence from other universities. To varying degrees, these were people who either said they wanted to work with us, or whom we persuaded to come. One large category was that of the research associates, whom we invited to come work with us on one of the research contracts. Many of these came in response to my request for a recommendation from a scientist I knew. They included several fine Japanese scientists recommended by my friend Professor Saburo Nagakura at the University of Tokyo.

Since much of my work was supported by research contracts, I should say something about how they were obtained. First, for each research project it was necessary to prepare and submit to the appropriate agency a proposal outlining the nature and duration of the contemplated research, together with a budget for the salaries of proposed research associates, typists and other necessary personnel; also for special equipment needed and not on hand. Sometimes a portion of the salaries of LMSS faculty members was included in the budget. As was mentioned above, several of our contracts were with military agencies. The first to award a contract to us was the ONR (Office of Naval Research). Our contract with ONR showed that what they wanted from us was nothing actually military, but only basic research of possible future background value. If the contract was approved, possibly after some revisions of the budget, we proceeded to obtain research associate appointments through university channels. Suitable reports (such as the Red Reports) were made during the life of the contract and frequently an extension or renewal was obtained. Reports on work done with NSF support were not included in the Red Reports. Instead, copies of reprints of all papers published in scientific journals and sometimes also preprints were sent regularly to NSF.

In the LMSS, there were, as already indicated, both students and postdoctoral people. The first of the latter was William C. Price, on leave from Imperial Chemical Industries, England, and later on the staff of King's College, London, where he became a professor. He was a friend with whom I had become well acquainted on English visits. He had an extensive record of fine spectroscopic work in the visible and ultraviolet regions. While he was here, we started some infrared work on boron compounds, largely because we could obtain them from Professor H.I. Schlesinger of the chemistry department.

There had long been arguments about the correct geometrical structure of B_2H_6. At one time an electron diffraction study seemed to indicate a trigonal structure like that of C_2H_6. But valence-wise this was not reasonable, and other structures had been suggested. Price in

119

his work here settled the matter. He showed by new work on the infrared spectrum that the structure is of D_{2h} symmetry like ethylene, with the two extra hydrogen atoms (as compared with ethylene) situated in a mid-plane position and each bonded to both boron atoms. Since that time a great many very complicated boron hydrides and other compounds with anomalous valence relations like those in B_2H_6 have been studied. While at Chicago Price also published papers on the infrared absorption spectra and ionization potentials of the hydrides and deuterides of sulfur, selenium, and tellurium, and on one or two other topics.

Clemens C.J. Roothaan, before long a faculty colleague at Chicago, came as a student in 1946 on a Netherlands-America Foundation fellowship. He had been well trained in physics and mathematics by Kronig at Delft, and soon began some interesting calculations. He and I presented a paper on some semiempirical LCAO-MO calculations on the twisting frequency of ethylene at a memorable American Chemical Society symposium at Northwestern University in December 1946. There I also discussed B_2H_6 and gave one more general paper. W.C. Price, Platt, and H.B. Klevens (an associate of Platt from the biochemistry department of the University of Minnesota) also gave papers.

At this time I advocated the use of semiempirical methods in molecular computations done by setting up a theoretical framework and at certain points in the calculation inserting experimentally determined quantities instead of certain integrals which were very difficult to compute. Later on I became converted to wholly theoretical ("ab initio") calculations.

Roothaan at my suggestion made a number of good semiempirical calculations on aromatic molecules, especially derivatives of benzene, but never published these.

Instead, he spent 1947–49 at the Catholic University of America in Washington, DC, where in Karl Herzfeld's department, he made great progress. He returned to Chicago in the summer of 1949 and received his Ph.D. in 1950. His thesis was his now classical paper on the all-electron self-consistent field (SCF) method, which laid the foundation for all subsequent "ab initio" calculations.

At the same time that Roothaan came to Chicago, C.N. Yang offered himself to me as a Ph.D. student in molecular structure or spectra, at the suggestion of his professor in China. When he showed me a paper he had written, it was clear that he was such a master of physical theory that I could not offer any useful suggestions. So he went to work at the Nuclear Institute, where he was first assigned experimental work, which was a mistake. (As Professor Allison sometimes remarked, "Where there's Yang, there's a bang.") Before long he earned a Ph.D. on a theoretical problem, and a few years later he won a Nobel Prize.

Charles W. Scherr, as student of Roothaan, did for his Ph.D. thesis the first all-electron computation for a molecule larger than H_2, namely for N_2. In this he was assisted by Tracy Kinyon who carried out the innumerable computations of one- and two-center integrals on one of the mechanical desk calculators (Marchants, Fridens, and Monroes) then available. Scherr's computations dealt not only with the ground state of N_2, but also with some important excited states. The ground state electron configuration is $1\sigma_g^2\, 1\sigma_u^2$ $2\sigma_g^2\, 2\sigma_u^2\, 1\pi_u^4\, 3\sigma_g^2,\ {}^1\Sigma_g^+$. Scherr's work also included the important set of six excited states of configuration . . . $1\pi_u^3\, 3\sigma_g^2\, 1\pi_g$ of the types ${}^3\Delta_u,\ {}^3\Sigma_u^+,\ {}^3\Sigma_u^-,\ {}^1\Delta_g,\ {}^1\Sigma_u^-,\ {}^1\Sigma_u^+$. He also computed the ${}^3\Pi_g$ and ${}^1\Pi_g$ states of configuration . . . $1\pi_u^4\, 3\sigma_g\, 1\pi_g$. These states and many others are now known experimentally, largely from work in our laboratory. Scherr's Ph.D. work was finished and published in 1955. Although Scherr used Slater rather than SCF AOs in his LCAO-MO expressions, and only a *minimal set* of these (i.e., one 1s, one 2s, one 2pσ and one 2pπ AO) we were very pleased at his accomplishment. Nowadays with a digital computer, the same computation can be done in a few minutes. In moving over to contemporary computer technology, we soon stopped making tables of integrals from which desired values were laboriously interpolated and thereafter computed integrals and everything else needed on digital computers directly for each molecule.

About 1950, when Roothaan's LCAO-MO method became available, we began to hope that it might become feasible to make genuine theoretical all-electron SCF calculations on relatively small diatomic molecules such as N_2. With our mechanical desk calculators, the process would be very slow. In the process it would also be necessary first to derive formulas for some difficult two-center interelectronic repulsion and other integrals. So Roothaan decided to concentrate on the problem of deriving the necessary formulas.

In August, 1950, he was joined in this attack by Klaus Rueden-berg, who had recently obtained his Ph.D. at Chicago with Professor Gregor Wenzel on quantum field theory problems. Although this was a distinctly different field from that of molecular integrals, it had given him very useful mathematical training. Ruedenberg came to LMSS following Professor Wenzel's generous suggestion that our program now looked more promising for future successful accomplishment than his own field theory work.

Incidentally, Robert Parr in his Ph.D. thesis with Crawford at Minnesota had computed some of these difficult two-center integrals. But instead of pursuing the matter further, Pariser and Parr in 1953, and independently Pople, developed fruitful semiempirical procedures which made it possible, with only moderate errors, to ignore the difficult integrals. Later several refinements of the method were developed, especially by Dewar.

However, Roothaan and Ruedenberg at Chicago continued on the trail of the difficult integrals until the problem was solved, at least for the two-center case applicable to diatomic molecules. Lennard-Jones in Cambridge developed a very different method which could be used for the two-center integrals and also for three-center and four-center cases, which occur for polyatomic molecules.

While the difficult integrals were being gotten under control, we heard reports of the beginning use of digital computers to increase greatly the speed of computations. As time went on, the method became steadily more rapid and more efficient and radically changed our viewpoint in favor of making machine computations. At first we constructed reference tables of integrals computed by machine. Earlier, about 1930, Kotani, in Japan, had computed and published tables of some of the more important integrals. But soon we learned that such tables were not needed when we could ask a machine directly for a desired result. Overlap integrals, for example, could now be very easily computed as input for the energy calculation, so tables were very little needed.

In and after 1947 Professor Platt with students and other collaborators published a number of valuable papers on hydrocarbon, flurocarbon, and related spectra. These and a number of later papers (1949–64) by himself and his associates were collected in two books published in 1964 by John Wiley and Sons. As time went on Platt's interests turned increasingly toward biophysics and social phenomena; he left Chicago for Ann Arbor in 1965.

One of the two 1964 books is a collection of 35 papers by Platt and his students and associates. The book is entitled "Systematics of the Electronic Spectra of Conjugated Molecules." It includes works which gave rise to good Ph.D. theses for three of Platt's graduate students: W.J. Potts, Jr., Ph.D. in Chemistry, 1955, with a thesis on low-temperature absorption spectra; M. Gouterman, Ph.D. in Physics 1959, with a thesis on porphyrin spectra; and J. Petruska in Chemistry 1961, with a thesis on perturbation theory for substituted cyclic polyene and substituted benzene spectra.

The second 1964 book consists of 21 papers and is entitled "Free-electron Theory of Conjugated Molecules." The papers are mostly by Platt and K. Ruedenberg, with several by N.S. Ham, while a few are joint papers by these authors and in some cases others at LMSS. The free-electron model, a favorite with Platt, is rather artificial and not rigorous but gives interesting and suggestive results similar to those of MO theory.

In and about 1947 I directed most of my attention to the preparation of papers on two subjects, one being that of overlap integrals, now to be explained. The other will be explained further on. In their papers on the quantum theory of valence, Slater and Pauling pointed out that the strength of the bond formed between two atoms should tend to be larger the more the regions of space occupied by the two electrons overlap. These regions of space are determined in valence-bond theory by the orbitals (AOs) occupied by the two electrons. The criterion for maximum strength is then that of *maximum overlapping* of these orbitals.

The best way to gauge the total amount of overlap of two orbitals as an index of bond strength is probably to write down a mathematical expression for each, to form the product of these, and then to take the integral of this product over all space (overlap integral). That is, if ϕ_a represents the expression for the orbital on one atom, and ϕ_b for that on the other, the overlap integral, which is commonly symbolized by S, is given by

$$S = \int \phi_a \, \phi_b \, dv \qquad (1)$$

Pauling had used a rather different and I thought less desirable procedure to evaluate the extent of overlap. Furthermore, in calculations made in those days it was usually customary to "neglect" overlap integrals, that is, put them equal to zero. For example, we explicitly neglected them in our big 1941 paper on hyperconjugation. However, in a subsequent brief note in 1941, we showed that the apparent complete neglect was actually only partial, although substantial. I will not try here to explain why, since the explanation is somewhat involved. The reader, if interested, should refer to our Note in *Journal of the American Chemical Society* **63**, 1770 (1941).

Convinced in any event of the importance of overlap integrals, Mrs. Rieke and I in 1949 obtained the collaboration of two students in mathematics, D. Orloff and H. Orloff, to obtain, first, useful mathematical formulas for various overlap integrals, and then, to compute mathematical tables for a number of important cases. Our results were published in the *Journal of Chemical Physics* in 1949 in a paper entitled "Formulas and Numerical Tables for Overlap Integrals." In this paper we gave formulas for S for all AO pairs involving ns, $np\sigma$, $np\pi$ AOs for n=1, 2, 3, and 5 using a set of AOs which had been proposed by Slater. (We chose n=5 instead of n=4 because in practice the size of n=4 AOs in actual atoms, as indicated by spectroscopic data, was nearer to what one would predict for n=5). Although it would have been more accurate to use SCF (self-consistent field) AOs, we did not have them at that time, and thought that the use of Slater orbitals would be good enough. Slater orbitals, although nodeless and therefore not properly representing the inner parts of the AOs, seemed acceptable because the overlaps we seek depend very largely just on the outer parts of the orbitals.

For the overlapping orbitals of any pair of atoms, the formulas and tables took account of the values of two important quantities which differ from case to case, namely the distance between the two atoms and the sizes of the two orbitals. We also took into account whether the two atoms are alike (homopolar bonds) or different (heteropolar bonds). Thus the tables cover a range of interatomic distances (or bond lengths) and of polarity of the bonds. A short preliminary paper published in May summarized the situation.

In a few subsequent papers I discussed related matters. Published in the *Journal of the American Chemical Society* in 1950, I discussed "Overlap Integrals and Chemical Binding." In the *Journal of Chemical Physics* in 1951, under the title "Overlap and Binding Power of 2s, 2p Hybrid Orbitals" are tables and figures to illustrate that "a little hybridization goes a long way," using tables of overlap integrals for hybrid orbitals. In a 1951 paper in the *Journal of Chemical Physics* entitled "Orthonormal Sets of LCAO Molecular Orbitals for Second-Row Homopolar Diatomic Molecules" I considered homopolar second-row LCAO MOs under the needed restriction that they form an orthogonal set, and showed that the requirement of orthogonality (that is, that the integral $\phi_1\phi_2 \, d\tau$ be zero if ϕ_1 and ϕ_2 are two MOs) causes a particular amount of 1s-2s-2p hybridization ("forced hybridization") among the AOs used in constructing the LCAOs. Thus in a diatomic molecule like N_2, where $1\sigma_g$, $2\sigma_g$ and $3\sigma_g$ MOs are occupied, their LCAO expressions must be orthogonal, and this produces forced hybridization. As I showed, this has the effect of weakening the bonding. A similar effect occurs with the $1\sigma_u$ and $2\sigma_u$ MOs.

Several years later, although our formulas and tables remained convenient, they became relatively trivial in view of the work of Roothaan and Ruedenberg on other much more difficult two-center integrals. This was true especially because of the increasing use of digital computers in molecular calculations. Integrals could now be computed directly without reference to tables.

In 1951 I wrote a paper entitled "Magic Formula, Structure of Bond Energies, and Isovalent Hybridization." This was published in the *Journal of Physical Chemistry* **54**, 295, (1952). Its purpose was to give approximate quantitative form to the Slater–Pauling criterion of maximum overlapping. It gives the energy of atomization D_0 as a sum of terms of which the principal ones are functions of overlap integrals (calculated theoretically), of atomic ionization potentials (experimental), and also of degree of hybridization where the latter can occur without a change of valence (isovalent hybridization). After calibration by fitting to three molecules, where the necessary information was known fairly accurately, it was found to fit seven other molecules within ± 0.3 eV.

This paper, about which I was somewhat enthusiastic when it was written, was essentially a semiempirical tour-de-force in which I had skillfully combined certain elements from LCAO-MO theory and valence-bond theory. At the time I was just on the verge of changing from an opinion favoring semiempirical to one favoring ab initio (purely theoretical) methods. Up to that time this had seemed too difficult for getting molecular wave functions and energies to be practical. The shift got under way following the Shelter Island conference in 1951. But when I wrote it, the magic formula and its by-products seemed a promising way to understand the component factors which contributed to the energy of formation of molecules from atoms, and other matters such as the nature and effects of hybridization.

My major activity for perhaps a year prior to 1948 was the preparation of a long report on some aspects of molecular orbital theory, to be presented at a big international meeting of chemists in Paris in April 1948. It was the first such meeting in France after the war, and was attended among others by practically all the chemical physicists active at the time. This was an important meeting and I felt I should go if at all possible. The only argument against going was that we were just then expecting our second child. Just three days before the Paris conference began, our daughter Valerie, named for my sister-in-law and also an Austrian aunt, was born on April 3, a healthy baby. My wife was much disturbed at my leaving so soon after this event but I felt I must go.

I went by Air France to Paris, with a heavy load of slides covering what I wanted to say. In those days, glass slides of size 3 $\frac{1}{4}''$ × 4″ were used. The conference chairman, Edmund Bauer, initiated the conference. I gave my lecture on molecular orbital theory with the help of my numerous slides. After I had discussed the contents of a slide in English, someone translated the discussion into French, with the result that the whole procedure took all morning. In the afternoon Linus Pauling explained valence-bond theory, again with numerous slides which were translated into French, so that it took all afternoon. On following days other people gave a variety of interesting talks.

All the papers were published in 1949 by the French *Journal de Chimie Physique*. For this purpose my papers were translated into French, with the title "Quelques Aspects de la Theorie des Orbitales Moleculaires." Publication was in vol. 46, pp. 497–542 for parts I–IV, and pp. 675–713 for part V, which was mostly an application to the benzene molecule.

Regarding my talk. I think there were some useful rather technical features, but nothing strikingly novel. One thing I did was to introduce the word spinorbital, an entity consisting of the product of an orbital and an electron spin function. Spinorbitals are necessary elements in constructing a properly antisymmetrical wave function, that is, one obeying the Pauli principle.

An especially pleasant feature of the conference was seeing old scientific friends and acquaintances, and meeting new ones. It was now 15 years since the last time I had been in Europe, and there were many new developments to discuss, both in theoretical and in experimental work. Besides myself and Pauling, there were only three other Americans at the conference. One other non-European was C.V. Raman from India. He had recently been studying the Raman effect and other characteristics of diamonds. He showed us large slices (three or four inches across as I remember it) of somewhat impure diamonds, for example, containing some nitrogen. The slices looked to me like slices of a vegetable such as rutabaga. Obviously these were not gem diamonds.

The most prominent French scientists in the realm of molecular electronic structure were Bernard and Alberte Pullman and Raymond and Pascaline Daudel. Husband and wife in each case, they were leaders in their scientific work. For some time the Daudels and Pullmans were rivals and not on the best of terms, but later they resumed friendly relations.

During the conference there were of course dinners and social events. I had lunch once with Professor and Madame Bauer. Most memorable for me was a party at the Pullman apartment, with endless bottles of champagne. The Pauling's daughter, Linda, put on a little solo dancing exhibition.

Among others present at the conference was Charles Coulson, who had studied at King's College, London, with Lennard-Jones, who, by 1948, was a professor at Cambridge. Coulson was already prominent for work on the theory of molecular structure and spectra. Another young man whom I met at the conference was H.C. (Christopher) Longuet-Higgins, who had also rather recently entered this field. He invited me to stay at his lodgings in Balliol College, Oxford. After the conference I took advantage of his invitation to visit with him at Balliol. During the few days I was there, he learned that his application for a fellowship, a Commonwealth Fellowship if I remember correctly, had been denied, quite wrongly in my opinion, in view of his promise and the excellent work he had done. I then told him that I had some ONR funds which I could use if he would care to come to Chicago and work with our group. He accepted and while in Chicago he published several good theoretical papers on MO theory of unsaturated hydrocarbons and aromatic amines, and other more general topics.

While at Oxford I was impressed by the brilliant group at the Physical Chemistry Laboratory, including Professor Cyril Hinshelwood, R.P. Bell, Tommy (H.W.) Thompson, E.J. Bowen, J.W. Linnett, Leslie Sutton, and Longuet-Higgins. Each had his own special line of research. I established friendly relations with all of them and became acquainted with their research activities. In the evening I enjoyed dinners at the "high table" of one or another of the colleges to which they belonged, followed by a taste of college news and gossip, good port, and perhaps a cigar. At one such dinner I especially enjoyed eating lampreys in the fish course, and recalled having read that King Henry VIII had died from "a surfeit of lampreys."

In England I also visited Manchester where there was another good center of chemical physics. They were doing research which interested me very much and broadened my ideas. Of the Manchester group, Skinner, Warhurst, and Swarc were at the Paris conference. Of course I spent some time in London, especially at University College, King's College, and Imperial College of the University of London, where I visited the spectroscopists and got better acquainted with them and their work. At University College I also visited Professor C.K. Ingold, the organic chemist well known especially for his classification of reaction mechanisms. His categories of nucleophilic and electrophilic reagents are considerably related to those of electron donors and acceptors. I had good discussions with him on this and later occasions. My best friend at King's College, Bill Price, was just then in Chicago with LMSS.

After England, I went to Belgium, where spectroscopy was active, in varying spectral regions at different centers. At Louvain I saw de Hemptinne and Manneback who were working on infrared and Raman spectra. At Louvain I also met Abbé Lemaitre who told me of the theory that the universe had started as a massive egg which exploded. Essentially this idea is now generally known, but in 1948 it was new to me, perhaps to nearly everyone. Abbé Lemaitre was one of the first, or perhaps the first, to entertain it. He had just come back from a visit at the Vatican. He told me that the spectroscopic group there had to be careful not to be too noisy, since their quarters were just under those of the Pope. There has long been a spectroscopic laboratory at the Vatican as part of the Vatican Observatory.

I was welcomed at Liège by Professor Louis d'Or, the chairman of the chemistry department, and others. I was given a bronze medal in appreciation of my work. This was my first medal. Spectroscopy of the kinds with which I was most familiar (emission spectra of molecules and radicals in the visible and near ultraviolet parts of the spectrum) was carried on actively at the University by P. Swings (Director of Astrophysics, with whom I got well acquainted), Boris Rosen, and Migeotte. Rosen I had first met in Berlin in 1925. Later, at Liège, he got out a valuable compendium of constants for diatomic molecules based largely on their spectra. Also at Liège was Jules Duchesne, who had been at the Paris conference. I, and later my wife, were good friends of his and knew his family, too.

Returning for a moment to the Paris conference, another scientist there was Miss Inga Fischer, who obtained her Ph.D. in work on molecular electronic structure problems. I think she worked with Professor Lennard-Jones when he was at King's College, London. Before long she married and became Mrs. Fischer-Hjalmars. She has been for some time a professor at the University of Stockholm working on quantum mechanics and its application to molecules. Anticipating events of some years later, I was delighted to find that just before I was presented to the King of Sweden to receive the Nobel Prize, it was she who gave the speech to introduce me with a survey of the work I had done that was deemed to make me worthy of the prize.

Until somewhat after the time of the Paris conference in 1948 most of our LCAO-MO calculations were made by the very empirical Hückel method. Further, they were generally confined to calculations on structure and spectra of the π electrons only. This limitation was somewhat justified by the fact that the most loosely held (easily ionized) electrons in unsaturated molecules, that is, organic molecules with double or sometimes triple bonds, are the π electrons in these bonds. Thus we could learn much by such calculations on these molecules. In doing so, following the lead of an important paper by Goeppart-Mayer and Sklar, we used an SCF (self-consistent field) method.

Our calculations in those days at LMSS were made laboriously by hand using mechanical desk calculators. They were done mostly by Mr. Tracy Kinyon, who had been paid by the government as a handicapped person since the Depression days. Tracy was a meticulous worker who carried out the calculations in duplicate with 6 to 8 figure precision. We counted on him for reliable and accurate calculations, and were grateful to him.

One feature of my Paris paper was an extensive analysis of the Hückel parameters α and β. In 1948–49, besides Longuet-Higgins and Mrs. Rieke, two other postdoctoral people were working with us at LMSS. One was Putcha Venkateswarlu from India as a Research Associate. He has long been a professor at the Indian Institute of Technology in Kampur. Putcha is an experienced experimental spectroscopist. Among other things, he has done much work on resonance series in the halogen molecule spectra. Two of his children were born in this country and have been having successful research careers here. In 1948–49, Putcha made a very interesting discovery, namely, an emission spectrum of the SiF_2 molecule.

The second Research Associate, at this time a National Research Council Fellow, was Harrison Shull. He published several papers on theoretical calculations which he made on intensities of electronic transitions in molecular spectra. These were along lines similar to those of my 1939–40 series on intensities. Harry Shull is now well known for his research and his successful graduate students in quantum chemistry, and for his work as a university administrator and in national science affairs. In 1982 he became Chancellor of the University of Colorado at Boulder, Colorado.

Dr. Robert G. Parr spent the summer of 1949 with me in some LCAO-MO calculations on π-electron energy levels of cis and trans butadiene (published 1950) and of resonance energies of benzene and butadiene (published 1951).

Every year in late April there is a meeting of the National Academy of Sciences, which I usually attended. In 1949 I was particularly interested in an abstract, published before the meeting, of a paper to be presented by Professor Joel Hildebrand of the University of California at Berkeley. He was reporting on a new absorption spectrum which he and his student H.A. Benesi had found when iodine was dissolved in benzene. Professor Hildebrand, an active chemist until he died at age 101 in 1983, was a well-known authority on solution spectra. Until 1919 I had concerned myself only with the spectra of molecules or radicals in the gas or vapor state, but not in substances dissolved in liquids. But as I have described earlier, I was much interested in the spectrum of iodine and related molecules, and was also interested in the energy levels of benzene. In fact Roothaan and I in 1948 had published a paper in the *Journal of Chemical Physics* (**16,** 118–22) entitled "Molecular Orbital Treatment of the Ultraviolet Spectra of Benzene and Borazole." Borazole is a molecule very like benzene except that three CH groups of benzene are replaced by N atoms.

The fact that an unexplained new spectrum appeared when iodine was dissolved in benzene intrigued me so much that when I met Joel Hildebrand at the meeting I said to him, "I bet I can explain that spectrum," and after trying for a year or so, I published in 1950 in the *Journal of the American Chemical Society* (**72,** 600-08) a paper entitled "Studies of Complexes Formed by Halogen Molecules with Aromatic and with Oxygenated Solvents." It had been known for some years that many molecules pair off with other molecules to form what are called molecular complexes. I assumed that benzene and an iodine molecule had gotten together in this way and that somehow the presence of iodine in the complex had made the benzene molecule produce a new spectrum. At the same time I tried to explain some new spectra which appeared when iodine was dissolved in alcohol or ether.

However, as it turned out, all my explanations were wrong. Fortunately, as it happened, Professor Hildebrand had been asked to plan a symposium on molecular complexes and their spectra at a meeting of the American Chemical Society in Chicago soon after my paper was finished, and he invited me to give a talk on the spectra of complexes. This got me to thinking again, very hard, and finally I came up with a new theory which turned out to be largely correct. I managed to put a short note on this theory into the tail end of my 1950 article during the process of checking the printer's proof of the article just before its publication.

My new theory assumed that when two molecules get together in a complex, there is a partial transfer of an electron from one (the donor) to the other (the acceptor). So I called such a complex a "charge-transfer complex." This aspect of the theory was not entirely new and, as it later turned out, I overestimated the extent of charge transfer in the ground state of the complex. However, the really most important aspect of the theory was that the new *spectra* which appeared when a complex was formed were "intermolecular charge-transfer spectra," where in the excited, upper, state of the complex pretty nearly a whole electron had been transferred from the donor to the acceptor molecule. Although the idea of partial charge transfer had been used before for atoms for example from a charged silver atom to a halogen molecule in the photographic process, and also in one of my interpretations of $N \rightarrow V$ spectra, the case here was different. My new theory said that the new spectrum which appeared only after a complex was formed and which did not occur for either of the two partners of the complex when alone was an *intermolecular* charge transfer spectrum. In this a quantum jump occurred during which the initial rather slight charge transfer, from donor to acceptor molecule, became pretty nearly complete resulting in a charge-transfer state which has nearly the character of a pair of oppositely charged molecular ions. I should add that the total spectrum of the complex also included all the spectra (perhaps slightly modified) which the two molecules that form the complex would show when alone.

Some time after this theory was published, G. Briegleb in Würzbug, Germany, published an excellent and comprehensive book describing his and his students' extensive work on molecular complexes, including spectra and other properties. He accepted my theory of intermolecular charge-transfer spectra so whole-heartedly that he dedicated his book to me. However, he did not accept my use of the name charge-transfer complexes for the ground states of complexes, but wisely spoke of electron donor-acceptor complexes.

Before long, several of us at LMSS were doing research on

donor-acceptor complexes and charge-transfer spectra, while other groups at various places also took up the subject. The studies were nearly all on complexes in liquid solutions. One result was, therefore, to get me to study solution spectra, as well as gas or vapor spectra. I said, "It got me into solution," putting me into company with Hildebrand and many other chemists.

My fascination with molecular complexes and electron transfer between molecules lasted for a long time. It was very strong in 1950–54, and I did not forget it while I was in England in 1955, and it continued in following years. Among students who worked in the field at LMSS was N.S. Ham, an Australian predoctoral fellow in 1952–55. Dr. H.M. McConnell came to Chicago to work on complexes, and was an NRC postdoctoral fellow in 1950–52. He worked on complexes between benzene and trinitrobenzene. Ham, Platt, and McConnell wrote a joint paper on complexes.

Dr. D.F. Evans from Imperial College, London, was an LMSS Research Associate in 1954. He made a thorough study, largely at very late evening hours, of solutions of iodine and bromine in various organic solvents in the rather far ultraviolet region of the spectrum. The spectrum of iodine when dissolved in solvents such as normal heptane showed pronounced absorption in the region 2200–2600 Å, in contrast to the fact that iodine vapor, likewise iodine, dissolved in a highly fluorinated solvent such as perfluoroheptane in which the hydrogen atoms of ordinary heptane are replaced by fluorine atoms, shows *no* absorption in this region. We did not find evidence that iodine and heptane molecules were held together even temporarily in a complex, but rather that a charge-transfer spectrum was produced by the two molecules momentarily in contact. When I was in London in 1955 I discussed this and similar cases with L.E. Orgel, and we published a paper together in which we introduced the name "contact charge-transfer spectra" for such spectra. Along with his work on iodine solutions, Evans found similar results with bromine solutions. One result of his work on both halogens was to show that highly flourinated hydrocarbons are truly inert solvents.

While I was in London in 1955, Orgel and I discussed the possibility of writing a book together on molecular complexes, and we accomplished some writing. Somehow, however, our approaches, or our styles, turned out to be so different that we gave up the attempt.

Meanwhile in Chicago, Saburo Nagakura, who had volunteered to come from Tokyo University to work on molecular complexes, was carrying on an excellent piece of work on the iodine complex of triethylamine. This was published in 1955. In later years he published an immense number of papers on complexes and a variety of related matters.

Nagakura is now director of a recently established research institute at Okazaki, some distance outside of Tokyo. He was instrumental in establishing that institute. He is internationally known and was once president of the International Union of Pure and Applied Chemistry. He is a good friend of many years, who has been very helpful to me on my visits to Tokyo, in spite of his busy schedule. My most recent visit was in 1982 during my induction as an honorary member of the Japanese Chemical Society. Since 1955 several of Nagakura's students have come to Chicago to do research on complexes. One of the first was H. Tsubomura, with whom I published a paper in 1960 on ultraviolet absorption spectra caused by the interaction of oxygen with organic molecules.

My pervasive interest in molecular complexes led me to give short talks on the subject at various places during 1944–45. These included a talk in Japan in 1953, one in France in 1954, one in Milan, Italy in 1952, and an article published in the journal *Nucleus* in 1964. I also published several much more comprehensive articles: in the *Journal of Physical Chemistry* (1952), in the McGraw–Hill Encyclopedia (1960); and in French *Journal de Chimie Physique* (1963). Also, jointly with Willis Person, who had spent some time with me in Chicago, there was a 1962 review article in *Annual Review of Physics*. Another review article presented the text of a Welsh Foundation lecture which I gave in Houston, Texas, in 1967. Further, jointly with Person, there was a long chapter in 1969 in vol. 3 of *Physical Chemistry*, published by Academic Press. These citations indicate that the subject had proved of extensive general interest.

One manifestation of interest in molecular complexes was the establishment of a Gordon conference on the subject. Gordon conferences are held each year, and at any one time a number of conferences on varied subjects are going on. The earliest Gordon conferences were held on an island in Chesapeake Bay, but New Hampshire proved more salubrious for summer. The conferences now make use of the dormitory, dining, and classroom facilities of a number of boys' schools which are not in session in the summer, but are leased for the Gordon conferences. Here the devotees of each subject gather for a week of informal talks, with the afternoon reserved for individual discussions or for exploration of the country.

An enjoyable procedure is to take a plane to Boston and there to rent a car to drive to the conference site and be free to roam from there. However, many conference attendants go in buses from the Boston airport. The Gordon conferences are excellent occasions for getting acquainted with fellow workers in one's field, and learning of their progress and new ideas. Any individual may be interested in more than one Gordon conference during the summer, for example I have been especially interested not only in the conferences on complexes but also in those on molecular electronic structure. Sometimes family members may be taken along and stay at a nearby hotel or the like. At one time that I remember, my daughter Valerie was in attendance with our two black cocker spaniel puppies recently brought from California. More recently, my older daughter Lucia and her husband John Heard came along to a meeting at a school on the shore of Lake Winnepesaukee.

The period of 1949–50 was characterized by growing emphasis on theoretical computations on molecular structure, and also by active experimental research on diatomic and polyatomic spectra. In 1950, Dr. Philip G. Wilkinson agreed to come as a Research Associate to work with the vacuum spectrograph which we had acquired from George Harrison of MIT in exchange for a diffraction grating ruling machine built in Chicago by Michelson. He had been for a few years working in spectroscopy at the Naval Research Laboratory in Washington, D.C., but in correspondence had expressed great interest in coming here to work with us and our vacuum spectrograph.

However, Wilkinson was a Naval Reserve Officer and when the Korean War broke out he felt he must go on active duty. To take his place, I persuaded Dr. Yoshio Tanaka, then a very fine young experimental spectroscopist to come on leave of absence from a position as Assistant Professor at the Tokyo University of Education. I had first met him when he and the well-known older Japanese spectroscopist, Professor Takamine, visited America just before World War II. At the time, our relations with Japan had been showing signs of strain, and Takamine discussed the problem with me. He wondered if we scientists on both sides couldn't do something to ameliorate the situation.

Tanaka reassembled the vacuum spectrograph and brought it into good working order. At last we had a high-resoluton vacuum spectrograph with a 15,000 and a little later a 300,000 line per inch grating. With this we obtained good spectra, although only down to a wave length of at best about 1000 Å, but often only to 1500 Å. In a vacuum spectrograph all the air has been pumped out because otherwise at wavelengths below about 2200 Å, the oxygen in the air absorbs practically all the light.

One day Tanaka told me that our old friend, Y. Fujioka, whom my wife and I had first met in Leipzig in 1930, was in town and wondered if we would be willing to see him now that the war was over. We had some people in to meet him. After a while he stood up and said, "I must go." Everyone else then left, but he came back and settled down for more drinks and some reminiscences.

At the end of two years in Chicago, I thought that Tanaka would expect to return to his position in Tokyo, but when I spoke of this he threw his hands in the air and said, "America is wonderful!" and told me that he was accepting a position at the Air Force Cambridge Research Laboratory near Boston and was bringing his family. For some years he remained there, making a long succession of fine contributions to experimental spectroscopy. Later T. Namioka (Ph.D. 1959) whose Ph.D. work at Chicago began with the theory of our vacuum spectrograph, whose design was somewhat unusual, became Tanaka's son-in-law. Some years later Tanaka moved to the University of California at Santa Barbara and continued to do novel and important work.

XX

The Shelter Island Conference: A Watershed

In April, 1950 at a Detroit ACS meeting, a group of chemists and physicists fell into a discussion of the inadequacies of valence theory and what might be done to improve it. The need felt most acutely was a reliable table of the difficult integrals which inevitably turn up in valence calculations. Everyone agreed that a conference on such integrals would be desirable. I undertook to organize a conference whose scope would emphasize the integrals problem but would also include a variety of other problems in chemical physics. In the planning I was aided by the advice and cooperation of D.A. MacInnes, chairman of the National Academy of Sciences committee on scientific conferences. And so, with the sponsorship of the Academy and the financial support and encouragement of the Office of Naval Research, the Conference on Quantum-Mechanical Methods in Valence Theory was held September 8–10, 1951 at Shelter Island, New York, close to the eastern end of Long Island. Invitations were issued to a number of chemists and physicists, both in the United States and overseas. Not everyone could attend, but 25 came, including five from England, one from Tokyo (M. Kotani), and one from Uppsala (P. O. Löwdin). Fifty-two papers were given, and were made available afterwards in a printed volume issued by the ONR. This includes a summary by R.G. Parr and B.L. Crawford, Jr., who acted as conference secretaries. This summary was published in June 1952 in the Proceedings of the National Academy of Sciences.

XX. The Shelter Island Conference: A Watershed

It would not be worth while here to go into detail about the papers presented and their discussion, since we have now progressed so far since 1951. However, for the sake of historical perspective, I will give a partial version of some major items in Parr and Crawford's summary. They state that the papers seem to fall into the following six groups.

(1) Applications of then currently used theory. Parr and Crawford include reference to Shull's work on the charge distribution in the CO bond of CO_2. They also say that the relatively small amount of discussion in this group of papers probably reflected a certain satisfaction with current π-electron theory. This was dominant then for calculations on structures and spectra, with little or no attention to the more numerous σ electrons. Wheland discussed magnetic anisotropy.

(2) The next group of papers dealt with quantum interpretation of chemical valence concepts, i.e., electron pairs, bond energies, bond orders, hybridization and chemical reactivity. Lennard-Jones especially discussed the role of electron pairs. T. Berlin pointed out that the space in a diatomic molecule can be precisely divided into binding and antibinding regions, the former tending to pull the nuclei together, the latter to make them fly apart. This formulation, although still valid and in my opinion a valuable one, has been relatively little used. Note here that binding does not mean the same thing as bonding. Coulson displayed some interesting maps of electron density in benzene, which showed the π electrons totally immersed in a sea of σ electrons. I discussed my "magic formula" and its indication that π-bonding contributions to the bond energies of multiple bonds are probably much larger than generally believed, and that isovalent hybridization and nonbonded inner shell exchange repulsions are often important in determining molecular stability. Coulson and I discussed various versions of the concept of bond order. Eyring emphasized the possible fruitfullness of quantum-mechanical calculations on activated complexes.

(3) Hirschfelder reviewed the problem of forces between molecules and between non-bonded atoms. Margenau told of some recent work in this area. Coulson discussed possible very long range forces postulated by some biologists. I presented intermolecular charge-transfer forces as a new type of force between electron donors and acceptors. Van Vleck discussed a new source of information on intermolecular forces, namely, line breadth in microwave spectra.

(4) When starting from either a valence-bond or an SCF LCAO-MO wave function, additional "configuration interaction" terms are required for an accurate function. The improvement in energy gained thereby is called correlation energy. Hartree rightly objected to the

137

term "configuration interaction" and instead spoke of "superposition of configurations." Roothaan and I believe we can use the simple term "configuration mixing" to meet Hartree's objection to "configuration interaction," but, regrettably, most workers in molecular structure still use the latter term. The improvement in a SCF wave function is properly described as "electron correlation." The improvement is obtained by forming a linear combination of the initial SCF function with other SCF functions, or, in other words, mixing these with the initial SCF function, which is the main term in the linear combination or mixture. The added functions are chosen subject to the condition of minimizing the calculated total energy so far as possible. With the passage of time, more and more sophisticated methods have been developed. The Shelter Island conference was just the earliest step in this direction.

(5) There were several mathematical developments. J.E. Mayer outlined a formulation of the Hartree–Fock equation employing the charge-density matrix, and P.O. Löwdin reviewed work on numerical integration schemes for these equations. Slater and Ufford reported that IBM computers were now in use for calculating atomic self-consistent fields. Computerized calculations on molecules were still in the future.

(6) Integrals were now considered explicitly. It was realized that accurate theoretical calculations could be done only if all integrals, including formerly neglected "small" integrals, were included. Among others, of course, overlap integrals, which are not always small, as had been assumed, must be included. Groups working circa 1951 on integrals included those at Cambridge, where Boys was systematically setting up to use automatic computing machinery. In Göttingen, Kopineck was compiling tables of two-center integrals. In Washington, D.C. at Catholic University, a program on two-center integrals initiated by Sklar was being continued using IBM machines. At Chicago, Roothaan and Ruedenberg, with the cooperation of Shull at Iowa State and the IBM group there, were at work computing and tabulating one and two-center integrals. At King's College, London, Coulson and Barnett had laid out a scheme for computing the desired integrals from a basic set of unit molecular integrals. In Tokyo, Kotani was extending his sets of tabulated two-center integrals. In Utah, Barker and Eyring's group was producing extensive tabulations of one- and two-center integrals. At Uppsala, Löwdin, and Lundquist were using direct numerical integration to evaluate integrals.

Finally, an informal integrals committee centered at the University of Chicago was established as a clearing house for information on integrals.

After the conference, Löwdin spent a month with us at Chicago.

After the Shelter Island conference, the two parts of LMSS, which I will call the downstairs and the upstairs groups, got to work on their respective tasks. Downstairs the experimentalists were photographing and analyzing molecular spectra. They had a large basement room in Eckhart Hall in which the grating spectrographs were located, with two or three side rooms for developing photographs and storage of plates, and so on. Across the hall were a few rooms used as home rooms for the students and visiting research associates, and a room for chemicals. The experimentalists preferred the basement because it was relatively free of disturbing vibrations.

The theorists (upstairs) were located on the third floor of Ryerson Physical Laboratory, one of the oldest university buildings, in which Millikan and Michelson had worked earlier. When I first arrived, Michelson had just retired, and I inherited his office. Michelson had worked in a basement area on perfecting ruling engines for the ruling of diffraction gratings for use in spectroscopy.

Roothaan, Ruedenberg, and Harvey Brimmer designed a cabinet of mathematical symbols and Greek letters which could be substituted in our IBM electric typewriter when needed. Thus our manuscripts could be prepared entirely in typescript, instead of having the special symbols written in by hand as was then usually done. We had a large conference room nearby for the presentation of progress reports and discussion of problems. Roothaan designed extensive enclosed shelves to hold boxes of the reprints which we had accumulated, both our own and others obtained by exchange with fellow workers elsewhere in the world. Close by there was a small room with running water and gas heat where coffee (or tea) could be made. My office was next to this, although much of my activity then was with the downstairs people. Nearby also there were rooms for students and postdoctorals, also a central room for a secretary-typist to deal with papers and report from both parts of LMSS. Later there were two or even three of them.

After the Shelter Island conference, Roothaan and Ruedenberg worked hard on the mathematical problem of obtaining formulas for the difficult integrals whose values needed to be computed. Their work was successfully completed before 1956. In 1955 Ruedenberg left LMSS for a professorial position at Iowa State University. The completion of the difficult integrals programs was a necessary prerequisite to the construction, beginning in 1956, of digital computer programs to make calculations of SCF wave functions and energies for diatomic molecules.

XXI

Advances in Molecular Spectroscopy

An important event for the downstairs group was the return of Phil Wilkinson as an LMSS research associate in 1952, when the Korean War was over. He took general responsibility for the experimental work of the LMSS after Tanaka's departure, and remained with LMSS until June 1960 when he returned to the Naval Research Laboratory, where he had been before he came to LMSS. He published a number of papers on emission and absorption spectra, some of them jointly with me. We cooperated joyfully in planning and carrying through the research program, with occasional time out for relaxation. Most of the papers were based on photographs taken with the vacuum spectrograph described above. Photographs were taken in various orders of the grating. Emission spectra were obtained in some cases down to 950 Å, but others only to about 1500 Å.

In the work on any absorption spectrum, a suitable continuous emission spectrum to serve as a background is needed. For this purpose, Tanaka and Wilkinson developed the use of continuous molecular emission spectra of the rare gases, each of these being of usable intensity over a different but limited range of wavelengths. Hence for an absorption spectrum, a suitable choice of background can be made. Moreover, because of its limited range, the choice can be made so as to use only one order of the grating. The ranges of rare gas continua are as follows: xenon, 1500–2500 Å; krypton, 1250–1650 Å; argon, 1070–1650 Å; neon, 744–790 Å. A helium continuum is also available at much shorter wavelengths.

140

Of the molecules studied at LMSS, diatomic nitrogen has been my greatest favorite. Among well-known N_2 spectra are the Lyman–Birge–Hopfield bands, involving an electronic transition between the lowest $^1\Pi_g$ and the $^1\Sigma_g^+$ ground state. They had earlier been studied by Lyman at Harvard, later by Birge at Berkeley and further by Hopfield there. Wilkinson was the first to find them in *absorption*, using our vacuum spectrograph (see *Journal of Chemical Physics* **30**, 773, 1959). They are well known as emission spectra even though the transition is forbidden by the usual electric dipole selection rules. This spectrum included some weak band lines which Wilkinson and I identified as being of electric quadrupole character (*Astrophysics Journal* **126**, 10, 1957). Other lines are either of electric quadrupole, of magnetic dipole character, or of both together.

Wilkinson studied high-resolution spectra of several important unsaturated hydrocarbons as follows. He photographed the absorption spectra of benzene (C_6H_6) and its deuterium isotope benzene-d_6 (C_6D_6) from 1300 Å to 1850 Å in the first order of the vacuum spectrograph. He examined four Rydberg series with over 100 vibrational bands. A valuable by-product was that these series converged to give the minimum ionization potentials of the molecules. These were 9.247 eV (electron volts) for benzene and 9.251 eV for benzene-d_6. Progressions of three vibrational modes were found associated with most of the 31 observed Rydberg transitions. Examination of one of the vibrational progressions led to the conclusion that the vibrationless nuclear configuration in the Rydberg state is of D_2h symmetry, that is, of a rectangular shape instead of the hexagonal symmetry of the ground state.

Wilkinson also photographed the absorption spectra of acetylene (C_2H_2) and its deutero-isomer C_2D_2 at high dispersion in the 1280–1520 Å region. He analyzed the vibrational structures of two transitions previously reported by Price. This indicated a linear structure of the molecule in two excited states just as in the ground state. However, he found a *trans*-bent excited state for a third transition and a *trans*-bent and twisted upper state for the fourth transition. He reported vibrational data for all the various states, as well as some rotational data.

He also photographed the absorption spectrum of ethylene (C_2H_4) and its isomer C_2D_6 in the 1300–1500 Å region in the first order of the vacuum spectrograph. He obtained vibrational constants for the stretching vibrations and the twisting vibrations in each of the five Rydberg states that are the upper electronic states of observed bands. He concluded that the molecule is bent or staggered in these states. Use of a torsional oscillator-rotator treatment gave 500–1200 cm^{-1} as potential barriers hindering free rotation in these states. Ethylene has long been one of my most favorite molecules, about which I shall have more to say later.

Although Putcha Venkateswarlu from India was a research associate at LMSS from 1949 to 1950, for unexplained reasons there is no record in the Red Reports of his presence. He is a very experienced spectroscopist who, among other things, had worked extensively on "resonance series" in the emission spectrum of the iodine (I_2) molecule. For some time, he was a professor of physics at the Indian Institute of Technology in Kanpur, India. However, he has spent much time in research at several other scientific laboratories. In these visits, his family has accompanied him. Two of his sons who were born in this country are now established as very competent research scientists in physics and mathematics. Putcha is now an old friend.

> The most interesting result of his stay at LMSS was the discovery of the emission band spectrum of the CF_2 (carbon difluoride radical). The resulting publication in 1950 in the *Physical Review* reports that the molecule has a triangular shape. It includes details of the bands, and a formula for the frequencies in terms of vibrational quantum numbers for the symmetric stretching and bending vibrations of the molecule, in both the lower and upper electronic states. A study of the sub-band heads (K-structure) shows that the light of the electronic transition involved is polarized with its direction parallel to a line through the two fluorine atoms. These CF_2 bands show resemblances to those of the CH_2 radical.

We have repeatedly returned to work on nitrogen, both theoretical and experimental, both by myself and others, notably work with Wilkinson in 1952 to 1960. However, as mentioned earlier, S.M. Naudé, from South Africa, was here and made the first analysis of the rotational structure of the important "first positive" bands of nitrogen in 1932. (He also discovered the isotope N^{15}.) More recently, while Wilkinson was still here, Alfred Lofthus came in 1954 on a Royal Norwegian Council fellowship. He published papers in 1956 and we published a joint paper in 1957 on a certain emission band spectrum of the nitrogen molecule. Later, Wilkinson and I wrote on this subject. In 1960, after his return to Norway, Lofthus published a magnificent detailed survey of all the work which had been done up to that time by anyone on the molecular spectra of nitrogen.

142

Kevin (P.K.) Carroll, on leave of absence from his professional position at University College, Dublin, came in 1961 to help carry forward the work on the nitrogen spectrum. He had previously made important contributions to our knowledge of this spectrum in research at Dublin. In 1962, he and I published papers on the $^5\Sigma_g^+$ (quintet sigma) state which can be obtained by the combination of two normal state nitrogen atoms. In 1965, we published a paper on $^3\Pi$ levels and predissociation of N_2 near the 12.135 eV dissociation limit. I have had pleasant visits with Kevin Carroll in Dublin at University College and at his home.

Related to the work on the nitrogen spectrum was some published work by William Lichten in the *Journal of Chemical Physics* in 1957 on "lifetime measurements of metastable states in molecular nitrogen." Lichten, who was a graduate student of John Platt, received a Physics Ph.D. on the basis of this work. Lichten used a molecular beam method to obtain the lifetimes of the $A^3\Sigma_u^+$ upper electronic state of the Vegard–Kaplan bands, and of the $^1\Pi_g$ upper state of the Lyman–Birge–Hopfield bands. Both of these band spectra are weak because forbidden by the rules for electric dipole radiation. For the lifetime of the $A^3\Sigma_u^+$ state he obtained a lower limit of 10^{-2} sec and for that of the $^1\Pi_g$ state, 1.7×10^{-4} sec.

Lucy Pickett of Mt. Holyoke College spent the summer of 1952 in Chicago. We studied hyperconjugation in the benzenium ion (benzene to which a proton has been added).

XXII

Oxford, Frankfurt and Tokyo, 1952–1953

For the year 1952–53 I had a Fulbright award for work at Oxford. While there I was temporarily a Fellow of St. John's College. This enabled me to take some part in the affairs of the college, and to gain understanding of the college life. I became a friend of a few of the Fellows and was loathe to leave.

Norbert Muller obtained a National Research Council Fellowship to work with me, so it was arranged that he also would do this at Oxford. We made semiempirical LCAO-MO calculations on hyperconjugation in the benzenium and other (mostly alkyl-substituted) ions.

Hyperconjugation in ions produces greater energy stabilization and other effects than occur in neutral molecules. I therefore called it "strong" hyperconjugation, in contrast to the relatively weak "sacrificial" hyperconjugation in the neutral case. The name strong hyperconjugation is in part a misnomer, because the effects are partly a result of shifts in charge distribution.

While I was in Oxford, John Platt had a Guggenheim Fellowship which he spent in England and Europe to good effect. Weldon Brown of the Chicago Chemistry Department and Clemens Roothaan, took care of the LMSS while I was away. However, I returned in January for a short visit in Chicago, Washington, and other places. Tanaka had just left after greatly improving our vacuum spectrograph, and Wilkinson had taken over.

A major reason for choosing 1952–53 to be in Oxford was that my daughter Lucia, after three years at Putney School in Vermont, was

18 and ready for new experiences. At Christmas she went with the Oxford–Cambridge ski team to Austria and made friends with students from both universities. During the year she was allowed to audit some graduate courses at the Institute of Social Anthropology at the university. She also learned some chemistry at the Oxford Technical College. But she learned most from her associations with Oxford (and some Cambrige) young people. She was very popular with them.

Sometimes some of them came to our apartment. This was on The High (High Street). The bedroom was incredibly noisy because of passing vehicles and a traffic light close to us. Thus sleeping was a problem. Yet the dining room and kitchen, a little further from the street, were quiet. The apartment was rented to me by Magdalene College, which was just down the road by the river. They let my wife plan the decorating before we moved in. One of the physical chemists, Dr. L.E. Sutton, and his wife lived nearby. At the end of the year Lucia was invited to Commemoration Balls at approximately six of the Oxford colleges. These were great events held annually.

In May I took Lucia on a trip to Amsterdam, then to Copenhagen, where we had lunch with Professor and Mrs. Bohr, then to Stockholm and Uppsala. During the trip of course I made scientific visits with old and new friends. Valerie meantime attended kindergarten at the Squirrel School in Oxford.

Early in June 1953 my wife and I visited Italy, where I gave lectures in Bologna and Milan on electron donor-acceptor interactions. Later in June we were in Paris for a conference on molecular spectroscopy. In July I made a two week trip to Germany, where I visited many universities and some government and industrial laboratories, spending about one day at each, and giving a number of lectures, speaking slowly in English. I moved according to a non-tiring schedule arranged through previous correspondence with someone at each place. My correspondents arranged hotel reservations and told me what train to take to go to the next place.

During my 1953 visits in Germany, I saw Hund in Frankfurt, where he was now a professor of theoretical physics. I stayed at his apartment, where on the wall was hanging a Japanese print which my wife and I had given him as a wedding present in 1932. I was rather amazed about this, since Hund had been in East Germany for most of the years since the war. I had read in the Chicago Daily News that the Russian authorities had put him out of his position as

Rector at Jena several years before, and was very interested to hear from Hund the story of what had actually happened. When the American soldiers came through Leipzig, before it was taken over by the Russians, apparently Hund was reluctant to give up his new house, and did not want to leave Leipzig as the Americans suggested. Thus he remained in East Germany, first at Leipzig and then at Jena. At Jena, one day he was summoned by the Russian commissar: "I am afraid I have some bad news for you. You have been elected Rector by the Senate, but any appointment as Rector has to have our agreement. I do not know what we are going to do about it." Hund then went away, but a week or two later he was summoned again by the commissar, who said in effect: "We have decided that we might as well go along with the Senate and agree to your appointment as Rector, provided you will agree to the 17 points listed in this document." Hund said he would think it over and went to talk with a friend who was a lawyer. The friend said that he might as well agree to the 17 articles, that they were just formalities, so Hund agreed. But some time later he apparently did not do what was expected for a visiting Russian dignitary, and it was this which led to his retirement as Rector, though he remained as professor.

However, some time later, he had an offer of an appointment at Frankfurt. At that time lecture visits of university people back and forth between East and West Germany, but not permanent transfers, were rather freely permitted. After some hesitation, Hund decided to accept the offer. He and each member of his family packed a suitcase. They all separately reached West Berlin, and went from there to Frankfurt. But of course all their furniture was left behind. Nevertheless, quite astonishingly, the authorities, who apparently always felt Hund to be not a bad fellow, six months later sent everything after him to Frankfurt. This was a sort of thing that did not normally happen to people who left East Germany in such an informal manner.

In August 1953 it was time to leave Oxford, but Valerie developed a severe infection from scratching her smallpox inoculation and, in a hectic last minute change of plans, Lucia and I returned by steamer to New York while Valerie (in the hospital) stayed in Oxford with her mother. After Oxford with a morning temperature of 42°F, and New York's 96°F, I bought a summer suit in Chicago and left shortly for hot, humid Tokyo to take part in a September meeting of the IUPAP (International Union of Pure and Applied

Physics). This was the first big post-war international conference in Japan, and everyone went all-out to make us welcome. Photographers and reporters were everywhere. There were meetings in Nikko, in Tokyo, and in Kyoto, interspersed and followed by sightseeing trips, dinners, a beer party at which there was dancing with the most beautiful movie stars, fascinating theatrical events, etc., etc. Again there were conversations with old and new friends, both on science and on much else. I gave talks in Nikko and Kyoto on electron donor-acceptor interactions and on the computation of approximate molecular energies.

We met so many mayors, provincial governors, deputy governors, and so on, that I developed the following generalization: the higher the rank, the greater the bulk. Mayors were slender, governors were very substantial, others were in between. One of the governors I recall was also the manager, or owner, of a brewery. Japanese beer we found to be excellent. For somewhat more formal occasions, sake was appropriate.

At one place which we visited we had the opportunity to paint a design on a clay plate which was then baked to become a finished piece of tableware. I decorated my plate with a strange animal and my initials. A photograph sent me subsequently by friends in Tokyo shows me looking pretty haggard. No wonder!

XXIII

Population Analysis

The following year (1954) was a good one for research at LMSS. That summer, however, instead of going as planned to a meeting in Sweden, I caught pneumonia; fortunately penicillin took care of it quickly. Nevertheless in 1954 I finished nine papers which were published in 1955. One on the vacuum ultraviolet spectrum of ethylene and deuteroethylene published in the *Journal of Chemical Physics*, was a joint paper with Wilkinson. There were also two rather general papers in the *Journal of the American Chemical Society;* one on the strengths of single bonds and on halogen molecule structure, the other on bond angles in water-type and ammonia-type molecules. Earlier, there was a joint paper with Professor Cyril Reid who was visiting us in Chicago in 1952–53 and worked on molecular complexes. Our paper, on complexes of pyridine and iodine, showed some unusually interesting features, including ion formation.

My 1954–55 work included a series of four papers on what I called "population analysis" on LCAO-MO wave functions. When a chemist looks at such a wave function he may wonder if it is possible to divide the LCAO expressions up so that he can divide the total electron population into populations on and between atoms. I found that this can be done in a way which, although not quite right, is very instructive.

The procedure, as presented in the first of the four papers, can be illustrated by the simple case of a diatomic molecule containing a

148

population of N electrons in one MO called ϕ. Let the MO be written in a normalized LCAO form, $\phi = a\phi_A + b\phi_B$, where ϕ_A and ϕ_B are AOs of atoms A and B. The population distribution in the MO can then be obtained as N times the square of the LCAO expression for ϕ. This is $N_a^2\phi_A^2 + N_b^2\phi_B^2 + 2N_{ab}\phi_A\phi_B$. I called N_a^2 the net electron population in ϕ_A on A, N_b^2 that in ϕ_B on B, and $2N_{ab}$ the overlap population, since $\phi_A\phi_B$ occupies the region of overlap of the two atoms. atoms.

A chemist may now want numbers for the total or "gross" populations on each atom. The gross population on A or B certainly includes the respective net population. But for each atom one must also include a part of the overlap population. The simplest procedure is to divide the latter into two parts, allocated one to A and the other to B. Arguing from the fact that the overlap population $2N_{ab}$ depends symmetrically on atoms A and B, even when a and b are unequal, I assigned just half of it, i.e., N_{ab}, to each atom. Adding this to the net population of either atom, a gross population, $N(A)$ or $N(B)$ is obtained. Note that $N(A)+N(B)=N$. The procedure is easily generalized to polyatomic molecules, and in other ways, for example to specify numbers of σ and π electrons in a molecule.

As reported in the Citation Index, my procedure has been very popular. This is in spite of the fact, which I have pointed out more than once, that the numbers it gives have only a somewhat approximate meaning and in some special cases border on nonsense. But fortunately such cases are rare. And even though the method is faulty, it has the insidious appeal of always giving definite numbers.

The sub-title of the second papers in the population analysis series is "Overlap Populations, Bond Orders, and Covalent Bond Energies." Various definitions of "bond orders" as measures of the strengths of chemical bonds have been given by various people, but it is argued in this paper that overlap populations are perhaps the best such measures.

This third paper discusses "Effects of Hybridzation on Overlap and Gross AO Population," and the fourth discusses "Bonding and Anti-Bonding in LCAO and Valence-Bond Theories."

A further activity which I finished in 1954, and which was published in the *Journal of Chemical Physics* in 1955, was an extensive "Report on Notation for the Spectra of Polyatomic Molecules." The purpose was similar to that for my 1930 report on notation for diatomic spectra, namely, to standardize notation and symbols so that scientists would understand one another more quickly when reading papers by other scientists. However, the problem was much more extensive for polyatomic than for diatomic molecules because of their much more complicated and more numerous types of motion including vibrations and rotations. My report was prepared at the request of the Joint Committee for Spectroscopy of the International Astronomical Union and the International Union of Pure and and Applied Physics, and was officially adopted as standard at a meeting in Lund, Sweden in July, 1954, while I was in Chicago with pneumonia. A humorous element was that in looking at the printer's proof of the article before publication, I forgot to add my name as the author.

XXIV

Science Attaché, London, 1955

The year 1955 I spent away from LMSS in a different kind of activity not wholly unrelated to science but also involving other things. I have always been much interested in international relations. For dealing with many of the problems in this field, our government has two main agencies, the State Department and what I think should be called the Military Department. This was originally called the War Department, and more recently the Defense Department. Either or both of these names is appropriate at certain times, but not all the time. Both departments, of course, must coordinate effectively with other departments and with the National Security Council and the President.

It had always seemed to me that we should, so far as possible, use the State Department, rather than the Military Department, in solving problems in our foreign relations. It seemed to me also that Congress tended to economize unduly on the already relatively small budget of the State Department. I thought also that Congress did not pay enough attention to efforts to make the Department more effective.

One important need, I thought, was that the State Department should know more about science and should include active scientific attachés at major posts, who should report to a high level science adviser in the State Department in Washington. With such thoughts in mind, when, through a friend, I was recommended for an appointment as Science Attaché or Scientific Attaché at the London Embassy in 1955 I readily accepted, even though this

151

interrupted an active period of research. I should like now to tell something of my experience as Science Attaché.

After about two weeks of briefing in Washington, I left with my wife and younger daughter Valerie for London in January. After some time we found a very attractive furnished house, No. One Culross Street in Mayfair, close to the Embassy. The house had four floors with a different heating system on each. Outside was a little garden. Once C.P. Snow came for a chat, and admired the house. Valerie attended the American school nearby. My older daughter Lucia was a student at Reed College in Oregon, but came to join us after the spring term was over.

My office was in the old embassy building on Grosvenor Square the present embassy was still in the future. I inherited the office used by my predecessor as Science Attaché, Ralph Wycoff, and also inherited his efficient secretary Carol Loden. My duties as Science Attaché were for the most part never clearly defined, aside from a few obvious things. Hardly anyone in the embasssy knew anything about science; some of those in the Economics Division came nearest to it. I was attached to the Political Division. However, I was responsible to the State Department's Science Adviser in Washington, who was then Mr. Walter Rudolph, an economist. Although it would have seemed logical that the Science Attaché should deal with current intergovernmental problems in nuclear energy, this function had been placed in the hands of representatives of the Atomic Energy Commission.

In the absence of suitable instructions about my day-to-day activities I tried to think of what might be appropriate. It seemed to me relevant to learn and report something on science-government relations in Great Britain. A consequence was that I had a number of very enjoyable luncheon discussions with Alex Todd (now Lord Todd), who was then chairman of the British government's Advisory Council on Scientific Policy. I also met with others at establishments such as the D.S.I.R. and the Research Councils. I had especially interesting conversations with Sir Harold Hartley and with Alexander King who was later one of the founders of the Club of Rome. On what I learned I sent reports to Mr. Rudolph.

I felt that pure science as such was being adequately taken care of by the normal contacts between American and British scientists, supplemented also by the special group of scientists maintained in London by the Office of Naval Research. Hence, I took only a little time for visits to fellow-scientists whom I knew at the universities.

I also visited Stockholm to compare notes with our Science Attaché there.

Day-to-day activities did of course include getting acquainted with fellow FSOs (foreign service officers). I, of course, was temporary. But I tried to understand how it was to be a regular FSO. It was generally agreed that the first year at a post is a period of getting acquainted with the situation and establishing one's local contacts, and that it took two or three years to become really efficient, which happened usually not long before transfer to another post. In finding local contacts, Dr. John G. Mallock, the Canadian Science Attaché, was very helpful to me, since he had been in London for a number of years and had accumulated a long list of contacts.

One obvious duty of the Science Attaché, a pleasant one, was helping visiting American scientists. I also had some enjoyable visits with David Martin, Secretary of the Royal Society, to discuss some official matters pertaining to American scientists. Toward the end of my stay, I gave a few lectures on nuclear energy to a small number of people in the Embassy, mostly from the Economics Division. Occasionally there were special requests or assignments from Washington. One of these was to attend the first Atoms for Peace Conference, in Geneva, as an observer.

Every week there was a staff meeting with the Ambassador, who was then Winthrop Aldrich. He called on each person in turn to report on developments in his sphere. Winston Churchill was then in his last term as Prime Minister. At one meeting, after I had been briefed earlier by Detlev Bronk, then President of the National Academy of Sciences, I disclosed that the United States was planning to launch a satellite—I called it a "little moon." The report was of course confidential. Unfortunately, the Russians sent up their Sputnik before our little moon was ready. Meantime, our government had decided that Science Attachés were an unnecessary luxury. The London office was closed after I left, along with the few others which then existed elsewhere. But after Sputnik, our government saw the light, and since then the usefulness of having Scientific Attachés in a number of places abroad is recognized.

One function of Embassy personnel is representational, which in my position included representing American science at various ceremonial occasions, for example at the annual dinner of the Royal Society, an enjoyable event. Another pleasant representational event was an evening party at Buckingham Palace, to which members of the London Diplomatic Corps, from all countries, with their wives, were invited at the Queen's command. At the proper time we were all lined up to be presented to the royal family: the Queen Mother, the Queen, Prince Phillip, Princess Margaret, and others. They all filed by and greeted us. I thought the Queen was very attractive, more so than photographs disclosed.

One appropriate representational activity was the entertainment of British scientists, for example at luncheon and at cocktail parties. My wife and I put on one magnificent party in our house for a distinguished group of British scientists and others, including some visiting Americans. To assist in entertaining, the Embassy personnel received a so-called "representation allowance." However, this was very meager. I think mine was $50, but perhaps it was somewhat more. All up and down the line the representation allowance was inadequate for a scale of entertaining which any American businessman would regard as essential in the furtherance of mutual understanding. Other governments were vastly more liberal. However, Congress, under the thumb of Congressman Rooney from New York, described the representation allowance as "the booze fund," and the public and the press supported this viewpoint. Everyone in the Embassy actually drew on his own funds to a considerable extent for the entertaining which he felt needed in his position. The Ambassador told me that entertaining cost him $25,000 a year; but, of course, he could afford it. However, the Minister (next in rank to the Ambassador) also had, I surmised, to dip heavily into his own pockets.

Besides governmental representatives inside and outside the Embassy, many representatives of business and other non-governmental organizations are stationed abroad. It seemed to me that all these people had rather similar interests and problems and would benefit by getting together occasionally. I discussed the matter with a colleague in the Economics Division and with Dr. William Q. Hull, who was then representing the American Chemical Society in London as European Associate Editor of Chemical and Engineering News. In July we started a luncheon group called American Scientific and Technical Representatives (in Europe), briefly ASTR. After lunch an invited speaker gave a talk.

Our membership consisted of citizens of North America who represented in Europe on a more or less full-time basis the interests of a scientifically based North American corporation or other organization or governmental agency concerned with technical and scientific developments. Among the governmental representatives, we chose a few from the Embassy, the ONR, and the Atomic Energy Commission. Meetings were usually held in London, but sometimes on the continent at the time of international conferences.

XXV

The Diatomic Molecule Project at LMSS, 1956–1966: Broken Bottlenecks

After I left the London embassy to return to Chicago, it took several months to get readjusted to the life of the laboratory; especially to pick up forgotten strands of thought. But before long we were again going strong.

The next few years (beginning in 1956) were a very active period for the LMSS, both upstairs and downstairs. My main interests in the experimental area were in two things: donor-acceptor complexes and their charge-transfer spectra, as already described, and the spectra of the nitrogen and other molecules.

In 1957 I published a paper on the energy levels of nitrogen which appeared in a publication called *The Threshold of Space*. In this I reviewed, and tried to assign MO electron configurations to, the energy levels of all the then known N_2 absorption and emission spectra. I also made several predictions on additional levels. The known absorption spectra included some distinctive so-called Rydberg series. The excited state of each member of a Rydberg series has an MO much larger than those in the ground state. The size of the MO increases as we go up the series to bands of higher frequencies. Each series converges toward a definite known state of the N_2^+ molecule. There were also miscellaneous bands leading to states which I did not succeed in identifying properly. Later all this was clarified by Dressler and by Carroll, who showed that the extra states are merely vibrational levels of identified Rydberg states. Later (1972) Alf Lofthus and P.H. Krupenie published a comprehensive review of the known N_2 spectra. Lofthus was with LMSS in 1944–45

156

as a Royal Norwegian Fellow and made valuable contributions to our knowledge of the N_2 spectrum.

Roothaan, who had become an assistant professor of physics, and his students were mainly interested in atoms and accurate calculations on small molecules, while I favored larger molecules, including those whose spectra were being studied downstairs. By 1956, Roothaan and Ruedenberg had solved for diatomic molecules the problems of the difficult two-center integrals which were mentioned above in the story of the Shelter Island Conference. This was a necessary prerequisite for theoretical calculations on diatomic molecules. At this point, Bernard J. Ransil joined the group. His appointment as a research associate followed some correspondence and an interview I had had with him at the Cosmos Club in Washington in April, together with a favorable answer to a proposal I had made to the NSF for a grant to do MO calculations using digital computers. Ransil was enthusiastic about undertaking these computations on molecules such as N_2, CO, and the diatomic hydrides.

Ransil had obtained a Ph.D. at Catholic University in October 1955 with a thesis on an LCAO-MO-SCF treatment of the H_3 molecule under Virginia Griffing, and had received one of the newly inaugurated National Academy of Science–National Research Council Postdoctoral Fellowships at the National Bureau of Standards (NBS). During that postdoctoral year he worked with staff members of the Bureau's digital computer (the SEAC) to develop a program for computing open-shell LCAO-MO-SCF wave functions on the H_3 radical. In October 1956, after the NSF proposal had been approved, Ransil arrived in Chicago to begin work at LMSS on the diatomic molecule project. Soon after his arrival, Roothaan went on concurrent Fulbright and Guggenheim fellowships for a year in Europe.

Two of Roothaan's Ph.D. students, Douglas McLean (who had come to Chicago form Western Australia) and Andrew Weiss, and his research assistant, Megumu Yoshimine, agreed to collaborate with Ransil during Roothaan's absence on the design and construction of an automated computer program (the first of its kind) to generate diatomic molecule wave functions in minimal orbital LCAO-MO-SCF approximation. The program would be written in machine language (computer languages such as Fortran were not yet available) for the UNIVAC (Remington Rand 1103) at Wright

Field Air Force Base, Dayton, Ohio, with which Roothaan and I had a contract for use of excess computer time not used by the base.

Ransil assumed responsibility for the overall design of the computer program, the production runs, and senior authorship of resulting publications. McLean, Weiss, and Yoshimine assumed responsibility for programming. The actual construction of the program proceeded on a collaborative team basis, with each team member contributing individual components that were designed through almost daily sessions at the big table and blackboard upstairs on the third floor of Ryerson.

> Using Roothaan's LCAO-SCF method, each LCAO-MO was set up as a minimal linear combination of AOs, for example, for N_2 only one 1s, 2s, 2pσ, and 2pπ AO. The AOs used are called a basis set. Later on, LCAO functions with many more AOs were used. For the diatomic molecule project, Ransil chose three different basis sets of AOs in which the exponents had different numerical values—Slater AOs (devised by Professor J. C. Slater at MIT), SCF AOs (obtained from Roothaan's atomic SCF program), and AOs specifically optimized for each molecule of the series, which included the first row homopolars, hydrides and LiF, CO and BF. The first two basis sets held good for the respective free atoms while the third was expected to provide a better approximate wave function for the bound molecule.

Over the next 18 months the project moved ahead rapidly with the team flying to Dayton, Ohio via TWA every two to three weeks in groups of two, three, or four, for two to three days (mainly evenings and nights) of computing. Here, and in the paragraphs which follow, I make use of a brief history of the project which Ransil kindly prepared for me in 1983. I took no part in the construction of the computer programs, but served mainly to applaud and encourage the work. However, I kept in touch in discussions with Ransil about the course of the program and on certain questions of nomenclature. Also, I carried on some theoretical work not or little related to the machine computations: I will describe this later.

When Roothaan returned from Europe in December 1957, the diatomic computing project was close to production-run status. It was agreed that the three graduate students would remain on the project until the program was fully debugged and operational. In the meantime, Wright Field switched to an 1103A (and later to an

1109), entailing a good deal of system rewrite work which Roothaan undertook with a new generation of graduate student assistants.

Approximately coincidental with the completion of the NSF molecular program during the first half of 1958 was the arrival of Serafin Fraga Sanchez on a Spanish Juan March Fund scholarship. I asked Ransil if he would take Fraga on the NSF molecule project as preparation for a small collaboration with me which was to follow in a few months' time. Ransil agreed and Fraga joined the team flying in and out of Dayton, adding additional verve and buoyancy to the operation.

The program became operational in the spring–summer of 1958, and as McLean, Weiss, and Yoshimine left the project to go on to Hartree–Fock quality atomic and molecular calculations with Roothaan for their Ph.D. theses, Fraga assisted Ransil in running the diatomic molecule production while working simultaneously on a project with me, an arrangement that continued until most of the projected computer runs had been completed.

By the winter of 1958–59 minimal orbital calculations had been performed for all the first row diatomics, hydrides, and the three heteropolars (BF, CO, and LiF). Production runs for population analysis, spectroscopic constants, and limited configuration mixing (CM), as Roothaan and I called it, were in the queue, waiting to be calculated, together with ground state functions and potential energy curves for H_2, He_2^{++}, and He_2.

By that time, the operational success of the computer program and the results it generated clearly heralded the dawn of a new era. It had become evident to everyone on the project that, as both computer speed and memory capacity improved, the main obstacle to obtaining accurate analytical wave functions and energies for small molecules would be how to give accurate analytical representation to electron correlation.

All other considerations—the nature of the basis sets, basis set expansion limits, and parametric optimization—were technical problems that would yield to the inexorable advance of computer technology. At the same time, the prospect of accurate numerical, rather than analytical, solutions was also seen as a distinct possibility and was actively pursued by Roothaan and Wlodzimierz Kolos, on leave from the University of Warsaw.

But human nature requires time to adjust to new ideas, and the tendency to think, model, and theorize in terms of limited orbital concepts predominated at the time, accompanied by the proliferation of terms and symbols in the literature (which was referred to in lighter moments as "alphabet soup") that was as intimidating (and often uninformative) to the uninitiated as it was confusing. This situation brought Ransil and me together in a series of discussions devoted exclusively to the development, from the nomenclature in then current usage, of a systematic glossary of terms and symbols for the LCAO formalism.

As the extent of our computations increased, we had several good secretary-typists to prepare our papers for NSF, from which we had a grant, and also the annual red-covered LMSS reports to our military supporters, with which we had contracts. Our secretary-typists were always interesting and sometimes intimidating; one was nicknamed Marilyn Monroe, another, Mata-Hari. In time, these were succeeded by Helen Griffith, who went on to a more responsible position in the Medical School. Still another now has a position in the physics department.

In 1959 I presented a paper entitled "Broken Bottlenecks and the Future of Molecular Quantum Mechanics" at the spring meeting of the National Academy of Sciences. This paper, jointly with Roothaan, was published in the *Proceedings of the National Academy of Sciences* (45, 394–398). It surveyed the progress made since the 1951 Shelter Island Conference in breaking two major bottlenecks which had been outstanding at that time.

First was that of the "difficult integrals" which had now been solved by Roothaan and Ruedenberg in Chicago, and Coulson and associates in England. Second was the previously excessively time-consuming process of using these integrals and other steps in computations to obtain the wave functions of molecular states. Here the bottleneck was broken by the use of digital computing machines as in the work of Ransil and others. Following this survey were predictions on the rapid future development of such digital machine computations, in which the need of adequate funds to pay for computing time was emphasized.

Simultaneous with all these activities came the call for papers for the Conference on Molecular Quantum Mechanics to be held at the University of Colorado at Boulder in June 1959, the first major meeting of its kind since the precedent setting Shelter Island meeting in 1951. LMSS was a beehive of activity and had much to contribute: Roothaan's SCF formalism for open-shell atomic systems and accurate calculations on atoms and two and three body systems (with W. Kolos, R.A. Sack, Lester Sachs, Andrew Weiss,

Douglas McLean, and Megumu Yoshimini), Ransil's results from the minimal orbital diatomic molecule project, my systemization (with Ransil) of LCAO nomenclature, and a study of coulomb energy in valence bond theory (which I made with Fraga). This last study was based on an idea which I then thought of considerable interest, about certain aspects of valence bond theory, which perhaps are still worth further attention. The proceedings of the Boulder meeting comprised the contents of the April 1960 issue of *Reviews of Modern Physics.*

I published another paper in 1960 on "Some Neglected Subcases of Predissociation in Diatomic Molecules." This I think made a worthwhile contribution to clarification of the subject of predissociation, earlier discussed by Herzberg.

Ransil presented two interrelated papers at the meeting. The first described the methodology and scope of the diatomic molecule project together with a summary of the results which consisted of a comparison (where possible) between the computed and the measured values of total energies, dissociation energies, dipole moments, and ionization potentials for the series of computed molecules. The second paper was a tabulation of the corresponding wave functions in minimal orbital LCAO-MO-SCF approximation for each of the three basic sets.

In all, the minimal orbital diatomic molecule project at LMSS produced eight published papers and four reports appearing in the LMSS Annual Report. For the series of twelve diatomic molecules it studied in uniform fashion, the project demonstrated that the single configuration minimal orbital approximation consistently (1) underestimated total molecular energies to 1% or less; (2) gave the correct sign of dipole moment and its correct order of magnitude; (3) estimated ionization potentials to one-figure accuracy; and (4) where experimental values of spectroscopic constants existed at the time, gave order of magnitude agreement in all comparisons, and 1 to 2 figure agreement in many. Because the dissociation energy was computed as the difference between two large numbers, both of which were underestimated by 1% or less, the computed dissociation energy usually underestimated the experimental value, but was considered to have little value for predictive purposes. Finally, it produced the first completely automated ab initio LCAO-MO-SCF interatomic potential curves for H_2, He_2^{++}, and He_2 using a 1s, 2s, and $2p\sigma$, $2p\pi$ basis set and both single configuration and CM (configuration mixing) functions.

The consistency of these results for a homologous series of molecules demonstrated the capability of ab initio molecular calculations in minimal orbital LCAO-MO-SCF approximation for predicting chemical and physical properties, and set lower limit estimates of what to expect for more accurate calculations. The project firmly established the role of the computer in ab initio molecular calculations, and set both a standard and a design prototype for subsequent numerical experiments.

Coincidental with the "milking" of the minimal-basis diatomic molecule program and publication of its results was the planning, design, and implementation of a second generation "extended basis set" diatomic molecular program, a development of the integrals calculations, Wright Field's acquisition of an even larger and faster computer, and the inexorable momentum toward "accurate Hartree–Fock" calculations generated by these developments.

As the second generation extended basis set program moved into the programming stage with the help of a new generation of programmers, all graduate students of Roothaan's, Ransil wrote up the remaining results for publication in the *Journal of Chemical Physics* and made plans both to enter medical school at the University of Chicago in September 1960 (where he received an M.D. in 1964) and to relinquish responsibility for the extended basis set work to Paul E. Cade (from Professor Hirschfelder's group in Madison). Cade took over in September 1961. At the time it was projected that he would follow a design similar to the prototype study, but would use an extended basis set LCAO-MO-SCF approximation. Tables of these functions were published in 1974 (P.E. Cade, A.C. Wahl, K. Sales, J.B. Greenshields and G. Mali, *Atomic Data and Nuclear Data Tables* **13**, 339 (1974)).

When Paul Cade came to us, he was very much a scholar. Later he astonished us after making a trip to Soviet Russia, by bringing back a bride from Estonia. They had met there when she was an official guide for touring visitors. After returning to America, he became a professor at the University of Massachusetts in Amherst, Massachusetts, where he and his wife have lived happily since then.

During the development and implementation of the computer calculations on larger diatomic molecules, Roothaan concentrated largely on accurate calculations on the hydrogen molecule. Cooperating with him was Professor Wlodzimierz Kolos who came here on leave from the University of Warsaw, Poland. He was with the

LMSS in 1957, on a Polish government fellowship to June 30, 1958, and then as a research associate until September of 1961. He returned again for three months in 1965 and in 1966, and for eight months in 1967–68. In 1963–64 his student L. Wolniewicz from Copernicus University in Torun, Poland came to carry on related work, in part together with Kolos. Dr. R.A. Sack, on leave from British Rayon Industries in 1958–59, collaborated in some of this work, and in 1964 published three mathematical papers relevant to diatomic molecule calculations. Kolos and Roothaan, with Sack, published in 1960, in *Review of Modern Physics*, a short paper on the ground state of three particles of various kinds with Coulomb interaction. Kolos and Roothaan published a paper on correlated orbitals for the ground state of the hydrogen molecule, using a wave function which involved a product of two occupied MOs times a function of the distance between the electrons. In another valuable paper they obtained accurate electronic wave functions for the hydrogen molecule in the ground and $^3\Sigma_u^+$, $^1\Sigma_u^+$, and $1\Sigma_g^+$ excited states, for a number of values of the distance between the nuclei; potential energy curves were then constructed. The calculations were more accurate than earlier ones of similar type, in particular those of James and Coolidge.

Kolos and Wolniewicz published in *Review of Modern Physics* in 1963 a paper on "non-adiabatic theory for diatomic molecules and its application to the hydrogen molecule." Most molecular calculations use "adiabatic" theory in which the total wave function is separated into a nuclear and an electronic part and the latter is computed only for fixed positions of the nuclei. The paper by Kolos and Wolniewicz does not make this separation and thereby, in the particular case of the ground state of H_2, they obtain much greater accuracy than before.

In 1965, in the *Journal of Chemical Physics*, Kolos and Wolniewicz extended their previous work to obtain good potential curves out to dissociation for the attractive ground state of H_2 and also for the low-energy repulsive $^3\Sigma_u^+$ state of two hydrogen atoms. They also obtained good curves for the lowest $^1\Pi_u$ state of H_2. In a following paper, Wolniewicz computed vibrational and rotational levels for H_2, HD, and D_2. In another paper, Kolos and Wolniewicz in an extremely accurate perturbation theory calculation calculated the energy, the dipole moment, and other properties of the ground and the first vibrationally excited states of HD.

XXVI

Moscow and Leningrad, 1958

In 1958 I visited Moscow and afterwards Leningrad in connection with the work of the joint spectroscopic committee of the International Unions of Astronomy and Physics. The occasion was primarily a meeting of the astronomers for whom, as is well known, a study of the spectra of celestial objects furnishes a great deal of astronomical information. I had, as mentioned earlier, prepared a report containing recommendations on nomenclature for polyatomic spectra and this was discussed by the joint committee.

On the way to Moscow, I stayed overnight in Copenhagen. While there I rented a car and made a trip to Hamlet's castle. I had some worries with this drive, since the car did not have the automatic transmission to which I had become accustomed. However, I got back safely. My worst moments were in edging into a stream of traffic on the way back, when I was afraid the car might stall as it had previously several times. However I took a chance, plunged in and by good luck successfully entered the traffic stream without stalling. That night in the hotel I dreamed of Hamlet's ghost.

In Moscow, aside from the joint spectroscopic committee meetings, I stayed away from most of the sessions since they were mainly devoted to astronomical questions outside my field of competence. However, one event of great interest on our program was a reception in the Kremlin. There on a series of tables along the immense Great Hall, was set forth to welcome us a feast of many delicacies. On one side at the far end of the hall we saw the room where the supreme council of the Soviets has its meetings. At the other end were many rooms of historic interest going back to the times of Peter the Great and the Romanoffs.

During my stay in Moscow I visited laboratories devoted to research problems in chemical physics. I had good discussions with chemists and physicists who were obtaining various new and valuable results. I also noted that some of the laboratories were so full of useful apparatus that there was hardly enough room for the experimenters.

In some of my spare time I looked at some of the new apartments which were being built, and exchanged stamps and coins with Russian boys. I also rode to the end of the line on one of the subways, and talked with a grandmother who hoped for peace with America.

I was impressed in Moscow and again later in Leningrad with the elegance of the subway stations, but even more with the fact of their great depth underground. This struck me especially in Leningrad, where the subways were far below the water level, which reached almost to the surface of the streets.

Living in the Hotel Ukraine, my general impression was one of inefficiency. On the day we were to take the train to Leningrad, I inquired repeatedly at the hotel desk, beginning after lunch, as to which of three trains to Leningrad that evening I would go on. The reply, long after dinner, was that they had not yet been able to find out. Finally our girl guide (who was wearing a University of Indiana sweater, and said she was studying Chaucer at the university) said it would be on the *last* train, the Red Arrow, and gave me a slip of paper to indicate this, but not a ticket for the trip, or anything about where I would sleep on the train. Those of us scheduled for this train got into the bus to go to the train station. The bus driver was impatient to leave, and finally started, apparently leaving behind the girl guide who had my ticket. She presumably was looking for some of the American passengers who had not yet shown up.

I arrived at the railroad station with no ticket or sleeping location, but they said "get on anyway." So I got on. Somewhat later a man from one of the "democratic republics" said they had a bunk where I could sleep, so I went there for the night.

After the train arrived in Leningrad the next morning, I got out and went with the others across the street to a hotel. On inquiring at the desk, I was told that this hotel was just for the people from the democratic republics. I was advised to wait for the arrival of the

165

next train, which had started earlier than the Red Arrow but arrived later. Sure enough, someone on this train knew where my hotel was and how to get there. Our girl guide appeared later. I don't know on which train she had come.

In Leningrad I visited the Institute of Professor Fock, well known for his work introducing electron exchange into the Hartree SCF (self-consistent field) theory of atomic structure to give what is known as the Hartree–Fock theory or SCF with exchange. I also visited the Hermitage museum, whose collection of French modern paintings is suprisingly similar to that in the Art Institute in Chicago. There is much else to see in the Hermitage Museum, but I did not have time for it.

I found it interesting to recall that my grandfather had spent the winter at Leningrad, then called St. Petersburg, just about a hundred years earlier, when his ship was frozen in the ice. My aunt once told me that a special skating figure which he executed there was named "the Mulliken."

On the way back from Russia, I stopped off in Sweden. Besides visits in Stockholm, I went to Volodalen to take part in one of Per-Olov Löwdin's summer symposia. Most of the time we were kept hard at work but we were allowed one day off to climb a moderate-sized mountain. Among others present at the symposium was Linus Pauling.

XXVII

Further Advances in Molecular Spectroscopy

In the spring of 1960 I bought a new car and drove with my wife and Valerie to Ithaca, where I had been appointed to the Baker Lectureship. My subject was Molecular Complexes. I should have written a book on this subject then, but didn't. However, Professor Willis Person, on leave of absence from the University of Iowa, came here in the fall of 1959 for a year to cooperate with me in writing such a book. This work was not finished until 1969 when I was in Tallahassee, Florida.

In September I went again to Stockholm to receive an honorary Ph.D. on the occasion of the inauguration of the former Institute of Technology as a university. The new doctors received a special gold ring and a special hat to be worn with formal evening dress. The diplomas were presented by the king.

In the summer of 1961 Dr. Albert Szent-Gyorgi, who had become enthusiastic about charge transfer in molecular complexes invited me to spend two weeks in the biological atmosphere of Wood's Hole. I drove there with the family. Others present included the Pullmans from Paris and J.R. Platt. I did some writing on a book about molecular complexes.

Concurrent with these activities were several important developments at LMSS. In LCAO-MO theory, the two lowest excited states of the H_2 molecule are the triplet $\sigma_g \sigma_u$ $^3\Sigma_u^+$ (T state) and the singlet $\sigma_g \sigma_u$ $^1\Sigma_u^+$ (V state) where the MOs $\sigma_g \sigma_u$ are respectively the normalized additive and subtractive linear combinations $1s_a \pm 1s_b$ of the 1s AOs of the two atoms, a and b, with each 1s of the form

$(\zeta^3/a_0^3\pi)^{1/2} e^{-\zeta r/a}_0$. If one uses $\zeta=1$ for both atoms, one gets very poor agreements between computed and observed energies for the T and V states and for the energy difference between them. Some years ago this was considered the "most conspicuous failure in simple LCAO-MO computing." In 1958 my student Paul Phillipson and I had published a short paper pointing out the really simple fact that if suitable, different values are used for ζ in the two states, agreements with observed energies can be obtained. Afterward we found that S. Huzinaga in 1957 had reached the same conclusion. Somewhat later Huzinaga reported a similar conclusion on the lowest singlet and triplet excited states of the ethylene molecule in which an electron has been excited from its normal bonding to the corresponding antibonding MO. Impressed by Huzinaga's work, I invited him to come here as a research associate of LMSS. He worked here in 1959–61. Later he became a professor in the University of Alberta in Canada.

Phillipson, now an old friend, obtained his Ph.D. in physics in 1961 for detailed calculations on the energy of interaction of two helium atoms at various distances apart.

One of the LMSS group in 1961–62 was Roberto Moccia, who came to LMSS from the University of Naples, Italy. His work was assisted primarily by a stipend under the Visiting Research Scientists Program supported by the International Cooperation Administration. I had thought it would be worthwhile to make ab initio calculations on molecules of the AH_n type using an expansion of the MOs in terms of a basis set consisting exclusively of AOs of the A atom. A few such computations had already been made elsewhere, but Moccia now carried out extensive computations on the ground states of HF, CH_4, SiH_4, NH_3, NH_4^+, H_2O, H_2S, and HCl. Moccia's results were good, although not as good as with LCAO-MOs using AOs of all the atomic centers. Although the single-center method has not been used in later calculations, I was glad to have given it a try.

Late in 1961, I learned that Dr. Marshall Ginter, then on a postdoctoral appointment in spectroscopy at Vanderbilt University, would be interested in coming to Chicago for postdoctoral work with me. He had obtained his Ph.D. in chemistry at Vanderbilt in 1960 on the basis of some spectroscopic research on atoms and molecules. I received very good letters of recommendation from his Ph.D. research professor and from my former research associate, Phillip Wilkinson, then at the Naval Research Laboratory. I sug-

168

gested that Dr. Ginter apply for a National Science Fellowship, which he did, but when this was not granted I wrote him that I would try to get a grant from the National Research Foundation which would make it possible to offer him a research associate appointment. I obtained the grant in time for Ginter to come to Chicago in 1962 with his wife who, like Ginter, had a Ph.D. in spectroscopy from Vanderbilt University.

At about this time I had become interested in the excited states of the helium molecule (He_2), a subject which had been dormant since 1932. In 1964 I sent off for publication a paper entitled "Rare Gas and Hydrogen Molecule Electronic States, Noncrossing Rule, and Recombination of Electrons with Rare Gas and Hydrogen Ions." In 1932 I had published potential curve diagrams for He_2 which included, for many repulsive states, curves that contradicted the "noncrossing rule" for potential curves of any one electronic species. At that time, the validity of this rule was not always respected as it has been since then. In the 1964 paper I corrected this error by presenting a new set of He_2 potential curves. I showed that a number of curves on their way to dissociation must go over a hump. I also concluded that the potential curves of some H_2 states must have similar humps.

In earlier work on He_2 excited states (which are Rydberg states) only a few of the theoretically expected states, and for these only a few vibrational bands, had been found experimentally. I now persuaded Ginter to look for more of these states. He was extremely successful in doing so, and found very many Rydberg states, as well as many vibrational levels for them.

In part with Mrs. Ginter, he later published a series of papers on the work done at LMSS and its continuation at the University of Maryland. In the later papers of the series they used Lu and Fano's 1970 application of Seaton's multichannel quantum defect theory. This is needed to understand the structures of the higher-energy Rydberg states of H_2.

The Ginters left Chicago for Maryland in September 1966. After leaving Chicago they spent a few months in Basel, Switzerland at the invitation of Professor Miescher, a well-known spectroscopist. They have since been active at Maryland in the study of a number of different atomic and molecular spectra.

Before Ginter left I began to look for a successor. Herzberg highly recommended Dr. Anthony J. Merer, who had been working with him in 1965. Merer was a D.Phil. of Oxford University, where he had worked in molecular spectroscopy with R.F. Barrow. Merer was then with K.K. Innes at Vanderbilt University as a visiting assistant professor. He had a job waiting for him in England at the University of East Anglia. However, this would not be available for over a year and it appeared that perhaps he could fill in at LMSS for the year 1966–67.

After some correspondence, Merer came to work with us in August 1966, in time to overlap briefly with Dr. Ginter who spent a few weeks here after getting back from Basel.

In my long 1932–35 series of papers on polyatomic molecules, ethylene (C_2H_4) and its derivatives are important. The ultraviolet absorption spectrum of ethylene near 2000 Å is a superposition of the spectra of two different electronic transitions. One, the N→V spectrum, is a broad intense region beginning near 2000 Å and rising to a flat maximum of intensity near 1630 Å. On this are superposed the sharp N→R bands, occupying a narrower range beginning at 1744 Å. A series of similar bands is seen at shorter wavelengths. The upper state V is identified as one differing from the ground state in the replacement of a bonding π MO by the corresponding antibonding π^* MO. The R state is the lowest energy of numerous Rydberg states, the spectra of transitions to which have been photographed by Wilkinson and others.

I persuaded Dr. Merer to turn his attention to the R←N bands. In doing this he was assisted by a graduate student in physics, L. Schoonveld. Merer and Schoonveld published a brief article in the *Journal of Chemical Physics* in 1968 on their results and conclusions.

They showed that the R←N bands consist of a short progression involving excitation of the R state C–C stretching vibration V_2, each member of which has 2→0 and 4→0 torsional frequency transitions associated with it. These are explained by the fact that when an electronic transition occurs, it is often accompanied by vibrational transitions but only if these are of a totally symmetrical character. Here this is true for the C–C stretching vibration but not of the twisting vibration. However, if the quantum number of the latter is excited by an even number of quanta (e.g. 2, or 4 here) the resulting total vibrational wave function is totally symmetrical and a transition to it becomes permitted, but usually weakly. However, the torsional bands here are highly irregular, both in position and in intensity. But, following earlier Hückel-type LCAO-MO calculations reported in 1947 by myself and Roothaan on the ground state of the $C_2H_4^+$ ion, including the effects of hyperconjugation, I concluded that the Rydberg states of ethylene are very probably of non-planar forms with the two CH_2 groups twisted relative to each other by about 30° as in $C_2H_4^+$.

170

Merer and Schoonveld investigated the C_2H_4 and C_2D_4 R←N absorption spectrum at high temperatures and obtained the 1,1 and 3,1 twisting band of each isotope. Their frequencies plus those of the $0{\rightarrow}2$ and $0{\rightarrow}4$ bands and the ground state torsional frequencies ν_4 (1023 cm^{-1} for C_2H_4 and 706 cm^{-1} for C_2D_4) permit computations of the R state torsional levels up to $\nu_4{=}4$ for C_2H_4 and C_2D_4, except for $\nu_4{=}3$ for C_2H_4. These very irregularly spaced levels for both isotopes suggest that a double-minimum potential may be involved.

Merer and Schoonveld therefore attempted to fit the energy levels using a potential function V of the form $V = \frac{1}{2}V_2 (1 - \cos 2\gamma) + \frac{1}{2}V_4 (1 - \cos 4\gamma) + \cdots$ to give a double-minimum situation. The equilibrium configuration of the molecule would then be slightly twisted out of plane, with a small potential barrier opposing inversion through the planar configuration, but a large barrier opposing internal rotation. The corresponding energy level and wave functions were computed for various values of the barrier. The parameters that gave the best fit to the experimental levels were $V_2{=}2317$ cm^{-1}, $V_4{=}{-}700$ cm^{-1}, $V_6{=}{-}292$ cm^{-1}; these values lead to a potential function in which the R state is twisted 26° out of plane, and the potential barrier to inversion is about 280 cm^{-1}. The barrier to internal rotation is about 2200 cm^{-1}. The potential maximum at the planar configuration lies between the levels $\nu_4{=}0$ and 1 for C_2H_4 and $\nu_4{=}1$ and 2 for C_2D_4.

I note here that the higher Rydberg transitions of ethylene as observed by Wilkinson are similar in appearance to the 1744 Å R←N transition.

In 1969 Merer and I published in *Chemical Reviews* a review on "Ultraviolet Spectra and Excited States of Ethylene and its Alkyl Derivatives." Also in 1969 in the *Journal of Chemical Physics*, Merer and I published "Vibrational Structure of the π^*-π Electronic Transition of Ethylene," meaning the V←N transition.

My interest in the V and R states of ethylene led me to continued studies which resulted in a brief Note in 1977 entitled "The Excited States of Ethylene" and in 1979 to another with the same title. Both were published in the *Journal of Chemical Physics*. In connection with these papers and with problems about the V state, I had extensive discussions and correspondence with other interested scientists. These included my friends Sigrid Peyerimhoff and Robert Buenker whom I visited several times in Bonn after one of the Nobel Prize alumni affairs in Lindau.

I should mention that Peyerimhoff had been at Chicago in 1963 on a German fellowship grant before she went to Princeton, where she first began her association with Buenker. While at LMSS, her work included computed wave functions and properties of HeH$^+$.

Further contributors to the study of the ethylene states were Ernest E.R. Davidson, who had made theoretical studies, and R. McDiarmid, who had contributed to an experimental understanding of these.

In the 1979 Note a somewhat revised classification is given of the spectral and other evidence for the four lowest-energy excited states of ethylene. The spectra include two transitions whose upper states Wilkinson had called 2R and $3R^1$. A third transition was brought to my attention by W.M. Flicker to whom I am much indebted for this and other helpful references and classifications.

My brief 1976 paper also gives data and interpretation for the weak T←N intersystem transition, where T is the lowest triplet state of the same configuration as V, the lowest singlet state. In T and V the π MO of the ground state is excited to the corresponding π^* antibonding MO.

Two other research associates doing experimental spectroscopic work in LMSS about 1961 were R.D. Verma and M. Aslam Khan. Verma had taken his Ph.D. in physics in work with Putcha Venkateswarlu at the Institute of Technology in Kanpur, India; he was at LMSS from 1959 to 1961. Verma and I published papers in 1961 on the spectra of CCl and CCl^+. Using an electrical discharge through helium containing a trace of CF_4, he soon found a CF^+ spectrum.

A little later in 1961 Verma found a new spectrum of unusual structure. In a paper by Verma and Mulliken this is analyzed and interpreted as due to a transition from a $^1\Sigma^-$ to a $^3\Pi$ state of SiO (silicon monoxide). The $^1\Sigma^-$ and $^3\Pi$ state are probably analagous to like-named states of carbon monoxide (CO) but the occurrence here was very surprising.

After leaving here, Verma became a professor of chemistry at the University of New Brunswick at Fredericton, N.B. He still lives there with his family and continues to do good research on molecular spectra. At his invitation I visited there not so very long ago to give a lecture.

Khan was with LMSS from 1961 to 1963. He came from the University of Pakistan and did research on the hydrides of magnesium and strontium.

One of my most favorite molecules, perhaps *the* most favorite, has been the nitrogen molecule (N_2). There are many reasons why people are interested in N_2 but my reasons have been mainly an obsession for understanding its structure and spectra scientifically; in other words, finding out what the electrons in it are doing, both when it is undisturbed in its ground state and when it is pushed into an excited, higher-energy state. Since there are infinitely many

172

excited states, it is necessary to be content with understanding a limited number. It is natural to choose those whose excitation energy is relatively small.

To secure the information which can be used to obtain such an understanding there are several methods. The most important is that of observing parts of the absorption and emission spectra. A number of spectroscopists over many years have advanced our knowledge of the nitrogen molecule spectrum. One who has contributed greatly to this endeavor in recent years is Kevin (Peter K.) Carroll, professor of physics at University College, Dublin. He and his students have refined the measurements and much advanced the analysis of previously known nitrogen molecule spectra, as well as discovering several new spectra.

For convenience of reference in the following discussion, I will give here some important lower-energy states of N_2. I first list for each state an informal letter symbol (such as X, A, B, a, c, etc.), then its species symbol describing the symmetry classification ($^3\Sigma_u^+$, $^3\Pi_g$, etc.) and finally its MO electron configuration, for example, $1\sigma_g^2\, 1\sigma_u^2\, 2\sigma_g^2\, 2\sigma_u^2\, 1\pi_u^4\, 3\sigma_g^2$ for the ground state. Spectral transitions from X to all of these states are now known as weak "forbidden" absorption spectra, found mostly at LMSS by Wilkinson.

Higher up are Rydberg states. Two important species of these are of the types $1\pi_u^3\, 3\sigma_g^2\, np\sigma_u$, $^1\Sigma_u^+$ and $1\pi_u^3\, 3\sigma_g^2\, np\pi^n$, $^1\Pi_u$, n=3,4,5 . . . . The MO $3p\sigma$ is identical with $3\sigma_u$ mentioned above. The MO $3p\pi$ can also be called $2\pi_u$.

Besides these Rydberg state series there are some very interesting fairly low-energy states called x, y, and k; x is of the species $^1\Sigma_g^-$ with configuration $1\pi_u^3\, 3\sigma_g^2\, 3p\pi_u$; y is of the species $^1\Sigma_g^-$ with configuration $1\pi_u^3\, 3\sigma_g^2\, 3p\pi_u$. More recently discovered in Carroll's laboratory is k, which has been diagnosed as half of a $^1\Pi_g$ state. By "half of a" $^1\Pi_g$ state, I mean that half of the rotational levels are missing so that it looks like a $^1\Sigma_g^-$ state, yet there is pretty convincing evidence that its rotational levels do belong to a $^1\Pi_g$ state. One piece of evidence is that it interacts strongly with the y state.

I have an extensive file of correspondence with Carroll dealing with questions and problems of mutual interest about N_2 spectra. Some of them were concerned with spectra which he had found and some with spectra that research associates and I (especially Wilkinson and later Lofthus) had studied at LMSS. Also I have a box of reprints, unpublished photographs, and manuscripts which

Carroll had prepared, as well as some manuscript items which we wrote jointly. One of the earliest of the latter, dated 1952, is on the first positive N_2 bands. This carries further the excellent analysis carried out earlier in my laboratory by Naudé and published in 1932. The reprints by Carroll include work on N_2+ and N_2++ as well as on N_2 spectra.

I have visited Carroll two or three times in Dublin. There I have met Professor Nevin, the head of the physics department, himself a spectroscopist; also Professor Wheeler and others, including students of Carroll.

On September 2, 1960, I sent a rather surprising letter to Carroll. It begins with a paragraph of our correspondence on N_2 and then goes on to an abrupt proposal which was bold, if not almost demanding, stating a time soon when Carroll could come to Chicago to work with me in LMSS. In reply, Carroll graciously agreed in principle but cited difficulties including scheduled teaching commitments. But soon everything was arranged. Professor Nevin agreed and arranged for a leave of absence and a substitute for student teaching. I obtained a letter of appointment for Carroll from the University of Chicago and he obtained a visa and managed other details. Carroll arrived in Chicago and began work on some N_2 problems.

One problem was concerned with the low-energy quintet $^5\Sigma^+$ of N_2. When two nitrogen atoms each in its normal $1s^2\,2s^2\,2p^3\;^4S$ quartet state get together, any one of four states of N_2 can result. Of these, the one of the lowest energy is the $^1\Sigma_g^+$ normal state. Next higher in energy is the $^3\Sigma_u^+$ triplet state, the lower state of the first positive bands. Higher is a quintet state which is not involved in any known spectra but which manifests itself in some perturbations in the rotational energy levels of the above-mentioned $^3\Pi_u$ state. Highest is a curve of $^7\Sigma_u^+$ species in which the two atoms repel each other more and more strongly as they approach each other.

The potential curve of the quintet state at large intermolecular distances is nearly flat for a long distance with a modest minimum and also a small maximum. Its form has been estimated in a paper published by Carroll using some experimental evidence and in another one by me based on theoretical MO arguments.

Kevin and I also published a joint paper entitled "The Predissociations in the $C^3\Pi_u$ state of N_2." The $C^3\Pi_u$ state is the upper state of the well-known "second positive" N_2 bands. When one gets a spark in the air, for example on a cold day from one's finger by rubbing it, the spectrum of the spark consists mainly of these bands. In the bands are two places where there is predissociation. One of these, we concluded is probably caused by a $^5\Pi_u$ state instead of by a $^3\Pi_u$ state as had been previously supposed. The second, whose potential curve mostly lies above that of the $C^3\Pi_u$ state, runs at first rather flat and, we concluded, over a hump, in the process of dissociating into two excited atoms, one of ^4S and the other of ^2D type. We explained several spectrum features, reported by various people, as vibrational energy levels whose electronic characters are mixtures of those of the C and C' states.

Carroll stayed with LMSS during 1961–63. He left in 1964 to continue work on diatomic molecular spectra at the Air Force Cambridge Research Laboratory in Cambridge, Massachusetts, where Tanaka had also been working. From Cambridge, he returned to Dublin.

Having realized in 1961 that I would reach the official retirement age at the University of Chicago, I became concerned about possibilities for an appointment elsewhere. In the fall of 1960 I visited the University of Indiana at Bloomington, where my friend Harrison (Harry) Shull was a Professor; he had been a Research Associate with LMSS in 1948–49. During my visit I received an extremely attractive offer for a professorship at Bloomington. However, the president of the University of Chicago, saying "That will never do," proposed a continuing appointment at Chicago, as Professor of Physics and Chemistry, that convinced me to remain.

XXVIII

India and Japan, 1962

Early in 1962, R.K. Asundi of the Atomic Energy Establishment Trombay, in Bombay, India, and President of the Indian Physical Society, arranged for me to spend seven weeks in India as a Visiting Professor. The Establishment, as well as the Tata Institute for Fundamental Research in Bombay, were under the directorship of H.J. Bhabha, who was also Chairman of the Atomic Energy commission. I left Chicago in time to spend Christmas in Athens with Lucia and her husband and two children, Wesley and Marina. She was now married to William W. McGrew, then a Foreign Service Officer with his first post in Athens. He and Lucia had first met as classmates in Reed College in Portland, Oregon.

On arriving in Bombay on December 27 early in the morning, the customs officer first required me to register the remains of a pint of whiskey, which I had taken along in the futile hope of getting some sleep on the plane. Foreigners, but not citizens of India, were permitted to have alcoholic drinks.

Soon after, I gave two lectures on molecular complexes in Bombay and then travelled, via Calcutta and Bhuvaneswar, to Cuttack on the east coast of India, where I took part in a spectroscopy symposium, followed by the Indian Science Congress. During these days there were also fascinating side trips to temples and other sights. Returning through Delhi, Indian friends took me to Agra to see the Taj Mahal, incomparably beautiful in itself and in the story of its creation. We also visited the magnificent palace of

176

the Moslem emperors. Before these visits, my friends went somewhere for an inexpensive lunch, leaving me to sit in a park with a picnic lunch put up by my hotel. As I ate, I had to share some it with monkeys, dogs, and human beggars.

Back in Bombay on January 11, I settled down to residence in the Taj Mahal Hotel, with daily trips to an office in the Atomic Energy Establishment's spectroscopic laboratory in Cadell Road. Here I saw much of Asundi, N.A. Narasimham, an excellent spectroscopist, and J. Shankar, the Head of the Chemistry Division, and others. Often I had lunch and discussions on the state of India and the world with Asundi and Shankar in the latter's office. Outside, almost tree-size poinsettias were blooming.

On some days I gave lectures on molecular orbital theory in the handsome new building of the Tata Institute, located close to the shore of the Indian Ocean in South Bombay. In the succeeding weeks excursions were arranged to nearby places of interest, and longer trips to university and other laboratories. The weather was warm, often hot, but one night the temperature fell to 55°F, causing big headlines in the newspaper: "Cold Wave. Fortunately No Deaths."

On January 26 I witnessed the magnificent ceremonies of Republic Day in New Delhi, and then left for Banaras, the ancient city on the Ganges. There I remained until the morning of January 29. At the Banaras Hindu University, I was the Guest of Honor at the Science College Day, with the unaccustomed duty of giving out the prizes to students who had distinguished themselves in scholarship or in athletics. I also visited what in this country would have been called the University Chapel. This is a very beautiful Shiva temple, tended by saffron-robed priests. Outside was some statuary, including a phallic symbol characteristic of the Shiva theology. On the walls are quotations from the Hindu classics. Most moving, I thought, were those from the Bhagavad Gita. Here Krishna, in poetic language, urges on one group of combatants in what might be called a civil war.

Another highlight was a visit to the Spectroscopy Department, where Professor Nandlal Singh made me welcome. Earlier Asundi had been the head of this department from the time it was first established in 1953. He had retired at age sixty, the normal retirement age for India. Banaras has been one of the very few universities in the world where spectroscopy has had an independent department or institute. On the walls of the laboratory were large photographs of Einstein, Herzberg, and myself—apparently the three gods of spectroscopy at Banaras.

With Nandlal Singh and students I went to call on the Maharajah of Banaras in his palace on the Ganges, up river from Banaras. The palace sits high above the river, and contains many memorabilia from royal visitors. While there, I was treated to a ride on the Maharajah's elephant.

From Banaras I made an excursion to nearby Sarnath, and saw the spot where Buddha preached his first sermon under a peepul or bo tree, a descendant of which now stands there. Not far away is a column set up by King Asoka who, after uniting much of northern India by bloody conquests, turned away from warfare to become famous as a benevolent and peaceful ruler.

In Banaras again, I made a very brief visit to the University art museum where, in just a few moments I got a vivid impression of their remarkably fine collection of colorful Indian miniatures. In the streets of Banaras, automobiles compete for passage with monkeys, dogs, camels, cows, and people. The automobile honks its way through.

From Banaras I returned to New Delhi, staying at the Asoka Hotel. I saw the impressive "Beating of Retreat," which marks the end of the Republic Day ceremonies. I visited the handsome American Embassy, where Earnest Watson, for many years a professor at the California Institute of Technology, was Scientific Attaché. I also visited the University and the National Physical Laboratory, and gave talks.

I learned that Emerson and Thoreau, and the Unitarian Church to which my mother belonged, had been much influenced by the Vedanta philosophy of ancient India and, as is generally known, that Gandhi developed his successful campaign to free India from British rule after he had read Thoreau's essay on "Civil Disobedience."

The next trip out from Bombay was to Andhra University at Waltair, on the Bay of Bengal. In the physics department at Waltair, I found a very active spectroscopic group, under Professor K. Rangadhama Rao. A week later I left for Karnatak University in Dharwar, where Professor N.R. Tawde had assembled an active spectroscopic group. On the way I passed the base of operations of the Indian army in their then recent takeover of Goa from the Portuguese. Another visit was to the National Chemical Laboratory and the University in Poona, southeast of Bombay. On my trips out from Bombay, Asundi and Narasimham rather regularly saw me off or welcomed me on my return.

From what I have said above, it can be seen that spectroscopy has been rather a favorite subject of research in India. However, most of this work, at least at the time of my visits, had been relatively old-fashioned in terms of equipment, and hence in its accuracy and its ability to detect and measure fine details.

One day I visited the Indian Institute of Technology (IIT) in Bombay. There are five IITs in India, each of which has had support from a different non-Indian organization: Kharagpur, UNESCO; Bombay, Russian assistance; Madras, West German; Delhi, British; Kanpur, American.

During these weeks I read some of the several English-language newspapers with much interest. It was my impression that their press was, if anything, freer than ours in America, in its comments and analyses. At this time a national election campaign was in full swing, and Nehru was travelling around the country making speeches for the Congress party candidates. His speeches were fully reported in the newspapers, and my impression was that they not only were very good, but were different at each different place.

Twice I heard Nehru speak, once in Cuttack at the Science Congress and once at the dedication of the Tata Institute in Bombay. On the latter occasion he intimated that he had a vague recollection of having been there eight years before to lay the cornerstone, and now wondered what Bhabha had been doing all this time (17). Nehru also indicated that he was pretty tired. However, as I read in the newspaper the next morning, he was not too tired to go down to a rally at the beach that evening and to denounce those young men of the party (They can go to hell, he said) who were opposing Krishna Menon, party candidate for re-election for the North Bombay district, and a favorite of Nehru. Menon, an America baiter, and anathema to some Indians too, was re-elected.

Before I left Bombay, I purchased copies of Nehru's *Discovery of India* and his *Introduction to World History* (These were based on letters which he wrote while he was in prison, to his daughter, who later succeeded him as Prime Minister of India.)

Near the end of my stay in Bombay, I was asked to give the first K.S. Krishnan Memorial Lecture of the Indian Physical Society. Krishnan, a very distinguished Indian physicist, a foreign Member

179

of our National Academy of Sciences, and a very humane person, had died in 1961. I had met him a number of times. I remembered particularly one lecture which he gave at the University of Chicago at which he skillfully demonstrated the phenomenon of critical opalescence. I also remembered how at the 1953 meeting in Tokyo he had told me about a great University at Takshashila in India which existed at about the time of Buddha.

In July with my wife and Valerie I drove to New Hampshire to take part in one of the Gordon conferences. Afterwards we went on to Ottawa where I visited with Herzberg, Ramsay, and others in the spectroscopic Mecca which Herzberg had created.

In September I took part in an International Symposium on Molecular Structure and Spectroscopy in Tokyo. I gave a paper on Molecular Rydberg States. This time my wife accompanied me; we stayed at the old Imperial Hotel, now most regrettably destroyed to make room for something modern. Scientifically it was a very good meeting (18), but also we met many friends, Japanese, European, and American. As usual, our Japanese hosts did everything they could to make us welcome at and after the meeting. In Tokyo there were among others: Kotani, Mizushima, Nagakura, and Fujioka; in Kyoto, Fukui, his wife, and others; T. Kubota in Osaka, where we also met Dr. and Mrs. Takeda (Takeda is Director of the Shionogi and Company Research Laboratory). We also visited Tsubomura in his native city of Nara, the earliest capital city of Japan. Nara is notable for its temples and for the numerous deer who roam freely in and outside a park in the center of the city. Nagakura, then Tsubomura, had spent some time in Chicago working on molecular complexes, and Kubota was just about to go there for a year.

Earlier in the year when I was in Bombay, Putcha Venkateswarlu had expressed the hope that I could give some lectures at the Indian Institute of Technology in Kanpur. While we were in Tokyo, he let me know that he had succeeded in arranging a visiting Professorship at IIT Kanpur for six weeks where I gave a series of lectures. Kanpur is an industrial city of a million or so people on the Ganges, between Banaras and Delhi. The IIT there had been a small institution. But now, with the advice and cooperation of a group of American professors representing a consortium of American universities, including MIT, plans had been made for a new and considerably larger Institute. This was to be located near Kalianpur, about six miles from Kanpur. In fact the Institute campus was already well on its way toward completion.

My wife and I proceeded from Tokyo to Kanpur, via Calcutta, with short stops in Hong Kong and Bangkok. The monsoon rains ended while we were in Calcutta, and from the moment we reached Kanpur there was bright sunshine every day, hot at noon, but cooler at night, a trifle less hot each succeeding day. There being no acceptable hotel in Kanpur, we were quartered in the Kamala Retreat, a palatial museum-like building in the midst of extensive gardens, owned by Padampat Singhania, a leading industrialist. There was a large swimming pool, with a wave-making machine which was a copy of one we had seen in Budapest in 1932. A young Rajput named Rawat cooked meals for us; after a while he got himself an assistant. Each morning we woke to hear the songs of the servants, based on singularly happy-sounding Indian movie music. In the trees there were green parrots and minah birds. One day my wife met a tall monkey in the garden; both were rather frightened.

Each day after breakfast I walked in the sunshine about a mile to my office for my lecture in the old IIT buildings, past goats and cows, water buffalo enjoying mud baths, and people. In the evening as the sun was setting, I returned for dinner, enjoying the distant unearthly howling of jackals in a large ring around the city.

One day on the banks of the Ganges we found an appealing dog which we adopted and took with us to the Retreat; Rawat took him home at night.

Early in our stay in Kanpur, we made a trip to Nanital, on a lake in the foothills of the Himalaya Mountains. Here D.D. Pant, a spectroscopist, was Professor at the D-S-B Government College. Pant and Hari Bist took us to Ranikhet, to witness the spectacle of sunrise over the Himalayas. During this trip we heard the news that the Chinese had begun an invasion of northern India. Somewhat later we visited Banaras and called on the Maharajah, who sent his barge for a trip up the Ganges to his residence. Jacqueline Kennedy had been a recent and popular visitor there.

When it came time to leave Kanpur, it so happened that it was Full-Moon-Day-of-the-Year, and about a million people had come to the river to bathe. The bridge over which our taxi had to cross was so jammed with people that we were delayed by an hour. We reached the somewhat distant airport just in time to see our plane already in the air, departing. (Commercial plane flights, suspended for some time because of the war, had just been resumed.) So we took an overnight train to Delhi and from there went to Bombay, for a few days and a lecture, before leaving India. On our way back to New York we stopped over in Athens to see Lucia and her family.

During the last weeks of this sojourn I had been having increasingly unpleasant symptoms, but no doctor knew what was wrong until we reached New York. There the diagnosis was hepatitis. The cure called for prolonged bedrest, accompanied by plentiful eating in spite of the fact that food tasted foul. The most striking initial symptom in India had been that dinner tasted bad; later also lunch, and finally even breakfast; also cigarettes. However, after several weeks in the hospital in New York, and then in Chicago, all was well; the liver had repaired itself.

XXIX

Quantum Chemistry in Florida.
Germany Again

Early in 1964 I spent a month in Tallahassee at the Institute of Molecular Biophysics of Florida State University (FSU) newly set up by Michael Kasha, with AEC (Atomic Energy Commission) assistance. Kasha had been at LMSS on an AEC fellowship in 1949–50. That spring I was almost persuaded to move to FSU as a Research Professor of Chemical Physics (19), but President Beadle intervened and I remained in Chicago after it was agreed that my appointment as Professor of Physics and Chemistry would continue as long as my health was good.

However, I also accepted the appointment at FSU for whatever time I could spare, and in 1965 began the practice of driving there in my car for the winter quarter with my wife.

Meantime Per-Olov Löwdin had established for himself an interesting international schedule: lectures and a conference on quantum chemistry in Florida in the late winter and in Sweden in the summer. He had appointments at the University of Florida in late fall or winter. He brought his wife and family with him. So my wife and they became good friends.

I have already mentioned how in returning from Russia in 1958 I attended one of Per-Olov's conferences in Sweden, at Volodalen. In the winter of 1965, as also in a few earlier and numerous later years, I participated in his Florida conferences on recent progress in quantum chemistry, which were held for many years in a hotel on Sanibel Island on the southwest coast of Florida. This very attractive location is especially notable for the great variety of sea shells which can be found on the beaches. At the conferences or symposia many papers were presented for discussion in the mornings and evenings, while afternoons were for swimming or other recreations, and for private conversations or discussions. The week of conferences was preceded by a week devoted to lectures on quantum mechanics and quantum chemistry for beginners in the field. Later the program also included a week of conferences on applications to problems of biological interest—roughly speaking, to quantum biology.

Löwdin always prepared a program including some invited speakers, and also invited many others to come as discussants or to present progress reports on their own work. To one invited speaker he gave a special designation as conference president. He also suggested topics for the invited speakers. In 1965 he designated me as conference president, and assigned the topic "Some fundamental problems in the theory of molecular structure and spectra." However, I said, "I am going to follow Professor Hylleraas' example of two years ago and give some reminiscences instead," and I did so. This talk was published later in 1965 in the *Journal of Chemical Physics* (**43**, 52–111), under the title "Molecular Scientists and Molecular Science: Some Reminiscences." Löwdin's Florida schools and conferences continued each year usually honoring some well-known chemist or molecular physicist. However, more recently they had to be moved to a location further north, on the Atlantic coast of Florida. At the time of the earlier meetings, Sanibel Island was accessible only by ferry, but the building of a bridge later made it too generally popular.

In the spring of 1965 I gave the Silliman Lectures at Yale, on molecular orbital problems, but did not write the hoped-for book.

In June, 1965, with my wife and Valerie, I spent some time in Amsterdam giving lectures on a new Visiting Professorship, making many interesting scientific and social contacts. We lived in a small pension and I rode to the University in a trolley car. On some weekends we visited friends in the country. Once we went to a museum devoted to paintings by van Gogh.

In July, I rented a Mercedes in Frankfurt and we drove to Bonn to visit Walter Weizel, whom we had not seen since 1931, then to Giessen to see Hans Kuhn, to Göttingen to see Hund and his family, and to Würzburg to see G. Briegleb who had (perhaps too generously) dedicated his book on donor-acceptor complexes to me.

184

From Würzburg we drove down the Romantische Strasse and on to Tübingen to renew my acquaintance with Kortüm. On the way to Tübingen we visited the Hechingen-Hohenzollern castle at the top of an eminence high above the surrounding forest. We thought that it had been here that my wife's grandfather Adolf Noé had for a time been physician for the Hohenzollern prince. He had then been in the service of the Austrian emperor, and received the title Noé von Archenegg from him with a distinctive new and gorgeous coat of arms, now in my possession. The word Archenegg in the title refers to Noah's ark, and this is depicted in the coat of arms. We also have a passport showing that he accompanied Metternich to Paris.

We stopped in Ulm so that I could visit the cathedral, which previously I had glimpsed only from afar; as a result of this visit and difficulty in finding my motel, I was almost too late for my lecture in Tübingen. The cathedral was immense but otherwise disappointing.

From Tübingen we went on to Heidelberg, and saw K.H. Hausser, who had been in Chicago at LMSS in 1956–57. Back in Frankfurt, we flew to Salzburg. After some sightseeing there I rented a car and we drove south across higher land and then down, to Klagenfurt. The road led through a snow bank remaining from winter and past an active glacier. In Klagenfurt we met a number of my wife's relatives including her aunt Lillie and her first cousin Herbert. One night she got them all together for an excellent dinner and the first reunion since our visit in 1932. From Klagenfurt we drove to Graz and Vienna. From Vienna we returned to Chicago.

Prior to about 1960, I had often been invited to give lectures, but had not received any special recognition in terms of awards or medals, except the bronze medal given me at Liège in 1948. As I have mentioned above in discussing my series of papers on polyatomic molecules published in 1934–35, I thought these papers were pretty good, but other people did not then seem much interested. However, in 1966, they were cited as a principal basis for a Nobel prize. This prize was the climax of a series of awards and beautiful medals which began in 1960. I have greatly appreciated and treasured each one. Each award provided the occasion for a pleasant visit, with new opportunities to learn about science and to meet fellow scientists. Five of the awards were from various sections of the American Chemical Society, to which I have belonged since 1918. Three of these awards honor chemists whom

I have known and greatly esteemed: the Gilbert N. Lewis medal of the California Section, the Peter Debye award of the California Section, the John G. Kirkwood award of the New Haven Section and of Yale University. The remaining two, the J. Willard Gibbs medal of the Chicago Section and the T.W. Richards medal of the Northeastern Section, also meant very much to me. Still another medal, from the City College of New York, gave me an occasion to get acquainted with an institution from which many of our best-known scientists have graduated.

XXX

Tallahassee

So far I have said relatively little about my life with Mary Helen during our winters at Tallahassee. Tallahassee, in the northwest corner of Florida, is the capital of the state. It lies on hilly ground some miles north of the Gulf of Mexico. A fascinating area near Tallahassee is that around Wakulla Springs. Here a flow of 200,000 gallons per minute of water comes out of the earth, to initiate a substantial river that flows southward to the Gulf. There are glass-bottomed boats in which one can see fish swimming below. On the banks of the river are many alligators, while several kinds of exotic birds fly among the trees.

In Tallahassee, politics and education at FSU are major activities. As a part-time professor, I had an office in the Institute of Molecular Biophysics, of which Michael Kasha is the Director. He had been a research associate with me in Chicago some years earlier. The physics and chemistry department buildings are close by and I often visited them for discussions or seminars. In the chemistry department there was for some years a fellowship for graduate students called the Robert S. Mulliken fellowship.

Mary Helen and I, with new friends there, had felt more and more at home in Tallahassee, and thought for a time of establishing ourselves more permanently there. We went so far as to bring some of our furniture and other family belongings from Chicago for our dwelling in Tallahassee. Further, we bought a tract of land (about three acres) on high ground at the juncture of two roads on which lived people we knew. Elise Duyall's house was adjacent down

187

Argonne Road. She was a friend who had rented to us some of the houses in which we stayed while in Tallahassee.

Our land was heavily wooded, mainly with tall pines below which grew interesting shrubs and vines. We found it thrilling to possess this piece of wild Nature. We talked about building a house there with the need to remove only a few of the pines. The land had earlier been part of a large area which had been given to Marquis de Lafayette by the first U.S. government in gratitude for his help in the American revolution. Finally, however, we sold this beautiful property.

In Tallahassee we often visited the Kashas (Michael, his wife Lilli, and their son Nicholas). Their house was on the top of a long grassy turf which sloped down to Lake Bradford, the largest of a chain of lakes. Michael had a sailboat in which we explored these. He and Nicholas made a treehouse in a tree by the lake. The Kashas often invited us and others for refreshments and talk at their house. Michael as a scientist worked on molecular problems but was also intensely concerned with the guitar and its history. He studied the physics related to its construction and succeeded in inventing an improved guitar, which found approval by a well-known master of the art of guitar playing.

Among other friends were Earle Plyler and his wife. He was chairman of the physics department. He was an expert in infrared spectroscopy, whose laboratory at the National Bureau of Standards in Washington in earlier days I had sometimes visited. We once wrote a small paper together on an iodine molecular complex. Once at the 1962 Spectroscopy meeting in Japan he had suggested my going to FSU after retirement at Chicago.

Others whom we saw rather often included Dr. and Mrs. Hans Gaffron. He was a biochemist who was a memeber of Kasha's Institute. He had earlier been with Franck in Chicago. He was a German who had been brought up in Peru. His full name was Hans von Pritwitz von Gaffron.

On one occasion, when the eminent Professor P.A.M. Dirac after he had retired at Cambridge was visiting Tallahassee, we drove to the Wakulla Springs. I have thought that the fascination of this area was one of the reasons why he became a professor at FSU. The excellent program in nuclear physics at FSU may also have been a reason.

We began 1966 with a winter quarter at FSU. Valerie was also there as a student at FSU High School until she graduated at the end of the quarter and then entered the university. Previously she had been for some time at the Woodstock Country School in Vermont, but was not happy there.

After the winter in Tallahassee, my wife and I returned to Chicago. There we had a visit from Hund, and also from John Slater who came to receive a Chicago Sc.D.

XXXI

The Nobel Prize, 1966

In September 1966 I had an intimation that I would receive a Nobel prize but did not take this seriously. That fall I had decided to begin the stay at FSU sooner than usual, in November. My wife and I arrived late on the evening of the fourth in Tallahassee after a drive from Chicago. We went at once to our motel for a night's rest. However, we were told that a man from Sweden had been looking for me. Early the next morning we had breakfast with this man, a representative of the Swedish press who told us the interesting news that I had been awarded the 1966 Nobel prize in chemistry. Other news representatives followed. My shoes were still covered with mud, an aftermath of an early snow storm in Alabama as we approached Tallahassee the day before. The reporters meticulously noted this fact, also that I was missing one button.

The news about the award of the prize gave rise to celebrations by friends in various places. FSU was especially pleased that one of their faculty members had won a Nobel prize, and I received both unofficial and official congratulations.

The University of Chicago and my friends there were also pleased, but perhaps wondered why I had chosen to be away just at that time. In any event, an additional cause for rejoicing was the news that my Chicago colleague Dr. Charles Huggins had also been awarded a Nobel prize in medicine.

Both of us were honored by a festive dinner in a downtown Chicago hotel on December 1. University colleagues and other Chicagoans as well as out-of-town people were invited to attend.

After dinner, Huggins and I were the featured speakers. Mayor Daley seemed to enjoy my speech, in which I said some pleasant things about Chicago, his favorite city.

A few days later, my wife and I and our two daughters travelled to Stockholm. People who saw the Swedish exhibit at the World's Fair in Montreal in 1967 reported seeing us all in movies of a reception at the royal palace, in which all the new Nobel prize winners were welcomed.

Sharing the great events which followed in Stockholm was Huggins. We and our families were made comfortable in the Grand Hotel. Leon Jacobson, our university colleague and sometime director of the university hospital, was also there to guard our health. He kept telling Huggins and me to "take it easy."

This visit was my seventh to Sweden. The first and second and some of the others have been mentioned above; all have been interesting. This one was the *most* interesting. I was thrilled at being presented to the King on December 10 to receive the prize, by Inga Fischer-Hjalmars (20), Professor of Quantum Chemistry at the University of Stockholm, a friend from earlier visits.

At the banquet in the palace on December 11, each of the women in attendance was given a slip of paper with the name of a man who would escort her in and be her dinner partner. Mary Helen was at first puzzled on finding that her escort and dinner partner would be H.M. Konung, but she was pleased to learn that in Swedish this meant the King.

On the 12th and 13th the prize winners gave their lectures; mine on the afternoon of the 12th. December 13 is a day which in Sweden is celebrated as Lucia day, a day when the darkness of winter is soon to begin to be lifted. In accordance with custom, we were awakened at 7 in our hotel room by the entrance of four young girls, each with a crown of lighted candles, bringing coffee and singing Santa Lucia in a most charming way. Also on Lucia day, Lucias from various countries come to Stockholm to help celebrate. It just so happened that our older daughter was named Lucia, which made it quite appropriate for her to be there.

At this point I must mention one by-product of our visit. While in Stockholm in 1932, my wife and I had been enchanted by the Swedish arts and crafts, and after many misgivings about the extravagance, had bought for $90 a beautiful modern Swedish wall hanging called Roda Hasterna (Red Horses). Then some years later in Chicago our very handsome but naughty black cocker spaniel chewed our lovely Red Horses, making two or three bad holes in it. For several years we had discussed the possibility of taking it back to Stockholm for repair, and on this visit we actually did so. The repairs cost as much as the original price of the hanging, but we were very happy about having it now restored to good condition.

Before leaving Sweden, we had a very pleasant visit with the Löwdins in Uppsala, and with the Edléns in Lund. From Lund we went to Copenhagen for a short visit; there we looked up my old friend Erik Hulthén, who was living in a suburb. I gave lectures in all these places. From Copenhagen we flew to England, and spent Christmas in Oxford, and from there went back to Tallahassee.

One of the happy consequences of the award of the prize had been a flood of congratulatory telegrams and letters. One which I especially cherished was a sympathetic and generous letter from Hund, with whom I would have been glad to have shared the prize.

One friend who had made a business of breeding dogs, Suzie Winnicke, to help celebrate the prize, gave us a beautiful little silky terrier. As "Mulliken's Miss Molecule" (briefly, Missy) she won a blue ribbon in the puppy class at the dog show in Tallasassee that winter.

XXXII

Post-Prize Activities

Early in January, 1967 I took part in Löwdin's annual symposium on Sanibel Island, which that year was in honor of John Slater. Later in the month I gave a talk at a special celebration in Tallahassee in my honor, in the presence of the governor, members of the Board of Trustees of the Florida University system, and friends. I think it was a good talk.

Earlier in January I had been scheduled to go to Bombay to introduce a comprehensive international symposium in spectroscopy, dedicated especially to honoring Asundi. However, my health had been causing some problems and I was finally persuaded that I should not go. I was very sorry, since I had wanted especially to pay my respects to Asundi. As at Tokyo in 1962, there was a very fine attendance at the symposium. Another event in early January which again I had to miss was an award, jointly with Huggins, as Chicagoan of the Year. This award was by the Press Club in Chicago.

The rest of 1967 included two hospital stays with excellent results and some other more interesting events. Returning from Tallahassee in late March, I went to Marquette University for an honorary Sc.D. In April I gave a talk entitled "Spectroscopy, Quantum Chemistry, and Molecular Physics," later published in *Physics Today* (**21**, 52, 1968), at a meeting of the Physical Society which President Johnson honored by his presence. In this talk I noted how the study of molecular spectroscopy was carried on mainly by physicists when I went into it in 1923, but since then had

193

gone more and more into the hands of chemists, who after all are the people most interested in molecules. For physicists, this work is part of "molecular physics," for chemists of "chemical physics" or "physical chemistry."

Early in June I signed the book as a Foreign Member of the Royal Society of London, to which I had earlier been elected. This happened in the friendly presence of a small group including Christopher Ingold and Sir Robert Robinson. After that I went to Cambridge to receive an honorary Sc.D., with the Todds as my hosts.

Late in June Mary Helen and I went to Versailles for a beautifully planned conference of the Institut de la Vie on "From Theoretical Physics to Biology," initiated by Dr. M. Marois. Many interesting people were there. The conference participants stayed at the Trianon Palace Hotel, in which the treaty of peace after World War I was worked out by Clemenceau and Lloyd-George and signed in 1919. The scientific conference sessions, emphasizing biological problems with some participation by physicists, were held in the Chateau de Versailles, the former royal palace. This conference was the first of a series of similar conferences organized by the Institut de la Vie every other year. Planning sessions accompanied by meetings with small symposia were held at various places in intermediate years. During each conference some excursions were made to neighboring castles.

From Paris we proceeded to the island city of Lindau on the Bodensee (Lake Constance). Here the city had arranged its annual symposium and festivities featuring Nobel prize winners, this year emphasizing the chemists. For two mornings there was a program of lectures by some of the prize winners for an audience composed largely of professors and students from (mostly German) universities. Professor R. Mecke of Freiburg in Breisgau, whom I had first met in Bonn in 1925, introduced speakers, and helped me by preparing and bringing along solutions which I used for demonstration in a talk on molecular complexes.

On another day, Count Bernadotte welcomed us at his castle, reached in an all-morning steamship excursion from Lindau up the lake. The castle was on a beautiful island (Insel Mainau). Here a hillside was covered with flowering plants in great variety. There were also numerous redwoods (Sequoia) that were brought some years earlier from California. At the castle we sat down to an excellent lunch. After saying good-bye we returned to the steamer, which crossed the lake for a visit to a nearby village, then down the lake to our hotel and to Lindau.

At night we stayed in the comfortable Hotel Bad Schachen across the lake from Lindau. One day we went at lunch time for a "Bavarian breakfast" which featured large white radishes. This took place in the Casino located at one end of the lake where railroad trains came in. After that there occurred the customary Maikafer (May bug) ceremony, an affair in which Count Bernadotte fancifully eulogized a large chocolate model of the May bug, while everyone received a smaller model of the bug.

On the steamer trip many students went along taking the opportunity for conversations with the prize winners and asking for autographs. Steurer, the mayor of Lindau, also came with us on the trip and the other events. He and his wife were especially charming.

Several times on the way home from Lindau, I have stopped off in Bonn to visit Robert Buenker and Sigrid Peyerimhoff. They have published a large number of excellent papers together and with students. These papers have reported the results of calculations on a variety of molecules. Peyerimhoff and Buenker had begun these joint publications as postdoctoral fellows at Princeton. Buenker then became a professor at the University of Nebraska, where I first met him, and was impressed with his work. Meantime, Peyerimhoff had become a professor and later a dean at Bonn University. Buenker was married and had three children; Peyerimhoff remained single. However, they continued to publish joint papers resulting from visits by him to Bonn or visits by her to Nebraska. More recently, he and his family lived in Bonn and now he continues his calculations as a professor at another university in Wuppertal, not far from Bonn. I have had good scientific discussions and correspondence with them both, especially on our common interest in the spectrum of the ethylene molecule. Peyerimhoff and I have visited with the Buenker family. I have had lunches with Peyerimhoff at a restaurant overlooking the Rhine and have visited Buenker and given a talk at his university in Wuppertal. We have all met now and then at other scientific conferences in Germany.

Thus far I have said relatively little about where in Chicago Mary Helen and I lived after our early enjoyment of a penthouse apartment. As time went on, we moved from one apartment to another but almost always remained near the university. Frequently our moves were occasioned by trips abroad.

We lived in a rented apartment except for a few years when we owned a share in a cooperative building with four apartments, at 5712 Kenwood Avenue. Here our co-owners included Weldon and Mildred Brown. Weldon had first come to Chicago, after a Berkeley Ph.D., to work with me on halogen molecule spectra, and later, was a professor of chemistry at Chicago. As I have already told above, we had many intensive discussions on facts and problems in organic chemistry, particularly on molecular complexes.

After several years Mary Helen and I sold our share in the cooperative (unfortunately just before prices went up sharply). We moved then to a very attractive lakeside apartment at 4800 Lake Shore Drive. But this proved inconveniently far from the university and we then moved to a newly constructed building at 5825 Dorchester Avenue, in which I lived until September 1985.

In December 1967, I gave a talk on molecular complexes at the annual Welsh Foundation Conference in Houston, Texas.

During January 1968, I was visiting Professor for a pleasant month at the University of California at Santa Barbara where I had an office and gave lectures in chemistry. Also I visited an old friend, Dr. H.P. Broida, in the physics building where he was doing some interesting spectroscopy. I had known him especially in visits to the National Bureau of Standards in Washington.

I also had a chat with Robert M. Hutchins, well-known former president of the University of Chicago, who was now located in Santa Barbara.

For February and March we went back to Tallahassee.

Carl Moser had arranged for me to give lectures at the University of Paris in the spring of 1968, also to do some research. My wife and I took up residence in the small Hotel Atala on the right bank, near l'Étoile. From there I could conveniently take the Metro to an office some distance away in Professor Daudel's center for quantum-mechanical computations in the Rue du Maroc.

I went to Paris by plane, and my wife followed by boat, bringing along Miss Molecule. My lectures were to be in the physical chemistry laboratory on the Rue Pierre Curie, where the 1948 conference had been held. Unfortunately this was the time of the student revolution. I reached the lecture room by walking up the Rue Gay-Lussac from the Boulevard St. Michel. Shortly before I gave my second lecture the entrance to the street had been barricaded by the students, and then as I walked up the street I passed the burned-out carcasses of many automobiles, while the street was littered with torn-up paving blocks. After that, we remained for some time in Paris hoping things would improve, but they got worse, and there were no more lectures. Transportation came to a halt; no Metro, no taxis, no trains, and the banks were closed.

Finally we became refugees, driving to Belgium with an American businessman from our hotel who succeeded somehow in renting a car and getting gasoline. We now settled down for some weeks in Liège, where at the University the physical chemists (especially Duchesne and d'Or) and the spectroscopists at the Observatory (especially Swings and Rosen) made me welcome. Our living quarters were at the Hotel Grande Bretagne. Here Miss Molecule had interesting adventures, including a flirtation with the waiters. (This had happened in Paris too.) Professors d'Or and Swings tried to persuade me to come back the following year on a new Visiting Professorship, but I decided against this.

We also spent some time in Brussels where I visited Prigogine's Institute in the Free University. Here the students had draped the Administration Building with the red flag of communism and the black flag of anarchy. However, research went on as usual in the laboratories. In Brussels Missy was not well, and we spent hours in the office of a celebrated veterinarian but our French was inadequate. Finally he recommended an operation, but after a sleepless night Mary Helen demurred, so we did not agree to it. Somehow Missy recovered.

Early in July we again went to Lindau, this time with the physicists. At the comfortable Hotel Bad Schachen we invited cousins of my wife from Austria to stay with us. Missy was also with us there and her picture, taken there, appears in my "Collected Papers" volume.

In August I lectured at Brookhaven, seeing among others the Freeds (Simon Freed had been on the faculty at Chicago), the Goldhabers and Stan Ehrenson who had been a postdoctoral with me at Chicago in the late 1950s.

In November I gave a lecture at Mt. Holyoke, honoring Lucy Pickett.

During the winter quarter at FSU in 1969, I took part in the Sanibel Island symposium honoring Henry Eyring. In March I made a brief trip to London to introduce a Royal Society discussion on photoelectron spectroscopy, which had been organized by Bill Price and D.W. Turner. I emphasized the fact that photoelectron spectroscopy has given increased reality to the previously rather abstract concept of molecular orbitals.

While in London I met Robert E. Mulliken and his family; he had written me after seeing my name in the news in 1966. He was possibly a distant relative, whose parents had lived in America, but later went to England.

Among the events in April there was a meeting of the International Academy of Quantum Molecular Science (IAQMS) in Baltimore, arranged by Robert Parr; usually they met in Menton, France.

Every year my native city of Newburyport celebrates one week in summer as Homecoming Week. During this week former natives return to be welcomed in varied festivities. In August 1969, my wife and I were invited by the mayor of Newburyport to come for the dedication of a new street to be called Mulliken Way. A welcoming party met us on our arrival at the Boston airport, and conducted us to a small plane which, flying at a low altitude, gave us a delightful panorama of cities and countryside, with salt marshes interspersed by creeks and rivers, on the way to Newburyport. At Newburyport we were guests at the home of Captain and Mrs. Claudius Pendill. He was a retired navy officer recently with a Newburyport corporation but now very busy in effective efforts to strengthen and build up the local Anna Jacques Hospital. One day the Pendills invited many of my former Newburyport friends and associates for reminiscences and a sociable afternoon visit.

The next day Mary Helen and I went to the dedication of the newly created Robert Mulliken Way. This is a street or road in a neighborhood being newly developed by the city for small business. It branches off Scotland Road, where I used to look for mushrooms (especially puffballs), and which led past the site of the old silver mines, marked by galena outcroppings, toward Byfield. One participant in the development on Mulliken Way is the Strem Chemical Company, which makes a great variety of special chemicals, some of which they supply for the research of my University of Chicago colleague, Jack Halpern.

After returning to Chicago I left on August 16 for Honolulu on the way to Sydney, Australia to participate in the XXII International

Congress of Pure and Applied Chemistry, in association with the XII International Conference on Coordination Chemistry. I gave one of the four plenary ICPAC lectures in a symposium on "50 Years of Valence Theory." The other speeches were by Coulson from England, Daudel from France, and Van Vleck from the United States. My talk at the symposium was entitled "The Path to Molecular Orbital Theory." In it I reviewed the early steps both before and after the advent of quantum mechanics. I also visited laboratories in Melbourne, Adelaide and Canberra. During my visit I also got acquainted with kangaroos, emus, Koala bears, the ornithorhincus, and other native Australian animals.

In May I visited the University of Nebraska for lectures mainly on molecular complexes, and talked with Professor Robert Buenker about his digital computer calculations on molecules. Later, as I have already mentioned, I have often visited with him and Sigrid Peyerimhoff in Germany. In October I went to the University of Iowa to give five lectures on molecular complexes.

In 1970, after driving to Tallahassee to spend January, Mary Helen and I went on to New Orleans for a Mardi Gras symposium with the quantum chemists of Louisiana State University and of Loyola University.

We then drove on to Austin, Texas where F.A. Matsen had arranged for me to spend three months as a Visiting Professor in Chemistry and Physics. There we met former Chicago colleagues (Judson Neff, Charner Perry and Charles Hartshorne) and their wives. J.S. Dewar was also there. I had first met Dewar when he was at Queen Mary College of the University of London. In 1960 he became a professor in the chemistry department of the University of Chicago. Increased funds for research before long took him to the University of Texas, where he and his students devoted themselves to computing molecular energies by semiempirical methods. Some years earlier I too had advocated the use of semiempirical methods. But, persuaded by the results of the Diatomic Molecule Project at LMSS and by the many more accurate molecular calculations subsequent to it, I had come to strongly favor ab initio methods using high-speed digital computers.

Dewar often seemed to me to delight in being annoyingly contrary. This was illustrated at a symposium at the University of Indiana in 1958. I was advocating hyperconjugation as the cause of somewhat shorter than usual bond lengths and other phenomena in certain molecules, while Dewar insisted that they can be fully explained by effects associated with hybridization. In papers published later, I agreed that he might be partly right, but that certainly hyperconjugation at least contributed to the observed effects.

In Austin, W.A. Noyes, Jr. was especially kind; I had first known him when he was a young instructor in the Chemistry Department at Chicago, and I was a postdoctoral fellow there just after getting my Ph.D.

During 1969 I had gathered a vast assemblage of reprints on the spectrum of iodine, as a basis for an intensive study. While in Austin I completed the resulting papers. One was a comprehensive review of facts and interpretations called "Iodine Revisited." I used this title because it seemed so highly appropriate in spite of the fact that I had an inner revulsion against reading about something "revisited."

My other paper on "The Role of Kinetic Energy in the Franck-Condon Principle" included a novel interpretation of the "McLennan bands" of iodine. I now explained these not as real molecular bands made up of overlapping band lines but as bits and pieces of a single continuum belonging to one particular electronic transition. I explained the existence of such a "structured continuum" by considering the role of kinetic energy in the application of the Franck–Condon principle. Herzberg had also observed a less extended structured continuum in the spectrum of molecular hydrogen. This had been discussed and explained in a paper by Dalgarno, Herzberg, and Stephens in the *Astrophysical Journal* (**162**, 49, 1970). The theory of this type of spectrum had earlier been briefly indicated in a paper by Condon who spoke of "diffraction bands" (*Physical Review* **32**, 55, 1928).

I discussed my new iodine papers at the Lindau chemistry meeting in late June. Newcomers there since the 1967 meeting included Onsager (1968 Nobel prize) and Eigen, Norrish, and Porter (1969 Nobel prize).

From Lindau my wife and I went to Menton for a gathering of the IAQMS presided over by Daudel. The Parrs, the Pullmans and Pople were among those in attendance.

After a Gordon Research Conference in August 1970, I went with my wife to San Jose, California for three months. Enrico Clementi had arranged that I could make some computations on the IBM 360/91 computer at the Research Laboratory, partly in collaboration with Franz van Duijenveldt and Bowen Liu. I greatly enjoyed this interaction with the big machine.

In 1971 we returned to California, this time for me to use the new 360/91 computer in the new Research Laboratory in San Jose. In my approaches to the computer I often felt as people must have in the old days on consulting the Delphic Oracle; I awaited the answers with eager anticipation and excitement and often with fear and trembling lest I had phrased my questions in a way that might be distasteful to the machine.

Some of the results of my computations were presented in two papers on BH and BeH in the *International Journal of Quantum Chemistry* in 1971. Based on computations we had made during my visit, Bowen Liu and I published in the *Journal of the American Chemical Society* in 1971 a paper on "SCF Wave Functions of P_2 and PO and the Role of d Functions in Chemical Bonding, and of s-p Hybridization in N_2 and P_2."

Another paper was on "The Nitrogen Molecule Correlation Diagram" published in *Chemical Physics Letters* in 1972 (Vol. 14, p. 137). Here I computed the energy of each of the MOs of N_2 in its ground state as a function of internuclear distance. Many years before I had published rough qualitative correlation diagrams for N_2 and other diatomic molecules, but now was very happy to be able to replace these by a quantitatively calculated diagram for N_2 (later also for CO).

During the time of my 1970 calculations on the IBM machine at San Jose, Mary Helen and I rented an apartment in the nearby town of Los Gatos, and I rented a car for the period of our visit. Every working day I drove in the morning to the IBM laboratory and back at night. In 1971 I paid to have my own car, a Plymouth Fury III driven from Chicago to Los Gatos for our use. That year we were in a different apartment, but as before I drove each day to the IBM laboratory.

While at San Jose in 1970 and 1971 we visited, among others, the Paulings and the Harden McConnells at Stanford, and the Tellers in Berkeley, where we also saw the Birges and the Hildebrands.

One scientific activity which I completed in Tallahassee was the manuscript of a book jointly with Willis Person entitled *Molecular Complexes, A Lecture and Reprint Volume* (published in 1969). Person had earlier visited Chicago when he was a professor at the University of Iowa and had made notes on my lectures on molecular complexes. We had also published two papers in this field, one a review paper. The "Lecture and Reprint Volume" included a revised version of my lectures, and a reproduction of some papers on molecular complexes which co-workers and I had published. We worked on the manuscript during visits of Willis to Tallahassee after he had driven down from Gainesville, where he had become a professor at the University of Florida.

Earlier, in 1971, Mary Helen and I had spent the winter quarter as usual at FSU, with a visit to Sanibel. In the spring, Peter Hammond from China Lake visited Chicago. That spring there was a planning meeting at Göttingen, in May, of the Institut de la Vie. During this visit there was also a symposium accompanying the dedication of the new Max Planck Institute for biophysical chemistry, with Eigen as its chairman and our host. Among people now established at the new institute were Albert Weller and Heinrich Kuhn. While in Göttingen I also saw Friedrich Hund, and we reviewed some of the changes which had occurred since my first visit in 1925.

During 1971 I had some correspondence with Joel Tellinghuisen who had been working in Berkeley on some of the iodine molecule bands whose assignment greatly interested me but was still problematical. At the time I first wrote him, he was doing research in Australia on a different subject but was returning to Berkeley in September. I wrote to ask whether he would then be willing to come to Chicago as a Research Associate with me to continue work on the iodine bands, provided I could obtain support for this project from the ONR (Office of Naval Research). I told him I was nearly but not quite certain I could obtain this support, and he agreed to come if I did.

By the time of his arrival in Berkeley in September the ONR had agreed. It was not time for me to return to Chicago after my work at the IBM San Jose Laboratory. My wife and Valerie returned to Chicago by plane while Joel Tellinghuisen and I undertook the drive back in my car. On the way back we had dinner and spent the night at a casino at Lake Tahoe. The management gave me a handful of coins to play with, and somewhat surprisingly, a small flood of coins came back to me. The next day we drove on, but at Kansas City I became rather sick of driving, so I took a plane to Chicago and let Joel drive the car home.

In Chicago the work on iodine continued, although with reduced space because the university had taken over most of my basement laboratory for an extension of the physics-mathematics library. This happened mainly because of a diminution in the output of experimental work from the spectroscopic laboratory. Joel Tellinghuisen however continued the iodine work. Before long he was joined by a New Zealand girl who came to be his bride. They got an apartment nearby where I had some pleasant visits.

Later after leaving here, Joel obtained a position at Vanderbilt University in Nashville, Tennessee. Here there had been a tradition of good spectroscopic work which he, as a professor there, has been carrying forward, with much good new work on the spectra of, among other things, rare gas halogen compounds. He also has made satisfying progress in solving the puzzles of the iodine molecule spectrum.

XXXIII

Some Family Matters

Back in Chicago, Mary Helen and I settled down in a new apartment on Dorchester Avenue. She arranged the placing of our furniture, pictures, and other belongings, and planned the decorating. The fourteen story building, at that time newly constructed, had two apartments on each floor, plus a few garden apartments on the ground floor. We were on the eleventh floor, on the east side, with views overlooking Lake Michigan.

But before Christmas Mary Helen became ill. After several weeks in hospitals, with hopes of rehabilitation, it finally proved no longer feasible for her to live at home. Lucia and I then found a good nursing home in a Chicago suburb where she could live comfortably in a friendly atmosphere. I drove out regularly to see her, usually with some of her Chicago friends or Valerie. Meantime, Valerie lived for a while in a boarding house while attending classes, but later with me in the Dorchester Avenue apartment. I now remained in Chicago except for short trips and gave up winter visits to Tallahassee.

At the nursing home Mary Helen made friends and took things philosophically. But in 1975 her conditions worsened although she remained cheerful. Lucia now came to be with me for a while. One day in March after we had had a good visit with her we received the sad news that Mary Helen had died. Since then I have been left with many memories of our life together.

One of the things that first attracted me to Mary Helen was the fact that she was a skilled artist. She had studied at the Art Institute of Chicago but did not graduate there; I don't know why. She did charming drawings and pictures, sometimes humorous. I tried to encourage her to work more at her art and to have an exhibit. But something inhibited her. I told her that she did not have to equal famous artists like Rembrandt or Michelangelo, but that she should be happy just being a good artist. I suggested sometimes that it would do no harm to do a few pictures which people might want to buy. I explained that I did *not* suggest this because I wanted her to supplement my income, but she gave me the impression that she thought that to try to sell her pictures would somehow be wrong. To support the family was a man's job, she seemed to believe.

But in contrast to this, we had good times together in going to auctions or sales to buy oriental rugs or paintings or beautifully crafted furniture at Colby's which was vastly marked down in price in the early depression years that occurrred after the great stock market crash about the time we were married.

We had some disagreements, notably when Mary Helen learned that I was paying off a debt which I owed to Mr. A.L. Loomis because he had kindly lent me several thousand dollars to satisfy an imperative demand which my Uncle Harry had made on me. Mr. Loomis strongly advised me against yielding to Uncle Harry's demand, but when I persisted, he agreed to lend me the money. Uncle Harry, my mother's brother, in the early days when I was a boy, had helped her out repeatedly in supplementing the rather limited income from my father's salary at MIT; further limited, I think, because he used some of it to help his mother and sister. Uncle Harry had had a very successful career as a manager with a mining company in Mexico, but after a while something must have gone wrong. He came to me (and my father) to demand money for reasons which he refused to explain. I sensed that there must be some kind of a scandal, but never learned more about it. At that time, he and his wife had become estranged as I witnessed once or twice; presumably she blamed him for getting into some kind of serious trouble such that (I surmised) he was being blackmailed. Anyway, after Mary Helen learned that I was paying off a debt which I had not told her about, and which seemed to her unjustified, she reacted by becoming rather extravagant where earlier she had been frugal. The strain of this situation lasted for many years, although it did no really serious damage.

During our years together in Chicago there were of course many occasions when we met with university colleagues, and sometimes there were visitors from outside Chicago, people whom Mary Helen or I had known, among them visitors from other universities. Sometimes we had people home for dinner. Mary Helen was an excellent cook and her dinners were notable, although sometimes late. She had a very large collection of cookbooks (perhaps about fifty). On special occasions she was an experienced and often witty conversationalist—so much so that I often did not try to compete. In my later years, however, I have made up for these earlier deficiencies and often enjoy a good conversation on the state of the world, or other matters, and occasionally can be classified as garrulous. Also, as I have described in recording my visit to San Diego with Lucia in 1983 to be initiated into the "Academy of Achievement," I gained a surprising reputation as a humorist.

In Mary Helen's life with me in Chicago, there were of course ups and downs in the impact of the external world on us. Mary Helen was normally in reasonable though not exuberant health. However, if a crisis occurred, she always rose at once to the occasion. She assumed full control of herself and the situation no matter how she had been feeling mentally or physically. I admired her for this superb exercise of will power.

In my previous references to Lucia, I told about visiting her and her husband William McGrew and their two children, Marina and Wesley, in 1962 in Athens, when he was there as a young Foreign Service Officer. My visits in Athens were on the way to and from India, alone on the way there and with Mary Helen on the return from Japan and India.

Since the time of my last Athens visit, Lucia had been divorced from Bill McGrew, although we all remained on friendly terms. A few years later Lucia married John Heard, who had come to America from Rhodesia—now Zimbabwe. At the very festive wedding, Mary Helen was there with Valerie and me. Among those present were Otis Mulliken, a cousin who came from the Lexington branch of the Mulliken family, and his wife, Jean. They both had had positions in the State Department and when I was in Washington I often went to see them.

Meantime, Lucia had become a high school teacher of English at the Dunbar School in Washington. She and John Heard bought a house in Arlington, Virginia, a twenty minute drive in her Volkswagen from the school in Washington. Since that time, when I visited Washington, for example, to attend the spring meeting of the National Academy of Sciences, I used to spend the night in

Arlington with Lucia and John. But more recently Lucia, John, and I have been living in a new and larger house in Arlington, Virginia which we bought in the fall of 1985. Marina and Wesley are now college graduates. Marina studied art and has, I think, much natural talent. Like my mother, she briefly taught art. Lucia too is accomplished as an artist. Marina is now married to Dirk Winkelmann, president of a corporation in Virginia. In 1983 they had a fine baby daughter, Rachele, my great-granddaughter. This was followed in 1985 by a second daughter, Kristina.

XXXIV

Selected Papers Volume.
Further Theoretical Work

A thick volume entitled *Selected Papers of Robert S. Mulliken* was published by the University of Chicago Press in 1975. It has 1127 pages. I call it "The Fat Book." It consists largely of a selection of my papers on molecular spectra and structure, published from 1930 on. Emphasis is on general or survey papers. A complete bibliography of papers published from 1919 through 1974 is included. Editors were D.A. Ramsay of Herzberg's Institute in Ottawa, and later also, Jürgen Hinze, who was for some time a colleague in the chemistry department at the University of Chicago.

The original impetus for the book came from Don Ramsay, who says "In my early career as an experimental spectroscopist, I became impressed by the frequency with which avenues of thought could be traced back to the theoretical papers of Mulliken and by the uncanny accuracy with which many new experimental results had been predicted or anticipated by Mulliken, sometimes twenty or thirty years earlier. I found that my colleagues referred with great regularity to the famous *Reviews of Modern Physics* articles (1931) by him, and indeed that Dr. Herzberg had a bound copy of these articles on his personal library shelf for ready reference. For these reasons it became clear that a reproduction of a selection of Mulliken's papers would provide a service to the reader as well as a fitting tribute to Professor Mulliken." During several years I travelled to Ottawa and alternately, Don Ramsay travelled to Chicago, to work on the plans for this book.

The initial selection of papers was mainly Ramsay's. I added some more historical and autobiographical writings. I also prepared introductory sections for each of the several chapters into which the book is divided. After a delay of about ten years, Dr. Hinze reviewed and continued the selection of papers and also dealt with the detailed biographical chapter. Into this he wove material from a 1974 interview with me by the well-known science historian Professor Thomas Kuhn.

To enliven the book, a few photographs were included as follows: Heisenberg, Dirac, and Hund on the occasion of their visit to the University of Chicago in 1928; three other scientists and I discussing nomenclature for diatomic molecules at Ann Arbor in 1928; the Paulings and Mary Helen; my graduate students and postdoctoral research associates in 1941; the participants in the first big post-war international conference on molecular structure at Paris in 1948; King Gustav of Sweden presenting the Nobel medal to me; our little dog, Miss Molecule, in Lindau, Germany.

After my computing experience in 1970 and 1971 with the IBM digital machine in San Jose, I decided to undertake some further computing. In 1954, Muller, Pickett, and I had made some semiempirical calculations bearing on the question of hyperconjugation in the benzenium ion $C_6H_7^+$. I felt that for a better understanding it would be desirable to make all-electron SCF calculations using a digital computer. In 1972 Hehre and Pople made such a calculation but with a somewhat limited basis set. I felt that a new calculation with a larger basis set including polarization functions would be worthwhile and might give an improved understanding of the role and importance of hyperconjugation. I then succeeded in obtaining support for such a computation from the Petroleum Research Fund, later supplemented by funds from the National Science Foundation and from a Joint Study agreement with the IBM Research Laboratory at San Jose. Meantime I persuaded Walter C. Ermler to come as a Research Associate to cooperate in the work here, while at San Jose, Doug McLean worked with us.

The results of our calculations were published in 1976. They included details of the geometrical structure of the benzenium ion, both sigma and pi (and pseudo-pi) electron populations, and charge distributions. We also obtained a value of the proton affinity of benzene in good agreement with an experimental value. Overlap populations and charges are shown in several diagrams in our paper. The overlap populations are measures of bonding between different parts of the ion. The MOs of benzenium are computed and compared with those of benzene. These results gave us, as we had hoped, a better understanding of the effects of hyperconjugation on the structure and energy of the benzenium ion.

Although the details are very interesting, they did not afford any radical new insights. The paper also includes an improved SCF computation on the benzene molecule.

In a 1978 paper Ermler and I reported the results of a similar study on the toluene molecule and its dipole moment and on the toluenium ion. The toluenium computations were made on one of four possible isomers which differ in the location of the methyl group. The results are interesting in throwing light on the role of the methyl group in adding a rather different type of hyperconjugation beyond that in the benzenium ion.

XXXV

Valerie's Death, 1983.
The Academy of Achievment

1983 was a year of both happy and very sad events. In Washington, Lucia was extremely busy at her teaching duties, as well as keeping her household going in Arlington, Virginia. Yet sometimes she found time for social events with John both at home and outside. The latter included some interesting affairs at the Smithsonian Institution in Washington.

Marina was busy with her husband Dirk Winkelmann and their active and altogether satisfactory baby daughter, Rachele, my great-granddaughter. They lived in a house just uphill through the back garden of John and Lucia's house. In Chicago, Valerie was living with me in the six-room eleventh floor apartment into which we had moved after returning from California in the late summer of 1971. The apartment had been freshly decorated under Mary Helen's supervision, and made home-like with our family pictures and furniture. Three times a week the very capable and sympathetic Mrs. Betty Easley came in as a part-time housekeeper.

Wesley was in his second year at the University of Chicago as a graduate student in economics. He at first lived in the International House very near us, but later shared an apartment a few blocks away. He came often to visit Valerie and me.

In 1983, Easter Sunday was Valerie's birthday, and Wesley and I were with her. Tragically, she became unwell. After a while her breathing stopped and she could not be resuscitated. Sadly, Valerie's friends and I, her father, and her other relatives were left with only fond memories of her. Some of the things I remember about Valerie are that she had many friends in Chicago and elsewhere, among both older and younger people. Everyone had a high opinion of her ability, including teachers in schools she had attended. She was very fond of small animals and had an extensive collection of Stief toy animals. She also collected dolls from foreign countries, some of which I had brought home from abroad. She was also much interested in coins and stamps. Of stamps from all over the world she had a collection of at least 50,000. At one time when one could not buy stamps from China in this country, I bought a considerable number of them for her in England.

But life must go on, and meanwhile, Wesley came to live with me. Also joining us was a graduate student in chemistry, Richard (Rick) Eng. Three times a week Mrs. E came to take care of the housekeeping. Our life now ran smoothly and harmoniously.

As I have written in previous pages, I had enjoyed being honored by awards and medals from a number of sections of the American Chemical Society. However, I had long wondered whether some time the Priestley medal, considered the Society's highest award, might come to me. Finally in March 1983, at the Society's meeting in Seattle, Washington I did receive this award.

In my acceptance speech, I began by saying that it was natural that the awards committee should have hesitated in giving this distinction to one who had for some years held a position as a professor of physics, whereas Priestley was a chemist. Thus, obviously, the award was intended to honor someone who had done good work on behalf of chemistry and chemists. I went on to say that eventually I had become a professor of physics *and* chemistry, which later on became mostly chemistry. Further, I had something special in common with Priestley in my work on the spectrum and the electronic structure of the oxygen molecule, for the discovery of which Priestley was famous.

In July of 1983 I received a very different sort of award from those received in the past. Edward Teller and Glenn Seaborg had written to me in January to ask if I would like to come to the Golden Plate dinner and award of membership in the American Academy of Achievement. I said yes, but completely forgot about the matter until I was reminded by a phone call in June from Wayne Reynolds, a son of the founder of this unique academy. I was invited to come with my spouse, but since that was impossible, they invited me to bring my daughter Lucia. The assembly that year took place at the Coronado Hotel in San Diego, California. We had a splendid three days there. In attendance were about three hundred high school honor students and about fifty new Golden Plate awardees, "captains of achievement" in just about every field of endeavor. Included were artists and singers, cartoonists and humorists, notable baseball coaches and owners of major baseball teams, presidents and chief executives of well-known corporations, the head of the well-known Perdue high-grade chicken industry, some of the best known bankers and lawyers, and politicians; in short, men and some women who had attained major success in practically every field of human activity. Each of the new awardees was requested to give the very brief account of things he had done. When my turn arrived, I arose to spend ten minutes (which was somewhat more than the allotted time) in a mixed assortment of reminiscences, beginning with high school. Somehow my small oration turned out to be unintentionally humorous, partly because of slips of the tongue such as saying "revolution" instead of "evolution" when remarking that "I had always accepted the theory of evolution as a fact rather than a theory." After I had stepped off the platform amid gratifying applause, I was told that I had received a standing ovation, which strangely I had not at all noticed, perhaps because I was too busy feeling that my fragmentary little talk was on the whole rather satisfactory. Later on, thinking over my performance, I felt that perhaps I had pretty well got rid of a long-standing inferiority complex, and that I could now hold up my head among the crowd of human beings who, each in his own way, could be considered as achievers. I also thought that now I can feel at home with the crowd of capable people. And I thought: I wish I had realized earlier that I could feel that easy self-confidence, and that I might have accomplished many and varied things that could have made me (and others) happier.

Chronology

Date	Event
1896	Born June 30, 1896, Newburyport, Massachusetts
1917	B.S., Massachusetts Institute of Technology, Cambridge, Massachusetts
1917–18	Junior Chemical Engineer, Bureau of Mines, U.S. Department of Interior, Washington, D.C. Research on war gases at American University
1918	Private First Class Chemical Warfare Service, U.S. Army, Washington, D.C.
1919	Assistant in Rubber Research, New Jersey Zinc Co., Palmerton, Pennsylvania
1920–22	Research on Isotope Separation, University of Chicago, Chicago, Illinois
1921	Ph.D., University of Chicago, Chicago, Illinois
1921–23	National Research Fellow, University of Chicago, Chicago, Illinois
1923–25	National Research Fellow, Harvard University, Cambridge, Massachusetts
1926–28	Assistant Professor of Physics, New York University, Washington Square, New York City
1928–31	Associate Professor Physics of University of Chicago, Chicago, Illinois

1929	Marriage to Mary Helen Von Noé, December 24, 1929
1930, 1932–33	Guggenheim Fellow, Germany and Europe
1931–61	Professor of Physics, University of Chicago, Chicago, Illinois
1934	Birth of daughter Lucia Maria, July 15
1939	Sc.D., Columbia University, New York, New York
1942–45	Director, Information Division, Plutonium Project, University of Chicago, Chicago, Illinois
1948	Birth of daughter Valerie Noé, April 3
1948	Bronze Medal Award, University of Liège, Liège, Belgium
1951–52	Fellow, American Physical Society
1952–54	Fulbright Scholar, Oxford University, Oxford, England
1952–53	Visiting Fellow, St. John's College, Oxford University, Oxford England
1955	Science Attaché, U.S. Embassy, London, England
1956–61	Ernest Dewitt Distinguished Service Professor of Physics, University of Chicago, Chicago, Illinois
1960	Ph.D. (Hon.), University of Stockholm, Stockholm, Sweden
1960	Baker Lecturer, Cornell University, Ithaca, New York
1960	Gilbert Newton Lewis Gold Medal, California Section of the American Chemical Society
1960	Theodore William Richards Gold Medal, Northeastern Section of the American Chemical Society
1961–85	Distinguished Service Professor of Physics and Chemistry, University of Chicago, Chicago, Illinois
1962	Lecturer, Indian Atomic Energy Establishment, Bombay, India; Lecturer, Indian Institute of Technology, Kanpur, India
1963	Peter Debye Award, California Section of the American Chemical Society
1964	John Gamble Kirkwood Award, New Haven Section of the American Chemical Society
1964–71	Distinguished Research Professor of Chemical Physics, Florida State University, Tallahasee, Florida

1965	Silliman Lecture, Yale University, New Haven, Connecticut
1965	Jan Van Geuns Visiting Professor, University of Amsterdam, The Netherlands
1965	J. Willard Gibbs Medal, Chicago Section of the American Chemical Society
1965	International Symposium on Atomic and Molecular Quantum Theory in Honor of Robert S. Mulliken, Sanibel Island, Florida
1965	Gold Medal and 15th Bicentennial Lecturer, City College of New York, New York, New York
1966	Nobel Prize for Chemistry, Stockholm, Sweden
1966	Chicagoan of the Year Award, Chicago Press Club, Chicago, Illinois
1967	Sc.D. (Hon.), Marquette University, Milwaukee, Wisconsin
1967	Sc.D. (Hon.), Cambridge University, Cambridge, England
1975	Sc.D. (Hon.), Gustavus Adolphus College, St. Peter, Minnesota
1975	Death of wife Mary Helen, March 3
1976	Session in Honor of Robert S. Mulliken, Ohio State Spectroscopy Symposium, Columbus, Ohio
1977	Tenth Midwest Theoretical Chemistry Conference in Honor of Robert S. Mulliken, Argonne National Laboratory, Argonne, Illinois
1978	Symposium in Honor of Robert S. Mulliken's Fiftieth Anniversary at the University of Chicago, Chicago, Illinois
1983	Death of daughter Valerie, April 3
1983	Golden Plate Award, American Academy of Achievement
1983	Priestley Medal
1984	Order of the Rising Sun, Second Class, Japan
1986	Died October 31, 1986 at Alexandria, Virginia
1989	Posthumous publication of his scientific autobiography *Life of a Scientist*

Memberships

American Academy of Arts and Sciences
American Chemical Society
American Philosophical Society
National Academy of Sciences

Memberships (*continued*)

Cosmos Club (Washington, D.C.)
Quadrangle Club (Chicago, Illinois)
Chemical Society of Britain (Hon.)
Indian National Academy of Science (Hon.)
Royal Society of London (Foreign Member)
Société de Chimique Physique (Hon.)
Royal Irish Academy (Hon.)
Chemical Society of Japan (Hon.)
Société Royal des Sciences de Liège
(Corresponding Member)

Bibliography

(Except where coauthors are listed, all articles are by R.S. Mulliken alone. This bibliography was compiled from the bibliography published in the *Selected Papers of Robert S. Mulliken* (#242); and from lists supplied by the University of Chicago Chemistry Department and by Lucia Mulliken Heard and John Heard, to whom the editor acknowledges his indebtedness and gratitude.)

1919

1. Tolman, R.C., Gerke, R.H., Brooks, A.P., Herman, A.G., Mulliken, R.S. and Smyth, H. DeW. Relation between intensity of Tyndall beam and size of particles. J. Am. Chem. Soc. *41*, 575–87 (1919).

1920

2. Norris, J.F. and Mulliken, R.S. Reaction between alcohols and aqueous solutions of hydrochloric and hydrobromic acids. II. J. Am. Chem. Soc. *42*, 2093–8 (1920).

1921

3. Harkins, W.D. and Mulliken, R.S. The separation of mercury into isotopes. Nature *108*, 146 (1921).

1922

4. Mulliken, R.S. and Harkins, W.D. The separation of isotopes. Theory of resolution of isotopic mixtures by diffusion and similar processes. Experimental separation of mercury by evaporation in a vacuum. J. Am. Chem. Soc. *44*, 37–65 (1922).
5. The separation of isotopes by thermal and pressure diffusion. J. Am. Chem. Soc. *44*, 1033–51 (1922).

6. Separation of liquid mixtures by centrifuging. J. Am. Chem. Soc. *44*, 1729–30 (1922).
7. The separation of isotopes by distillation and analogous processes. J. Am. Chem. Soc. *44*, 2387–90 (1922).

1923

8. The separation of isotopes. Application of systematic fractionation to mercury in a high-speed evaporation-diffusion apparatus. J. Am. Chem. Soc. *45*, 1592–1604 (1923).
9. The vibrational isotope effect in the band spectrum of boron nitride. Science *58*, 164–66 (1923).

1924

10. Isotope effects in the band spectra of boron monoxide and silicon nitride. Nature *113*, 423–24 (1924).
11. The isotope effect as a means of identifying the emitters of band spectra: Application to the bands of the metal hydrides. Nature *113*, 489–90 (1924).
12. The isotope effect in line and band spectra. Nature *113*, 820 (1924).
13. The band spectrum of boron monoxide. Nature *114*, 349–50 (1924).
14. Electronic states of the CN molecule. Nature *114*, 858–59 (1924).

1925

15. The isotope effect in band spectra. Part I. Phys. Rev. *25*, 119–38 (1925).
16. The isotope effect in band spectra. II. The spectrum of boron monoxide. Phys. Rev. *25*, 259–94 (1925).
17. A band of unusual structure probably due to a highly unstable calcium hydride molecule. Phys. Rev. *25*, 509–22 (1925).
18. The isotope effect in band spectra. III. The spectrum of copper iodide as excited by active nitrogen. Phys. Rev. *26*, 1–32 (1925).
19. Mulliken, R.S. and Turner, L.A. Ultra-violet arc lines of iodine. Phys. Rev. *25*, 886 (1925).
20. The excited states of the CuI molecule, and the band spectra of certain salts. Phys. Rev. *25*, 887 (1925).
21. The isotope effect in band spectra. IV. The spectrum of silicon nitride. Phys. Rev. *26*, 319–38 (1925).
22. A class of one-valence-electron emitters of band spectra. Phys. Rev. *26*, 561–72 (1925).

1926

23. Systematic relations between electronic structure and band-spectrum structure in diatomic molecules. I. Proc. Natl. Acad. Sci. *12*, 144–51 (1926).

24. Systematic relations between electronic structure and band-spectrum structure in diatomic molecules. II. The ZnH, CdH and HgH molecules and their spectra. Proc. Natl. Acad. Sci. *12*, 151–58 (1926).
25. The electronic states of the helium molecule. Proc. Natl. Acad. Sci. *12*, 158–62 (1926).
26. Systematic relations between electronic structure and band-spectrum structure in diatomic molecules. III. Molecule formation and molecular structure. Proc. Natl. Acad. Sci. *12*, 338–43 (1926).
27. Electronic states and band-spectrum structure in diatomic molecules. I. Statement of the postulates. Interpretation of CuH, CH and CO band-types. Phys. Rev. *28*, 481–506 (1926).
28. Electronic states and band-spectrum structure in diatomic molecules. II. Spectra involving terms essentially of the form $B(j^2-\sigma^2)$. Phys. Rev. *28*, 1202–22 (1926).

1927

29. Electronic states and band-spectrum structure in diatomic molecules. III. Intensity relations. Phys. Rev. *29*, 391–412 (1927).
30. Electronic states and band-spectrum structure in diatomic molecules. IV. Hund's theory; second positive nitrogen and swan bands; alternating intensities. Phys. Rev. *29*, 637–49 (1927).
31. Jenkins, F.A., Barton, H.A. and Mulliken, R.S. The β bands of nitric oxide. Nature *119*, 118–19 (1927).
32. Intensity relations and electronic states in spectra of diatomic molecules. Phys. Rev. *29*, 211 (1927).
33. Electronic states and band-spectrum structure in diatomic molecules. V. Bands of the violet CN (^{2}S-^{2}S) type. Phys. Rev. *30*, 138–49 (1927).
34. Jenkins, F.A., Barton, H.A. and Mulliken, R.S. The β bands of nitric oxide. I. Measurements and quantum analysis. Phys. Rev. *30*, 150–174 (1927).
35. Barton, H.A., Jenkins, F.A. and Mulliken, R.S. The β bands of nitric oxide. II. Intensity relations and their interpretation. Phys. Rev. *30*, 175–88 (1927).
36. Kemble, E.C., Mulliken, R.S. and Crawford, F.H. The Zeeman effect in the Angstrom CO bands. Phys. Rev. *30*, 438–57 (1927).
37. Electronic states and band-spectrum structure in diatomic molecules. VI. Theory of intensity relations for Case b doublet states. Interpretation of CH bands $\lambda\lambda$ 3900, 4300. Phys. Rev. *30*, 785–811 (1927).

1928

38. Interpretation of the atmospheric oxygen bands; electronic levels of the oxygen molecule. Nature *122*, 505 (1928).
39. The heat of dissociation of nitrogen. Nature *122*, 842–43 (1928).
40. Structure of the OH bands. Phys. Rev. *31*, 310 (1928).

41. The assignment of quantum numbers for electrons in molecules. I. Phys. Rev. 32, 186–222 (1928).
42. Van Vleck, J.H. and Mulliken, R.S. On the widths of σ-type doublets in molecular spectra. Phys. Rev. 32, 327 (1928).
43. Electronic states and band-spectrum structure in diatomic molecules. VII. $^2P \rightarrow {}^2S$ and $^2S \rightarrow {}^2P$ transitions. Phys. Rev. 32, 388–416 (1928).
44. The assignment of quantum numbers for electrons in molecules. II. The correlation of molecular and atomic electron states. Phys. Rev. 32, 761–72 (1928).
45. Interpretation of the atmospheric absorption bands of oxygen. Phys. Rev. 32, 880–87 (1928).

1929

46. Monk, G.S. and Mulliken, R.S. Fine structure in the helium band lines. Nature 124, 91 (1929).
47. Band spectra and chemistry. Chem. Rev. 6, 503–45 (1929).
48. Band spectra and atomic nuclei. Trans. Faraday Soc. 25, 634–45 (1929).
49. Formation of MH molecules; effects of H atom on M atom. Phys. Rev. 33, 285–86 (1929).
50. Electronic states and band-spectrum structure in diatomic molecules. VIII. Some empirical relations in σ-type doubling. Phys. Rev. 33, 507–11 (1929).
51. The assignment of quantum numbers for electrons in molecules. III. Diatomic hydrides. Phys. Rev. 33, 730–47 (1929).
52. Mulliken, R.S. and Monk, G.S. Fine structure and Zeeman effects in helium band lines. Phys. Rev. 34, 1530–40 (1929).

1930

53. The interpretation of band spectra. I, IIa, IIb. Rev. Mod. Phys. 2, 60–115; Additions and corrections, ibid 506–8 (1930).
54. Electronic states and chemical linkage in diatomic molecules. Z. Elektrochem. 36, 603–05 (1930).
55. Report on notation for spectra of diatomic molecules. Phys. Rev. 36, 611–29 (1930).
56. Interpretation of the visible halogen bands. Phys. Rev. 36, 364 (1930).
57. Electronic states in the visible halogen bands. Phys. Rev. 36, 699–705 (1930).
58. Correlation of atomic J values and molecular quantum numbers, with applications to halogen, alkaline earth hydride, and alkali molecules. Phys. Rev. 36, 1440–50 (1930).

1931

59. Interpretation of band spectra. IIc. Empirical band types. Rev. Mod. Phys. 3, 89–155 (1931).

60. Bonding power of electrons and theory of valence. Chem. Rev. 9, 347–88 (1931).
61. Note on the interpretation of certain $^2\Delta$, $^2\Pi$ bands of SiH. Phys. Rev. 37, 733–35 (1931).
62. Note on the visible halogen bands, with special reference to ICl. Phys. Rev. 37, 1412–15 (1931).
63. Electronic energy levels of neutral and ionized oxygen. Phys. Rev. 37, 1711–12 (1931).
64. Mulliken, R.S. and Christy, A. Λ-Type doubling and electron configurations in diatomic molecules. Phys. Rev. 38, 87–119 (1931).
65. Note on the interpretation of the beryllium fluoride bands. Phys. Rev. 38, 836–37 (1931).
66. Jenkins, F.A. Roots, Y.K. and Mulliken, R.S. The red CN band system. Phys. Rev. 38, 1075–77 (1931).

1932

67. Interpretation of band spectra. III. Electron quantum numbers and states of molecules and their atoms. Rev. Mod. Phys. 4, 1–86 (1932).
68. Jenkins, F.A., Roots, Y.K. and Mulliken, R.S. The red CN band system. Phys. Rev. 39, 16–41 (1932).
69. Electronic structures of polyatomic molecules and valence. I. Phys. Rev. 40, 55–62 (1932).
70. Electronic structures of polyatomic molecules and valence. II. General considerations. Phys. Rev. 41, 49–71 (1932).
71. Electronic structures of polyatomic molecules and valence. III. Quantum theory of the double bond. Phys. Rev. 41, 751–58 (1932).
72. Interpretation of the rotational structure of the CO_2 emission bands. Phys. Rev. 42, 364–72 (1932).
73. Quantum theory of the double bond. J. Am. Chem. Soc. 54, 4111–12 (1932).

1933

74. Electronic structures of polyatomic molecules and valence. IV. Electronic states, quantum theory of the double bond. Phys. Rev. 43, 279–302 (1933).
75. Electronic structures of polyatomic molecules and valence. Magnetism of B_2H_6. Phys Rev. 43, 765 (1933).
76. Mulliken, R.S., and Stevens, D.S. New O_2^+ bands. Dissociation energy of O_2^+ and ionization potential of O_2. Phys. Rev. 44, 720–23 (1933).
77. Electronic structures of polyatomic molecules and valence. V. Molecules RX_n. J. Chem Phys. 1, 492–503 (1933).

1934

78. Symbols and names for the hydrogen isotopes. Science 79, 228–29 (1934).
79. Hopfield's Rydberg series and the ionization potential and heat of dissociation of N_2. Phys. Rev. 46, 144–46 (1934).
80. The halogen molecules and their spectra. J-J-like coupling. Molecular ionization potentials. Phys. Rev. 46, 549–71 (1934).
81. Electric moments and infrared spectra and the structure of CO. J. Chem. Phys. 2, 400–402 (1934).
82. Note on electric moments and infrared spectra. A correction. J. Chem. Phys. 2, 712–13 (1934).
83. New electroaffinity scale; together with data on valence states and on valence ionization potentials and electron affinities. J. Chem. Phys. 2, 782–93 (1934).

1935

84. Structure, ionization and ultraviolet spectra of methyl iodide and other molecules. Phys. Rev. 47, 413–15 (1935).
85. Electronic structures of polyatomic molecules and valence. VI. On the method of molecular orbitals. J. Chem. Phys. 3, 375–78 (1935).
86. Electronic structures of polyatomic molecules. VII. Ammonia and water type molecules and their derivatives. J. Chem. Phys. 3, 506–14 (1935).
87. Electronic structures of polyatomic molecules. VIII. Ionization potentials. J. Chem. Phys. 3, 514–17 (1935).
88. Electronic structures of polyatomic molecules. IX. Methane, ethane, ethylene, acetylene. J. Chem. Phys. 3, 517–28 (1935).
89. Electronic structures of molecules. X. Aldehydes, ketones and related molecules. J. Chem. Phys. 3, 564–73 (1935).
90. Electronic structures of molecules. XI. Electroaffinity, molecular orbitals and dipole moments. J. Chem. Phys. 3, 573–85 (1935).
91. Electronic structures of molecules. XII. Electroaffinity and molecular orbitals, polyatomic applications. J. Chem. Phys. 3, 586–91 (1935).
92. Electronic structures of molecules. XIII. Diborane and related molecules. J. Chem. Phys. 3, 635–45 (1935).
93. Electronic structures of molecules. XIV. Linear triatomic molecules, especially carbon dioxide. J. Chem. Phys. 3, 720–39 (1935).

1936

94. Absorption processes in the halogen spectra. J. Chem. Phys. 4, 620–21 (1936).
95. The low electronic states of simple heteropolar diatomic molecules. I. General survey. Phys. Rev. 50, 1017–27 (1936).

96. The low electronic states of simple heteropolar diatomic molecules. II. Alkali metal hydrides. Phys. Rev. *50*, 1028–40 (1936).

1937

97. Low electronic states of simple heteropolar diatomic molecules. III. Hydrogen and univalent metal halides. Phys. Rev. *51*, 310–32 (1937).
98. Science and the scientific attitude. Science *86*, 65–68 (1937).
99. Solved and unsolved problems in the spectra of diatomic molecules. J. Phys. Chem. *41*, 5–45, and discussion on pp. 299, 305, 315, 318 (1937).
100. Some proposals concerning nomenclature and symbols for polyatomic molecules. J. Phys. Chem. *41*, 159–73 (1937).

1938

101. Absolute intensities in halide spectra. Phys. Rev. *55*, 239 (1938).

1939

102. Electronic states of diatomic carbon, and the carbon-carbon bond. Phys. Rev. *56*, 778–81 (1939).
103. Recent progress in the interpretation of molecular spectra and in the study of molecular spectra in celestial objects. Intensities of electronic transitions in molecular spectra. Astrophys. J. *89*, 283–88 (1939).
104. Aston, F.W., Bohr, N., Hahn, D., Harkins, W.D., Mulliken, R.S. and Oliphant, M.L. International table of stable isotopes for 1939. Union Intern. Chim. *1939*, 3–14.
105. Intensities of electronic transitions in molecular spectra. I. Introduction. J. Chem. Phys. *7*, 14–20 (1939).
106. Intensities of electronic transitions in molecular spectra. II. Charge-transfer spectra. J. Chem. Phys. *7*, 20–34 (1939).
107. Intensities of electronic transitions in molecular spectra. III. Organic molecules with double bonds. Conjugated dienes. J. Chem. Phys. *7*, 121–35 (1939).
108. Intensities of electronic transitions in molecular spectra. IV. Cyclic dienes and hyperconjugation. J. Chem. Phys. *7*, 339–52 (1939).
109. Intensities of electronic transitions in molecular spectra. V. Benzene. J. Chem. Phys. *7*, 353–56 (1939).
110. Intensities of electronic transitions in molecular spectra. VI. Molecular refractivities of organic compounds. J. Chem. Phys. *7*, 356–63 (1939).
111. Intensities of electronic transitions in molecular spectra. VII. Conjugated polyenes and carotenoids. J. Chem. Phys. *7*, 364–73 (1939).

112. Intensities of electronic transitions in molecular spectra. VIIIa. Odd-numbered conjugated polyene chain molecules and organic dyes (with notes on optical anisotropy and Raman intensities). J. Chem. Phys. 7, 570–72 (1939).

1940

113. Intensities of electronic transitions in molecular spectra. IX. Calculations on the long wave-length halogen spectra. J. Chem. Phys. 8, 234–43 (1940).
114. Intensities in molecular electronic spectra. X. Calculations on mixed-halogen, hydrogen halide, alkyl halide, and hydroxyl spectra. J. Chem. Phys. 8, 382–95 (1940).
115. Halogen molecule spectra. II. Interval relations and relative intensities in the long wave-length spectra. Phys. Rev. 57, 500–515 (1940).
116. McMurry, H.L. and Mulliken, R.S. Mechanism of the long wavelength absorption by the carbonyl group. Proc. Natl. Acad. Sci. 26, 312–17 (1940).

1941

117. Correlation of energy levels of linear and bent triatomic molecules, and the ultraviolet CS_2 absorption spectrum. Phys. Rev. 60, 506–13 (1941).
118. Species classifications and rotational energy level patterns of non-linear triatomic molecules. Phys. Rev. 59, 873–89 (1941).
119. Mulliken, R.S., Rieke, C.A. and Brown, W.G. Hyperconjugation. J. Am. Chem. Soc. 63, 41–56 (1941).
120. Mulliken, R.S. and Rieke, C.A. Improved computations on conjugation and hyperconjugation. J. Am. Chem. Soc. 63, 1770–71 (1941).
121. Mulliken, R.S. and Rieke, C.A. Molecular electronic spectra, dispersion and polarization. Theoretical interpretation and computation of oscillator strengths and intensities. Phys. Soc. Rept. Prog. Phys. 8, 231–73 (1941).

1942

122. Nature of electronic levels in ultraviolet spectra of hydrogen and alkyl halides. Phys. Rev. 61, 277–83 (1942).
123. Mulliken, R.S. and Teller, E. Interpretation of the methyl iodide absorption bands near λ2000. Phys. Rev. 61, 283–96 (1942).
124. Electronic structures and spectra of triatomic oxide molecules. Rev. Mod. Phys. 14, 204–15 (1942).
125. Mulliken, R.S. and Rieke, C.A. Rev. Mod. Phys. 14, 259 (1942). Abstract only.
126. Structure and ultraviolet spectra of ethylene, butadiene, and their alkyl derivatives. Rev. Mod Phys. 14, 265–74 (1942).

Bibliography

1945

127. Remarks on a possible division of spectroscopy in the American Physical Society. Rev. Sci. Instr. *16*, 42–43 *(1945)*.

1947

128. Quantum-mechanical methods and the electronic spectra and structure of molecules. Chem. Rev. *41*, 201–06 (1947).
129. The structure of diborane and related molecules. Chem. Rev. *41*, 207–17 (1947).
130. Mulliken, R.S. and Roothaan, C.C.J. The twisting frequency and the barrier height for free rotation in ethylene. Chem. Rev. *41*, 219–31 (1947).

1948

131. Roothaan, C.C.J. and Mulliken, R.S. Molecular orbital treatment of the ultraviolet spectra of benzene and borazole. J. Chem. Phys. *16*, 118–22 (1948).
132. Molecular orbital method and molecular ionization potentials. Phys. Rev. *74*, 736–38 (1948).

1949

133. Mulliken, R.S., Rieke, C.A., Orloff, D. and Orloff, H. Overlap integrals and chemical binding. J. Chem. Phys. *17*, 510 (1949).
134. Mulliken, R.S., Rieke, C.A., Orloff, D. and Orloff, H. Formulas and numerical tables for overlap integrals. J. Chem. Phys. *17*, 1248–67 (1949).
135. Quelques aspects de la théorie des orbitales moléculaires. Parts I-IV. J. Chim. Phys. *46*, 497–542 (1949).
136. Quelques aspects de la théorie des orbitales moléculaires. Part V. J. Chim. Phys. *46*, 675–713 (1949).

1950

137. Parr, R.G. and Mulliken, R.S. LCAO self-consistent field calculation of the π-electron energy levels of cis- and trans-1,3-butadiene. J. Chem. Phys. *18*, 1338–46 (1950).
138. Structures of complexes formed by halogen molecules with aromatic and with oxygenated solvents. J. Am. Chem. Soc. *72*, 600–608 (1950).
139. Overlap integrals and chemical binding. J. Am. Chem. Soc. *72*, 4493–4503 (1950).

227

1951

140. Lewis acids and bases and molecular complexes. J. Chem. Phys. *19*, 514–15 (1951).
141. Overlap and bonding power of 2s, 2p-hybrid orbitals. J. Chem. Phys. *19*, 900–912 (1951).
142. Orthonormal sets of LCAO molecular orbitals for second row homopolar diatomic molecules. J. Chem. Phys. *19*, 912–22 (1951).
143. Mulliken, R.S. and Parr, R.G. LCAO molecular orbital computation of resonance energies of benzene and butadiene with general analysis of theoretical versus thermochemical resonance energies. J. Chem. Phys. *19*, 1271–78 (1951).

1952

144. A comparative survey of approximate ground state wave functions of helium atom and hydrogen molecule. Proc. Natl. Acad. Sci. *38*, 160–66 (1952).
145. Molecular compounds and their spectra. II. J. Am. Chem. Soc. *74*, 811–24 (1952).
146. Overlap integrals and molecular energies. Record Chem. Progress *13*, 67–77 (1952).
147. Magic formula, structure of bond energies, and isovalent hybridization. J. Phys. Chem. *56*, 295–311 (1952).
148. Molecular compounds and their spectra. III. The interaction of electron donors and acceptors. J. Phys. Chem. *56*, 801–22 (1952).

1953

149. Pickett, L.W., Muller, N. and Mulliken, R.S. Hyperconjugation in $C_6H_7^+$ and other hydrocarbon ions. J. Chem. Phys. *21*, 1400–1401 (1953).
150. Glusker, D.L., Thompson, H.W. and Mulliken, R.S. Infrared spectra of solutions of iodine. J. Chem. Phys. *21*, 1407–8 (1953).

1954

151. On approximate computation of molecular energies. Symposium on molecular physics; Nikko, Japan, 1953, (1954), pp. 17–22.
152. The interaction of electron donor and acceptor molecules. Symposium on Molecular Physics; Nikko, Japan, 1953 (1954), pp. 45–51.
153. Intermolecular charge-transfer forces. Proc. Intern. Conf. Theoret. Phys. Kyoto and Tokyo, 1953 (1954), pp. 622–27; discussion, pp. 627–28.
154. Forces intermoléculaires de transfert de charge. J. Chem. Phys. *51*, 341–44 (1954).
155. Intermolecular charge-transfer forces. Rendiconti del Seminario Matematico e Fisico di Milano 1952–53 *24*, 3–9 (1954).

156. Reid, C. and Mulliken, R.S. Molecular compounds and their spectra. IV. The pyridine-iodine system. J. Am. Chem. Soc. 76, 3869–74 (1954).

157. Muller, N., Pickett, L.W. and Mulliken, R.S. Hyperconjugation and spectrum of the benzenium ion, prototype of aromatic carbonium ions. J. Am. Chem. Soc. 76, 4770–98 (1954).

1955

158. Structures of the halogen molecules and the strength of single bonds. J. Am. Chem. Soc. 77, 884–87 (1955).

159. Bond angles in water-type and ammonia-type molecules and their derivatives. J. Am. Chem. Soc. 77, 887–91 (1955).

160. Molecular compounds and their spectra. V. Orientation in molecular complexes. J. Chem. Phys. 23, 397–98 (1955).

161. Electronic population analysis on LCAO-MO molecular wave functions. I. J. Chem. Phys. 23, 1833–40 (1955).

162. Electronic population analysis on LCAO-MO molecular wave functions. II. Overlap populations, bond orders, and covalent bond energies. J. Chem. Phys. 23, 1841–46 (1955).

163. Wilkinson, P.G. and Mulliken, R.S. Far ultraviolet absorption spectra of ethylene and ethylene-d_4. J. Chem. Phys. 23, 1895–1907 (1955).

164. Report on notation for the spectra of polyatomic molecules. J. Chem. Phys. 23, 1997–2011 (1955).

165. Electronic population analysis on LCAO-MO molecular wave functions. III. Effects of hybridization on overlap and gross AO populations. J. Chem. Phys. 23, 2338–42 (1955).

166. Electronic population analysis on LCAO-MO molecular wave functions. IV. Bonding and antibonding in LCAO and valence-bond theories. J. Chem. Phys. 23, 2343–46 (1955).

1956

167. Molecular complexes and their spectra. VI. Some problems and new developments. Rec. Trav. Chim. Pays-Bas 75, 845–52 (1956).

1957

168. The energy levels of the nitrogen molecule. The Threshold of Space, Ed. M. Zelikoff. Pergamon Press, New York and London, 1957. pp. 169–79.

169. Orgel, L.E. and Mulliken, R.S. Molecular complexes and their spectra. VII. The spectrophotometric study of molecular complexes in solution; contact charge-transfer spectra. J. Am. Chem. Soc. 79, 4839–46 (1957).

170. Lofthus, A. and Mulliken, R.S. Emission band spectra of nitrogen. Kaplan's first and second systems. J. Chem. Phys. 26, 1010–17 (1957).

171. Wilkinson, P.G. and Mulliken, R.S. Dissociation processes in oxygen above 1750 Å. Astrophys. J. *125*, 594–600 (1957).
172. Wilkinson, P.G. and Mulliken, R.S. An electric quadrupole electronic band system in molecular nitrogen. Astrophys. J. *126*, 10–13 (1957).

1958

173. The lower excited states of some simple molecules. Can. J. Chem. *36*, 10–23 (1958).
174. Phillipson, P.E. and Mulliken, R.S. Improved molecular orbitals (Computations on H_2). J. Chem. Phys. *28*, 1248–49 (1958).
175. Muller, N. and Mulliken, R.S. Strong or isovalent hyperconjugation in some alkyl radicals and their positive ions. J. Am. Chem. Soc. *80*, 3489–97 (1958).

1959

176. Conjugation and hyperconjugation: A survey with emphasis on isovalent hyperconjugation. Tetrahedron *5*, 253–74 (1959).
177. Bond lengths and bond energies in conjugation and hyperconjugation. Tetrahedron *6*, 68–87 (1959).
178. Research at the Laboratory of Molecular Structure and Spectra, University of Chicago. Zhurnal Optika i Spektroskopia *6*, 437 (1959).
179. Mulliken, R.S. and Roothaan, C.C.J. Broken bottlenecks and the future of molecular quantum mechanics. Proc. Natl. Acad. Sci. *45*, 394–98 (1959).
180. Plyler, E.K. and Mulliken, R.S. Molecular complexes and their spectra. IX. Infrared absorption by iodine in its pyridine complexes and in benzene. J. Am. Chem. Soc. *81*, 823–26 (1959).
181. Wilkinson, P.G. and Mulliken, R.S. Forbidden band systems in nitrogen. II. The $a^1\Sigma_\mu^- \leftarrow X^1\Sigma_g^+$ system in absorption. J. Chem. Phys. *31*, 674–79 (1959).
182. The electron affinity of O_2. Phys. Rev. *115*, 1225–26 (1959).

1960

183. Self-consistent field atomic and molecular orbitals and their approximations as linear combinations of Slater-type orbitals. Rev. Mod. Phys. *32*, 232–38 (1960).
184. Fraga, S. and Mulliken, R.S. The role of coulomb energy in the valence-bond theory. Rev. Mod. Phys. *32*, 254–65 (1960).
185. Hausser, K.H. and Mulliken, R.S. The ultraviolet absorption spectrum of chloranil. J. Phys. Chem. *64*, 367–68 (1960).
186. McLean, A.D., Ransil, B.J. and Mulliken, R.S. Charge distribution, hybridization, and bonding in acetylene and carbon dioxide. J. Chem. Phys. *32*, 1873 (1960).

187. Some neglected subcases of predissociation in diatomic molecules. J. Chem. Phys. 33, 247–52 (1960).

188. Phillipson, P. and Mulliken, R.S. Note on Hurley's "Improved molecular orbitals and the valence-bond theory." J. Chem. Phys. 33, 615–16 (1960).

189. Lowest triplet states of ethylene. J. Chem. Phys. 33, 1596–97 (1960).

190. The interaction of differently excited like atoms at large distances. Phys. Rev. 120, 1674–84 (1960).

191. Tsubomura, H. and Mulliken, R.S. Molecular complexes and their spectra. XII. Ultraviolet absorption spectra caused by the interaction of oxygen with organic molecules. J. Am. Chem. Soc. 82, 5966–74 (1960).

192. Molecular structure and spectra. McGraw-Hill Encyclopedia of Science and Technology 8, 547–56. McGraw-Hill, New York, 1960.

193. The interaction of electron donors and acceptors. Nucleus, June (1960).

1961

194. Verma, R.D. and Mulliken, R.S. Rotational structure of the band spectrum of CCl molecule. J. Mol. Spect. 6, 419–37 (1961).

195. Verma, R.D. and Mulliken, R.S. A $^1\Sigma^-$ -$^3\Pi_r$ spectrum of SiO. Can. J. Phys. 39, 908–16 (1961).

1962

196. Molecular orbitals. Encyclopaedic Dictionary of Physics 4. Pergamon Press, New York and London, 1961–62.

197. Discussion in "An Epistologue on Carbon Bonds." Tetrahedron 17, 247–54 (1962).

198. Criteria for the construction of good self-consistent-field molecular orbital wave functions, and the significance of LCAO-MO population analysis. J. Chem. Phys. 36, 3428–39 (1962).

199. Low-energy $^5\Sigma_g^+$ states of the nitrogen molecule. J. Chem. Phys. 37, 809–13 (1962).

200. Mulliken, R.S. and Person, W.B. Donor-acceptor complexes. Ann. Rev. Phys. Chem. 13, 107–26 (1962).

201. π-Delocalization in butadiene and cyanogen. J. Phys. Chem. 66, 2306–09 (1962).

1963

202. The interaction of electron donors and acceptors. J. Chim. Phys. 60, 20–38 (1963).

1964

203. The Rydberg states of molecules. Parts I-V. J. Am. Chem. Soc. 86, 3183–97 (1964).
204. Rare-gas and hydrogen molecule electronic states, noncrossing rule, and recombination of electrons with rare-gas and hydrogen ions. Phys. Rev. 136, A962–65 (1964).

1965

205. Carroll, P.K. and Mulliken, R.S. $^3\Pi$ Levels and predissociations of N_2 near the 12.135 eV dissociation limit. J. Chem. Phys. 43, 2170–79 (1965).
206. Molecular scientists and molecular science: some reminiscences. J. Chem. Phys. 43, 52–111 (1965).
207. Discussion following Nesbet's paper. J. Chem. Phys. 43, S33 (1965).
208. Discussion following Cohen and Roothaan's paper. J. Chem. Phys. 43, S39 (1965).

1966

209. The Rydberg States of molecules. VI. Potential curves and dissociation behavior of (Rydberg and other) diatomic states. J. Am. Chem. Soc. 88, 1849–61 (1966).
210. John Clarke Slater, His Work and a Bibliography. Quantum Theory of Atoms, Molecules, Solid State. Ed. P. Löwdin. Academic Press, New York, 1966. pp. 5–13.
211. The Bonding Characteristics of Diatomic MO's. Quantum Theory of Atoms, Molecules, Solid State. Ed. P. Löwdin. Academic Press, New York, 1966. pp. 231–41.

1967

212. The assignment of quantum numbers for electrons in molecules. Intl. J. Quantum Chem. 1, 103–17 (1967).
213. Spectroscopy, molecular orbitals, and chemical bonding (Nobel Lecture). Science 157, 13–24 (1967). Angew. Chem. 79, 541–554 (1967), in German. Successes in the Physical Science 94, 585–606 (1967, Academy Sci. U.S.S.R.), in Russian.
214. Electrons, what they are and what they do (High School Essay). Chemistry 40, 13–15 (1967).

1968

215. Spectroscopy, quantum chemistry and molecular physics. Physics Today 21, 52–57 (1968).
216. Electron-donor acceptor interactions and charge-transfer spectra. Proceedings of the Robert A. Welch Foundation Conference on Chemical Research, December 1967. XI, 105–50 (1968).

1969

217. Mulliken, R.S. and Person, W.B. Electron donor-acceptor complexes and charge-transfer spectra. Physical Chemistry. Ed. D. Henderson. Academic Press, New York, 1969. Vol. 3, pp. 537–612.
218. Mulliken, R.S. and Merer, A.J. Vibrational structure of the π^*-π electronic transition of ethylene. J. Chem. Phys. 50, 1026–27 (1969).
219. The charge-transfer band of the pyridine-iodine complex. J. Am. Chem. Soc. 91, 1237 (1969).
220. Mulliken, R.S. and Person, W.B. Molecular compounds and their spectra. XXI. Some general considerations. J. Am. Chem. Soc. 91, 3409–13 (1969).
221. The Rydberg states of molecules. VII. J. Am. Chem. Soc. 91, 4615–21 (1969).
222. Merer, A.J. and Mulliken, R.S. Ultraviolet spectra and excited states of ethylene and its alkyl derivatives. Chem. Rev. 69, 639–56 (1969).
223. Mulliken, R.S. and Person, W.B. Molecular complexes: A Lecture and Reprint Volume. John Wiley and Sons, New York, 1969.
224. Mulliken, R.S. and Itoh, M. Singlet-triplet absorption bands of methyl-substituted ethylenes. J. Chem. Phys. 73, 4332–34 (1969).

1970

225. Potential curves of diatomic rare gas molecules and their ions, with particular reference to Xe_2. J. Chem. Phys. 52, 5170–80 (1970).
226. The role of kinetic energy in the Franck-Condon principle; with application to the iodine molecule emission spectrum. Chem. Phys. Letters 7, 11–14 (1970).
227. The path to molecular orbital theory. Pure Appl. Chem. 24, 203–15 (1970).
228. Introductory remarks at Royal Society discussion on photoelectron spectroscopy. Phil. Trans. Roy. Soc. London A 268, 3–5 (1970).

1971

229. Iodine revisited. J. Chem. Phys. 55, 288–309 (1971).
230. The role of kinetic energy in the Franck-Condon principle. J. Chem. Phys. 55, 309–14 (1971).
231. Politzer, P. and Mulliken, R.S. A comparison of two atomic charge definitions as applied to the hydrogen fluoride molecule. J. Chem. Phys. 55, 5135–36 (1971).
232. Mulliken, R.S. and Liu, B. SCF wave functions of P_2 and PO, and the role of d functions in chemical bonding, and of s-p hybridization in N_2 and P_2. J. Am. Chem. Soc. 93, 6738–44 (1971).
233. The lowest excited states of BeH. Int. J. Quant. Chem. 5, 83–94 (1971).
234. The ground state of BeH. Int. J. Quant. Chem. 5, 95–101 (1971).

1972

235. The nitrogen molecule correlation diagram. Chem. Phys. Letters *14*, 137–40 (1972).
236. Rydberg and valence-shell character as functions of internuclear distance in some excited states of CH, NH, H_2 and N_2. Chem. Phys. Letters *14*, 141–44 (1972).

1974

237. Through ZPG to NPG. Bull. At. Scientists *30*, 9 (1974).
238. Mixed V states. Chem. Phys. Letters *25*, 305–7 (1974).
239. Potential energy curves and radiative transmission probabilities for rare-gas molecules. Radiat. Res. *39*, 357–62 (1974).
240. Molecular orbitals of N_2 at small internuclear distances. Int. J. Quant. Mech. 8, 817–21 (1974).

1975

241. William Draper Harkins. Biographical Memoirs. Natl. Acad. of Sciences XLVII, 49–82 (1975).
242. Selected Papers of R.S. Mulliken. Eds. D.A. Ramsay and J. Hinze. University of Chicago Press, Chicago, 1975.
243. The centrality of science and absolute values. Proc. Fourth Int. Conf. on the Unity of the Sciences, New York (1975).

1976

244. Rydberg states and Rydbergization. Accts. Chem. Res. 9, 7–12 (1976).
245. Predissociation and Λ-doubling in the even-parity Rydberg states of the nitrogen molecule. J. Mol. Spectr. *61*, 92–99 (1976).
246. Ermler, W.C. and Mulliken, R.S. Energies and orbital sizes for some Rydberg and valence states of the nitrogen molecule. J. Mol. Spectr. *61*, 100–106 (1976).
247. Ermler, W.C., Mulliken, R.S. and Clementi, E. Ab initio SCF computations on benzene and benzenium ion using a large contracted gaussian basis set. J. Am. Chem. Soc. 98, 388–94 (1976).

1977

248. The excited states of ethylene. J. Chem. Phys. 66, 2448–2451 (1977).
249. Rydberg and valence-shell states and their interaction. Chem. Phys. Letters *46*, 197–200 (1977).
250. Ermler, W.C. and Mulliken, R.S. Molecular orbital correlation diagrams for He_2, He_2^+, N_2, N_2^+, CO and CO^+. J. Chem. Phys. *66*, 3031–38 (1977).
251. Mulliken, R.S. and Ermler, W.C. Diatomic Molecules: Results of Ab Initio Calculations. Academic Press, New York, 1977.

1978

252. Ermler, W.C. and Mulliken, R.S. Ab initio SCF computations on toluene and the toluenium ion using a large contracted gaussian base set. J. Am. Chem. Soc. *100*, 1647–1653 (1978).
253. Chemical Bonding. Ann. Rev. Phys. Chem. *29*, 1–30 (1978).

1979

254. The excited states of ethylene (Rev.). J. Chem. Phys. *71*, 556–557 (1979).

1980

255. The cold war. Bull. At. Scientists. October, 8–9 (1980).

1981

256. Mulliken, R.S. and Ermler, W.C. Polyatomic Molecules: Results of Ab Initio Calculations. Academic Press, New York, 1981.

1982

257. Ermler, W.C., McLean, A.D. and Mulliken, R.S. Ab initio study of valence state potential energy curves of N_2. J. Chem. Phys. *86*, 1305–14 (1982).

Posthumous

258. Ermler, W.C., Clark, J.P. and Mulliken, R.S. AB initio calculations of potential energy curves and transition moments of $^1\Sigma_g^+$ and $^1\Sigma_\mu^+$ states of N_2. J. Chem. Phys. *86*, 370–375 (1987).
259. Life of a Scientist. Ed. B.J. Ransil. Springer-Verlag, Heidelberg, 1989.

Footnotes

[1] Concerning Mrs. Jane Marcet see *Notes and Records of the Royal Society of London,,* Volume 22, p. 169. The "Conversations" was first published about 1809, inspired by Sir Humphrey Davy's lectures at the Royal Institution. Michael Faraday's interest in chemistry was first awakened by reading it. Ed. Note: Mrs. Marcet's *Conversations on Chemistry,* is the subject of an article by M. Elizabeth Derrick in *Journal Chemical Education,* **62,** 749 (1985) who comments that while the chemistry is dated it has "something of value to say" to modern chemists about how to teach the subject (as reported in *Chemical and Engineering News,,* December 2, 1985).

[2] In 1956 my wife and I called on a Newburyport man of 106 years, Mr. Henry Bailey Little, who told us he had seen my grandfather bring his bride to church in 1860, at the time of Lincoln's election campaign. I had gone to kindergarten with Mr. Little's youngest daughter.

[3] The room above a room in the rear of the house, near the kitchen, where firewood was stored.

[4] John Gyles, *Memoirs of Odd Adventures, Strange Deliverances, Etc. in the Captivity of John Gyles, Esq. Commander of the Garrison on St. George's River,* S. Kneeland and T. Green. Boston, 1736. For a fictional version of his experiences as a slave of the Maliseet Indians, see Stuart Trueman, *The Ordeal of John Gyles,* McClelland and Stewart, Toronto/Montreal, 1966.

[5] For example, see Sarah Elizabeth Mulliken, *Boys and Girls in Colonial Times,* Ginn and Co., N.Y., 1928; and *The Voyage of the Anna Smith,* Bobbs Merrill, N.Y., 1940.

[6] Editor's Note: This may be rendered alternatively: "He is a sly fox" or "He is a deep one."

[7] For a cultural background, Harvard was then certainly much broader than M.I.T., which was an excellent scientific and engineering school. Nowadays MIT has greatly broadened its cultural horizons and ambitions.

[8] Robert S. Mulliken. Science and the Scientific Attitude. *Science,* **86,** 65–68 (1937).

[9] In 1775, according to my Aunt Sarah, he from his pulpit called for volunteers to fight the British.

[10] On large scale this is the best that can be done. In experiments on an extremely small scale, it is possible to separate individual atoms of isotopes. J.J. Thompson and F.W. Aston did this with the mass spectrograph, and thus proved the existence of isotopes. But this is not practical on a larger scale.

[11] I have written an obituary, published in *Biographical Memoirs. National Academy of Sciences* **XLVII,** 49–82 (1975).

[12] Before World War I, this region of the Dolomites had belonged to Austria but after the war it was transferred to Italian rule.

[13] HX molecules seemed to show some discrepancies from this behavior but in better work some years later they were removed.

[14] Robert S. Mulliken. *Science,* **86,** 65–68 (1937).

[15] On the events of this period, see *A Peril and A Hope: the Scientists' Movement in America 1945–47,* by Alice Kimball Smith, The University of Chicago Press, 1965.

[16] Division IV of the National Nuclear Energy Series. The numerous volumes of this series were published by McGraw–Hill beginning in 1948.

[17] Bhabha was much interested in art, and himself did some painting.

[18] The Proceedings of the symposium, published by the Science Council of Japan in December 1962 consists mainly of preprints of the numerous papers which were presented.

[19] Professor E.K. Plyler had already asked me at the Tokyo meeting in 1962 whether I would like to come to Florida State University. I had known Plyler at the National Bureau of Standards in Washington, and had once published a paper with him.

[20] For her talk, and much else about the occasion, see *Les Prix Nobel in 1966,* published in 1967 by the Nobel Foundation. The beautiful diploma and gold medal are illustrated there.

Photographs

Robert Sanderson Mulliken at one year, 1897. (Credit: Russell, Quincy, Massachusetts)

L. to R. Katherine, (Mrs.) Katherine Wilmarth Mulliken, Robert and Gyles (sitting) Mulliken, early 1900s, Newburyport. (Credit: Noyes, Newburyport)

Samuel Parsons Mulliken, Robert's father, Washington, D.C. 1917–18. (Credit: Clinedinst Studio, Washington, D.C.)

241

Mulliken's birthplace. 46 High Street, Newburyport, Massachusetts.

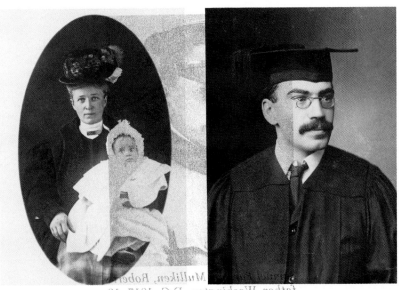

Mary Cullaton Noé and daughter Mary Helen.

Adolf C. Noé, Mary Helen Mulliken's father. (Credit: W.J. Root, Chicago)

242

Robert S. Mulliken, graduation from Newburyport High School. (Credit: Thompson, Newburyport, Mass.)

Robert S. Mulliken, MIT graduation. (Credit: Otto Sarony Co.)

Mulliken's Isotope Factory, U. of Chicago, 1922.

Robert and Mary Helen Mulliken. Believed to have been taken at the time of their marriage, December, 24, 1929.

Robert S. Mulliken, undated; approximately 1940s.

LMSS Group, July, 1949. Back Row: Charlene Scott, Secretary, Robert G. Parr, Robert S. Mulliken, John R. Platt, Harrison Shull. Front Row: Clemens C. J. Roothaan, Putcha Venkateswarlu, H. Christopher Longuet-Higgins.

244

Participants at Shelter Island Conference, September 8–10, 1951. Left to Right Standing: Ruedenberg, Berlin, Barnett, Crawford, MacInnes, Margenau, Pitzer, Kimball, Ufford, Mulliken, Van Vleck, Löwdin, Lennard-Jones, Eyring, Slater, Coulson, Hirschfelder, Wheland, Shull, Sutton, Parr. Seated: Mayer, Moffitt, Roothaan, Kotani.

Mary Helen, Valerie and Robert Mulliken, London, 1955. (Credit: Fujioka)

L. to R. Per-Olov Löwdin, F.A. Matsen, Robert S. Mulliken, Linus Pauling, Valadolen, Sweden, August 1958.

Robert S. Mulliken burns the midnight oil. U. of Chicago, December, 1959. (Credit: M. Yoshimine)

Robert S. Mulliken, Bernard J. Ransil and Clemens C.J. Roothaan, LMSS, U. of Chicago, December, 1959. (Credit: M. Yoshimine)

Robert S. Mulliken, 1960.

Robert S. Mulliken and Inga Fischer-Hjalmars, Nobel Prize Ceremony, 1966. (Credit: Reportage-bild, Stockholm)

L. to R. Valerie, Lucia and Mary Helen Mulliken, Mrs. Per-Olov Löwdin and daughter, Uppsala, 1966. (Credit: Uppsala-Bild)

Robert S. Mulliken, Stockholm U., December 1967.

Robert S. Mulliken and Gerhard Herzberg, Lindau, July 1974. (Credit: Bild-Photo-Pfeiffer, Kressbronn)

Robert S. Mulliken and Miss Molecule (Missy), U. of Chicago, 1976.

Name Index

The assistance of Paul E. Cade in the construction of this index is gratefully acknowledged. Roman numerals refer to page numbers of the introductory material. Page IX and pages denoted by *italics* contain photographs.

251